The Descendants of James Campbell and Christy MacDonald

ISBN 978-1-926494-42-5
Copyright © by John Westlie 2022

Selkirk Stories™ and the image of a heart and three stars are trademarks of Selkirk Stories, Cornwall, Prince Edward Island, Canada.

The cover image is a map of Lots 49 and 50 from *Meacham's Atlas* (1880), used with the gracious permission of the Robertson Library, University of Prince Edward Island, and islandimaged.ca.

A Campbell Family of Prince Edward Island

The Descendants of James Campbell and Christy MacDonald

Research by Roy and Maida Campbell
and Jean MacLean

Edited and Organized by John Westlie

Selkirk
STORIES

Table of Contents

Publisher's Preface   vii

Introduction   x

Overview: the Descendants of James Campbell and Christy MacDonald   14

A1. The Descendants of Malcolm Campbell and Janet Murchison   65

A2. The Descendants of John Campbell and Euphemia Murchison   98

A3. The Descendants of Margaret Campbell and Alexander Stewart   123

A4. The Descendants of Sarah Campbell and Samuel Martin   126

A5. The Descendants of Donald Campbell and Christy MacLeod   160

A6. The Descendants of Ann Campbell and Donald Murchison   165

A7. The Descendants of Christy Campbell and Joseph Beers   174

Appendix: Obituaries, Weddings, Other Documents   177

Index of Names   226

Publisher's Preface

When Roy Campbell and Maida Campbell approached me earlier this year with the material making up this book, I was pleased to agree to publish it. This account of the descendants of James Campbell and Christy MacDonald, both immigrants from Skye to Prince Edward Island, is based on research done by Jean MacLean and printed on a home computer in 2004, which was later complemented and completed by Roy and Maida Campbell and similarly printed in 2010. By publishing it, Selkirk Stories hope to make this genealogical information available to a wider public, fulfilling our mission of telling the stories of Prince Edward Island.

However, the material the Campbells provided required reorganization and editing to make it easily accessible to readers. The remainder of this preface explains this reorganization.

Family Trees

Following an introduction written by Roy and Maida Campbell, readers will find an overview of the entire family tree of the descendants of James Campbell and Christy MacDonald. There are no dates of birth and death, no biographical details, simply names of descendants and their spouses or partners. The family tree is organized in a hanging indented style, so that the each of the children of James and Christy Campbell, the first generation, is assigned a letter (A) designating the generation, and a number (1, 2, 3, etc.) indicating the order of birth. Each of their children is similarly designated (B1, B2, etc.), and so on until each generation is accounted for.

Each of the children of the original couple is then given a separate section, which includes all biographical information available, such as dates of birth and death, newspaper and obituary accounts, careers, and so on. The same organizational scheme is followed. The first generation (children of James Campbell and Christy MacDonald) is A, their children are B, their grandchildren C, and so on.

Biographical Information

When biographical information is available, it is presented in the following order: date and place of birth, baptismal information, date of death, place of burial. The same information is often provided about spouses and is presented in the same order. Details about careers and about marriage (such as date and place, officiating clergy, witnesses and bondsman) follow. If there is more than one marriage, they are designed as (1), (2) and so on. For the sake of brevity, full sentences are not always used. A typical entry might read:

> Donald Campbell, b. February 22, 1850, Uigg, d. August 3, 1938, Kinross, buried, Orwell Head. Donald was a farmer, shoemaker and tanner. He m. Flora MacLeod, b. May 17, 1855, Murray Harbour Road, baptized July 23, 1855, Orwell Head Church of Scotland, d. February 22, 1941, Uigg, in the residence of her daughter Edith, buried, Orwell Head. Donald and Flora were married on August 3, 1875, at the residence of James Campbell by the Rev. John Goodwill.

Written in full sentences, this would read:

> Donald Campbell was born on February 22, 1850, in Uigg, Prince Edward Island, and died on August 3, 1938, in Kinross. He is buried in Orwell Head. Donald was a farmer, shoemaker and tanner. He married Flora MacLeod, who was born on May 17, 1855, on the Murray Harbour Road and baptized on July 23, 1855, in the Orwell Head Church of Scotland. She died February 22, 1941, in Uigg, in the residence of her daughter Edith. She is buried in Orwell Head. Donald and Flora were married on August 3, 1875, at the residence of James Campbell by the Rev. John Goodwill.

A shorter entry might simply read: "James Campbell, b. 1960, m. Mary MacPherson, July 23, 1988." This would mean: "James Campbell was born in 1960 and married Mary MacPherson on July 23, 1988."

Appendix

An appendix at the end of the genealogical tables contains death notices, obituaries, wedding announcements, press clippings and other documents of interest to genealogists and Campbell family members. If there is an entry in the appendix, the corresponding section of the genealogical table is marked with an asterix, thus: C2*.

Place Names

Towns, villages and place names given without any further information (such "Uigg" and "Murray Harbour Road" above) should be assumed to be in Prince Edward Island. If not, the current postal abbreviations are used for Canadian provinces (ON for Ontario, BC for British Columbia) and American states

(CA for California, MA for Massachusetts). Other locations are indicated in full (England, Scotland, China, etc.).

NAMES

The abbreviation [?] indicates an unknown name. "Flora [?]" means Flora, last name unknown; "[?] MacDonald" means a MacDonald whose Christian name is unknown. In a few cases, children's names are given without a family name, even though the names of the parents are known. This is how the original text presents them, and we have chosen to respect the original researchers' choice.

When an individual is known by a name other than his or her given name, that name is indicated in parentheses following the surname. This is often a nickname or a middle name. For example: "Euphemia Campbell (Effie)" is an example of a nickname, while "Ronald James Campbell (James)" is an example of a man known by his middle name.

INDEX

The index of names includes all occurrences of the names of the descendants of James Campbell and Christy MacDonald. However, it does not include other names found in this book, such as witnesses at weddings, officiating clergymen at weddings and funerals, and other names that may be included in biographical information or press notices.

We hope that this publication is useful to members of the Campbell family, their descendants, and all those interested in the history of Scottish immigration to Canada.

John Westlie
Publisher, Selkirk Stories
2022

Introduction

James Campbell, b. ca. 1795, Skye, Scotland, d. June 6, 1839, Uigg, PEI, buried Uigg Pioneer Cemetery. James m. Christy MacDonald, b. ca. 1801, Skye, Scotland, d. March 14, 1883, Uigg, PEI, buried Uigg Pioneer Cemetery.

The following is a general and fragmentary summary of information about James distilled from a variety of sources. Some of the evidence is, of course, speculative in nature.

Birth and Death of James Campbell

James emigrated from Skye on the *Mary Kennedy* in 1829 and died aged about 44. The inscription on his headstone reads: James Campbell. Died June 6, 1839, Ae. 44. He was a native of Skye, Inverness Skire, Scotland, and emigrated to P.E.I. in 1829. He is said to be the first person buried in the Uigg Pioneer Cemetery. Some suggested he died of injuries received from a falling tree, and others that he died of cancer. Since injuries in the woods were common in those days, it is probable that a non life-threatening injury was associated in their minds with some form of cancer, since death from falling trees was normally quicker than his death seems to have been. Family tradition has it that he was ailing for a year before he died.

James' Sibling on PEI

According to a "Pedigree" of the MacDonalds of the Belfast/Orwell Cove area, compiled by Margaret (Murchison) Finlay in 1937, James had at least one sibling on PEI: a sister, Flora, who came out with the Selkirk settlers in 1803. She was married to a John MacDonald who settled in Pinette. They had twenty-two children. However, contact with these Campbell/MacDonald relatives has not been maintained over the years.

Was Margaret Campbell a Sister?

While it was commonly known in both the MacKinnon and Campbell families that there was a relationship between Margaret Campbell (sometimes mistakenly referred to as Ann) and James, the precise nature of that relationship has been lost over time. Margaret (or Ann) Campbell was married to Malcolm MacKinnon of Uigg, who came out with the 1829 settlers. The early death of James Campbell would also tend to weaken the relationship between the two families.

In a conversation some years ago, Margaret's great grandson, William MacKinnon (Billy), thought Margaret might have been a sister of James, but was not sure. Edith Campbell Hume, 1898-1990 (a great granddaughter of James), lived in the community all her life and was very knowledgeable about the history of the family. She also thought that Margaret was perhaps a sister of James. However, we have no concrete evidence to support this specific link.

On the contrary, we have seen recent evidence from a MacKinnon family tree, brought from Skye, that Margaret's father's name was William. This would mean that William was also the name of James' father if he and Margaret were brother and sister. If that were true, one would expect James to follow the old Scottish custom of naming the eldest son after the grandfather. But the name William was not given to any of his sons. The evidence, then, suggests that Margaret was more likely a cousin than a sister. And given the prevalent Scottish custom of naming the oldest son after the paternal grandfather, one might reasonably infer that since James named his oldest son Malcolm, that was likely his own father's name.

Scottish Ancestry of James Campbell

Following up on this speculative hunch, and having no luck in finding information on James in a search of Scottish records in Skye, we thought it might be worthwhile to peruse the MacDonald rent rolls in the Uig area of Skye for the 1820s, the period before James left for PEI. In the 1970s and 1980s, we checked out the Glen Conan Campbells and could find no common link between James Campbell and the Campbells residing on the south side of Glen Conan. The most likely croft that we could fit him into was one in Earlish (just outside Uig) in the parish of Snizort, Trotternish. In 1823, the croft was listed under the name of: the Widow of Malcolm Campbell. Other information obtained indicated that her maiden name was Margaret Beaton. A later rent roll indicated that the croft was listed under the name of John Campbell, most likely her son, as his father's name is listed as Malcolm in another document. We are speculating that John, who was married to a Marion Ferguson, was probably James' brother. John died in 1883 and had the following children: Malcolm, Mary, Kenneth, Catherine and Christy. Except for Kenneth, these are familiar names in James' family tree. Kenneth was the name of John's wife's mother. Malcolm was also the name given to James' oldest son.

Christy MacDonald Campbell

Christy emigrated in 1829 with her husband and three of the children. The fourth child, Sarah (Marion), seems to have been born during or very shortly after the crossing. Christy also had a brother, Hector, a veteran of Waterloo, who came out in 1829 and settled in nearby Grandview. A sword that he brought from Waterloo was used for years in the ceremonies of the local Orange Lodge, but the lodge closed down many years ago. Although a trace of the sword was attempted several years ago, it could not be located. An old sword was found, but it was not the Waterloo sword, for it had a date of 1829 inscribed on it, considerably later than the 1815 battle.

The notice of Christy's death in *The Examiner* of March 27, 1883, is as follows:

> At Uigg, on the 14th instant, Mrs. Campbell, widow of the late Mr. James Campbell. She leaves a large number of friends and relatives, by whom she was very highly esteemed. She had seven children, seventy-eight grandchildren, and twenty-seven great grandchildren, besides a great number of relatives and connections. She lived a consistent Christian life. All who knew her respected her highly.

According to Edith Campbell Hume, Christy's great granddaughter, Christy was buried next to her husband, but her name never got onto James' stone. The stone is actually of such a size and nature that it does not readily lend itself to additional names. In addition, a new cemetery was opened next to the church in Orwell Head in 1867, and burial largely ceased in the Pioneer Cemetery. (Christy died in 1883.)

Roy and Maeda Campbell

Their Arrival from Scotland

> 84 immigrants including women and children from the Isle of Skye arrived here on Sunday. They left their native place about six weeks ago in a ship for Cape Breton along with a number of settlers for that Island. They seem all to be in high health and, judging from appearance, in easy circumstances.
>
> With prudent foresight characteristic of their race they came provided with 12 months' provisions and an ample stock of warm clothing. They have all relatives already settled on the Island, chiefly about Belfast and, with the exception of one family, it is, we understand, their intention also to locate in that thriving settlement.

The PEI Register and Gazette, Tuesday, June 2, 1829

Uigg, where the settlers ended up, is about eight or nine miles from Belfast. As indicated above, James had a sister Flora in Belfast, who came out in 1803 with Selkirk.

Their children were:

- A1   Malcolm Campbell, b. September 10, 1821.
- A2   John Campbell, b. May 24, 1823.
- A3   Margaret Campbell, b. 1826.
- A4   Sarah (Marion) Campbell, b. May 14, 1829.
- A5   Donald Campbell, b. ca. 1831.
- A6   Ann Campbell, b. 1833.
- A7   Christy Campbell, b. October 27, 1839.

Overview: The Descendants of James Campbell and Christy MacDonald

A1   Malcolm Campbell, m. Janet Murchison (Jessie).
- B1   James Campbell, m. Harriet Elizabeth Gilmour.
  - C1   Malcolm Neil Campbell, m. Ida Frohmander.
    - D1   Maynard V. Campbell, m. Vera Howard.
      - E1   Malcolm Campbell.
    - D2   Myrna Campbell, m. Eric Beavon.
      - E1   Harold Beavon.
      - E2   Fred Beavon.
      - E3   Chester Beavon.
      - E4   Everyl Armson Beavon, m. Evelyn Wismer.
        - F1   Frederick John Malcolm Beavon, m. Spoar [?].
          - G1   Cindy Beavon.
        - F2   Donald Neil Beavon, m. Sheila Murphy.
          - G1   Brianne Beavon.
          - G2   Samantha Beavon.
          - G3   Terra Beavon.
          - G4   Anapuma Beavon.
        - F3   Trudy Lee Ann Beavon, m. Nils Lee.
          - G1   Justin Ryan Lee.
          - G2   Erin Lee (twin of Erica).
          - G3   Erica Lee (twin of Erin).
    - D3   Laura Campbell.
  - C2   Laura Elizabeth Campbell, m. Warren Smith.
    - D1   James Smith, m. Irene Lois Kitchcock.
    - D2   Warren Smith.
    - D3   Dorothy Smith, m. [?] Gould.
    - D4   Donald Smith.
    - D5   Robert Smith.
  - C3   Chester Gilmore Campbell, m. Margaret Ann Downey.
    - D1   Marian Elinor Campbell, m. Edwin Cone.
      - E1   Donald Campbell Cone, m. Virginia [?].
        - F1   Kevin Cone.
        - F2   Bryan Cone.
      - E2   Bruce Eldridge Cone, m. Beverly [?].

				F1	Cindy Cone.
				F2	Ronda Cone.
				F3	Sean Cone.
			E3	Gratia Cone, m. Kenneth Hersey.	
				F1	Melissa Hersey.
				F2	David Hersey.
				F3	Allyson Hersey.
			E4	Edwin A. Cone, m. Julie [?].	
				F1	Jennifer Cone.
				F2	Daniel Cone.
			E5	Ann Elizabeth Cone, m. David Vining.	
				F1	Jessica Vining.
				F2	Jacqueline Vining.
		D2	Margaret Campbell, m. [?] Garland.		
		D3	Janet Irene Campbell.		
		D4	Ruth Campbell.		
	C4	Janet Campbell, m. William Frohmander.			
		D1	Kathryn Frohmander.		
		D2	Ruth Frohmander.		
		D3	Malcolm Frohmander.		
		D4	William Frohmander.		
	C5	Albert Campbell, m. Mildred Shaw.			
		D1	Marjorie Campbell.		
	C6	Herbert Campbell, m. Catherine Hastings.			
		D1	George Campbell.		
		D2	Katherine Louise Campbell, m. [?] Koch.		
		D3	Laura Campbell.		
		D4	Melvin Campbell.		
		D5	Latba Campbell.		
		D6	Janet Campbell, m. [?] Kirk.		
		D7	Norman Campbell.		
	C7	Irene Harriet Campbell, m. Ernest Uriah Ayars.			
		D1	Dorothy Carolyn Ayars, m. Kenneth Harvey Emerson.		
			E1	Anita Inez Emerson, m. Robert Stanley Folkenberg.	
				F1	Robert Stanley Folkenberg, m. Audrey Ann Gibson.
					G1 Robert Stanley Folkenberg.

                G2   Randall Thomas Folkenberg.

                G3   Katelyn Ann Folkenberg.

          F2   Kathi Lynne Folkenberg, m. David Arnold Jensen.

                G1   Michael Allan Jensen.

      E2   Robert James Emerson, m. (1) Mary Catherine Konevich, (2) Linda Kaye Knolls.

          F1   Traci Lynn Emerson, m. (1) Mark Edward Berault.

                G1   Joshua Alan Berault.

                G2   Brittney Lynn Berault.

          Traci Lynn m. (2) Aaron Stanford.

                G3   Megan Ashley Stanford.

          F2   Robert Kenneth Emerson.

          Robert James m. (3) Peggy Neal.

      E3   Richard Kenneth Emerson, m. (1) Sharon Paige, (2) Sandra Charlene Clayton.

          F1   Ariel Elizabeth Rebecca Emerson.

          F2   Alison Hilary Kaitlyn Emerson.

    D2   Ernest James Ayars, m. Carleen Louise Siems.

      E1   Karen Ayars.

    D3   Mildred Ayars.

B2   Euphemia Campbell (Effie), m. Murdoch MacKinnon.

  C1   Neil Campbell Garrett, m. Florence Melva Acorn.

    D1   Katherine Margaret Garrett, m. Waldo Keith MacLeod.

      E1   Kelli Margaret MacLeod.

      E2   Karla MacLeod.

    D2   Marjorie Faye Garrett, m. Kenneth MacDonald.

    D3   Arthur Daniel Garrett, m. Sheila Marlene MacKenzie.

    D4   John Caleb Garrett, m. Shirley Dianne MacKenzie.

    D5   Ada Garrett (Valerie), m. David Wallace Garrett.

B3   Donald Campbell, m. Flora MacLeod.

  C1   Hector Campbell, m. (1) May Ferguson, (2) Laura Clark.

  C2   Mary C. Campbell, m. Angus Alexander MacLeod.

    D1   Walter MacLeod (Gordon), m. Mabel MacLeod.

      E1   Wayne MacLeod.

           E2   Elaine MacLeod.
     D2   Willard Campbell MacLeod, m. Catherine Martin
           (Muriel), see A4-B11-C4, p. 55.
     D3   Angus MacLeod (Allistair), m. Constance Belya.
           E1   David MacLeod.
           E2   Ian MacLeod.
     D4   Donald MacLeod (Everett), m. Susan Alma Reid.
           E1   Pat MacLeod.
           E2   Madeline MacLeod.
           E3   Douglas MacLeod.
           E4   Ross MacLeod.
     D5   William MacLeod (Sinclair), m. Elsie MacGregor.
           E1   Mary MacLeod, m. Gordon [?].
           E2   Lee MacLeod, m. Cathy [?].
           E3   Bruce MacLeod, m. Cheryl [?].
           E4   Karen MacLeod, m. Allen [?].
C3   Janette Campbell (Jessie), m. William P. Dempsey.
     D1   William Dempsey.
     D2   Malcolm Dempsey.
     D3   Frances Dempsey.
     D4   Florence Dempsey.
C4   William Malcolm Campbell.
C5   Euphemia Campbell, m. Owen Crouse.
     D1   Walter Crouse (also known as Walton Crouse).
     D2   John Everett Crouse.
     D3   Florence Crouse.
C6   Stella Dyan Campbell, m. William Cummings.
     D1   Douglas Lee Cummings.
     D2   Beatrice Cummings, m. Clayton Stephens.
C7   Ann Evaline Campbell, m. Albert Murphy.
     D1   Albert Murphy.
C8   Christina Laura Campbell, m. Alexander Martin.
C9   Edith Rachel Campbell, m. Samuel Hume.
     D1   Donald William Hume, m. Margaret Shaw.
           E1   John William Hume, m. Linda Bieren.
                 F1   Cathy Lynn Hume, m. Sheldon
                       Stewart.
                       G1   Alyssa Jane Stewart.
                       G2   Braeden John Stewart.
                 F2   Donald William Hume, m. Kelly
                       Smyth.

                    G1   Ethan William Hume.
                    G2   Kieren Blaine Hume.
B4   Sarah Ann Campbell (Marion), m. Donald Stewart.
     C1   James Alex Stewart, m. Mary Lamont (Masie).
          D1   Mabel F. Stewart.
          D2   Sadie Stewart, m. [?] MacKinnon.
     C2   John Goodwill Stewart.
     C3   Janet Euphemia Stewart, m. James Donald Murchison (see A6-B11, p. 170).
     C4   Margaret Priscilla Stewart, m. Nelson Cantelo.
     C5   Malcolm Campbell Stewart, m. Lillian Burt Main.
     C6   Euphemia Margaret Stewart (Effie), m. William McInnis.
          D1   Arthur McInnis.
     C7   Roderick MacLean Stewart.
     C8   Malcolm Hector Murchison Stewart, m. Catherine MacPherson.
     C9   Allan Campbell Stewart, m. Euphemia Campbell (Etta).
          D1   Hazel Mae Stewart, m. Norman MacLeod.
               E1   Anne Bernice MacLeod, m. John Milton Andres.
                    F1   Jamie Stewart Andres, m. Michael Eric Larsen.
                         G1   Declan Phillip Andres-Larsen.
                    F2   Paul MacLeod Andres, m. Jeni Ann Reiz.
                         G1   Clara Jane Andres.
                         G2   Charles Alexander Andres (Alex).
                    F3   David Allan Andres, m. Susan Faye Meyer.
                         G1   Emma Anne Andres.
                         G2   Adam John Andres.
                         G3   Grau Alice Andres.
                    F4   Phillip Campbell Andres, m. Caroline Gray Schless.
                         G1   Margaret Gray Andres.
                         G2   Catherine Jean Andres.
               E2   Norman Stewart MacLeod, m. Caroline Ruth Lee.
                    F1   Norman Scott MacLeod, m.

Gabrielle Isabella Marent.
    G1   Norman Conner MacLeod.
    G2   Caitlin Marie MacLeod.
F2   Shawn Allen MacLeod, m. Alicia Golleher.
    G1   Callie Leah MacLeod.
    G2   Caitlin Ayn MacLeod.
    G3   Carrick Ian MacLeod.
F3   Leah Alyse MacLeod, m. Robert Albert Irwin.
    G1   Ceylor Alyse Irwin.

E3   Allan Kenneth MacLeod, m. (1) Valeria Mavis Lygon.
    F1   Laurie Ann MacLeod, m. Alex Ramirez.
        G1   Jenna Brianne Ramirez, m. Ron Hulsey.
            H1   Lauryn Marie Hulsey.
        G2   Brandon David Ramirez.
        G3   Tara Karissa Ramirez.
        G4   Jacob Allen Ramirez.
        G5   Danielle Alyssa Ramirez.
        G6   Levi Samuel Ramirez.
    F2   Kerry Lynn MacLeod, m. (1) Kelly Michael Reaves.
        G1   Joshua Reaves, m. Angela Bishop.
        G2   Brittany Leeanne Reaves.
    Kerry Lynn m. (2) Rick Lutrell, (3) Mark Evans.
Allan (E3) m. (2) Carolyn Rummens, (3) Linda [?], (4) Lynn [?], (5) Linda Marie Templeton.

E4   Mary Ferguson MacLeod, m. Paul Michael Saint.
    F1   Matthew Paul Saint.
    F2   Andrew Michael Saint, m. Christy Breanna Pierce James.
        G1   Aiden James Saint.
        G2   Gavin MacLeod Saint.

G3 Bryson Saint.
E5 Donald Campbell MacLeod, m. (1) Victoria Qualls, (2) Nancy DeVore.
F1 Julie Anne MacLeod.
F2 David Campbell MacLeod, m. Erin C. Wilkinson.
G1 Dawson Lauder MacLeod.
G2 Cameron Donald MacLeod.
G3 Lauren Ellie MacLeod.
Donald m. (3) Wiescia Salanardi, (4) Katherine Heaston.
D2 Edison Campbell Stewart (Cam), m. Mary Elizabeth Sandall (Betty).
E1 Maryl Elaine Stewart.
E2 John Sandall Stewart (Sandy), m. Edith Morrison.
F1 Angus John Stewart, m. Danita Aspin.
G1 Charlie Angus Stewart.
G2 Laney Rose Stewart.
F2 Eric Donald Stewart.
E3 Donald Campbell Stewart, m. Elizabeth Gough Azmier.
F1 Benjamin Campbell Stewart.
F2 Morgan Allen Stewart, m. Andrew Mears.
E4 David Allan Stewart, m. Diane Lynn Piper.
F1 Catherine Melissa Stewart (Cathy), m. Eric Terrance Nordgren.
G1 Flynn Eric Nordgren.
G2 Anika Nordgren.
F2 Shawna Lee Stewart, m. Dale Philip Melvin.
G1 Isabelle Anne Melvin.
G2 Olivia Melvin.
E5 Elizabeth Anne Stewart (Anne), m. (1) Bob Baden. She had a child by Alexander [?].
F1 David Alexander Stewart.
E6 Robert Clifford Stewart (Cliff), m. Ann Michele Smyth.

    F1 Georgia Mary Stewart.
D3 Donald Arthur Stewart, m. Winifred Georgina Anne Robertson (Win).
  E1 Allan Robertson Stewart, m. Sharon Barrie Harmer.
  E2 Robert Livingstone Stewart, m. Audrey Cecilia Thornton.
    F1 Aaron Michael Stewart.
    F2 Todd Donald Stewart, m. Elysia Dhyana Meen.
  E3 Georgina Anne Campbell Stewart, m. Michael Angelo Manuel Manchon.
    F1 Alexander Stewart Manchon.
    F2 Nicholas Velandi Manchon, m. Andrea Kathleen Freer.
    F3 Melissa Maria Manchon.
D4 Allan Stewart (John), m. Margaret Esplin (Jean).
  E1 James Allan Stewart (Jim), m. Sharrin Catherine Beruschi.
    F1 Abigail Jean Stewart, m. Brent Petterson.
      G1 Matthew James Petterson.
    F2 Catherine Marie Stewart, m. [?] Murphy.
      G1 Olivia Anne Murphy.
  E2 John Alexander Stewart, m. (1) Randise Gail McLaughlin (Randy).
    F1 Jesse Alexander James Stewart, m. Lora Lau.
      G1 Emily Stewart.
    F2 Colin John Stewart.
   John m. (2) Jean Garrie.
    F3 Hayley Stewart.
    F4 Benjamin Stewart.
  E3 Kenneth Esplin Stewart, m. Donna Jean Belden.
    F1 Ian James Stewart, m. Nicole Brassard.
      G1 Nathan James Stewart.
      G2 Logan James Stewart.
    F2 Amy Leanne Stewart, m. (1) Patrick

Novak, (2) Jay Thorbourn.
- E4 Roberta Jean Stewart, m. Hatto Heinrich Horn.
- E5 Daniel Maynard Ross Stewart, m. (1) Darcy [?].
  - F1 Travis Stewart.
  - F2 Ashley Stewart.
  - F3 Kayla Stewart.

  Daniel m. (2) Kristine Findlay.
  - F4 Claudia Piper Stewart.
  - F5 Henry Daniel Stewart.

  Daniel has a son with a First Nation woman to whom he was not married.
- E6 Heather Ruth Stewart, m. Glen Arthur Lynskey.
  - F1 Torin Stewart Lynskey.
  - F2 William John Lynskey.

C10 Christy Ann Stewart, m. William Ross.
C11 Donald or Daniel Stewart, m. Ida Louise Keith.
- D1 Bernard Stewart.
- D2 Richard Stewart (Dickie).
- D3 Donald Stewart (Donnie).

B5 Margaret Campbell, m. (1) Malcolm Archibald MacPherson.
C1 Malcolm James MacPherson, m. Ella Mabel Stavert.
Margaret m. (2) Neil MacPherson.
C2 Daniel MacPherson.
C3 Janet Florence MacPherson (Jenny), m. John Thomas Mellish.
- D1 Clarence William Mellish.
- D2 Ruth Amelia Mellish, m. Simon Alexander Campbell (see B8-C3, p. 25).
- D3 Margaret Florence Mellish, m. Robert Alexander Munn (Bob).
  - E1 Merrill Munn, m. Georgina Penny.
    - F1 Lisa Margaret Munn.
    - F2 Penny Michelle Munn.
    - F3 Lincoln Merrill Munn.
  - E2 Boyd Munn, m. Leona Anstie.
    - F1 Robert Fitzpatrick.
    - F2 Ronald Boyd Munn (Ronnie).
    - F3 Lindsay Margaret Munn.

- E3 Blair Douglas Munn.
- D4 Elsie May Mellish, m. Charles Frederick Carver (Fred).
  - E1 Evelyn Joyce Carver, m. Richard Black.
  - E2 Margaret Jean Carver, m. (1) Elmer Gillis.
    - F1 Terry Lynn Gillis, m. Jim Renn.
      - G1 Shannon Renn.
    - F2 Kevin Frederick Gillis.

Elsie m. (2) Douglas Kitchen.
  - E3 Mary Jeanette Carver, m. Basil Higginbotham.
    - F1 Cindy Lynn Higginbotham, m. Donald MacMillan.
      - G1 Tiffany MacMillan.
    - F2 Patricia Ann Higginbotham, m. Robert Carver.
      - G1 Samantha Marie Carver.
    - F3 Michael Higginbotham, m. Christa MacSwain.
      - G1 Mary Hannah Higginbotham.
      - G2 Hope Higginbotham.
    - F4 Marilyn Higginbotham, m. Wade MacLean.
      - G1 Topanga Sea MacLean.
  - E4 Muriel May Carver, m. David Augustine Power.
    - F1 Adam David Power, m. Tray Landry.
    - F2 Kelly Rose May Power, m. Troy Griese.
      - G1 Kirsten Rose May Griese.
  - E5 Judith Elizabeth Carver, m. Donald Gordon Nicholson (Gordon).
    - F1 Mary Christine Nicholson.
    - F2 Raymond Donovan Nicholson.
    - F3 Donald Matthew Nicholson.
- C4 Sarah Catherine MacPherson.
  - D1 Chester MacPherson, m. Rosalie Favell.
    - E1 Joyce MacPherson, m. James Wilson (Jim).

                    E2   Gloria June MacPherson, m. Peter S. Boyle.
                            F1   Debbie Boyle, m. John Quon.
                                    G1   Brian Quon.
                                    G2   Lori Ann Quon.
                                    G3   Jacquelin Quon.
                            F2   Diane Boyle, m. Randy Alex.
                                    G1   Ricky Alex.
                                    G2   Shaun Alex.
                                    G3   Breeanna Alex.
            C5   Euphemia MacPherson (Phemie), m. Adrian Hiram Reynolds.
                    D1   Arthur Stroud Reynolds, m. Elizabeth Weir (Betty).
            C6   Mary Ann MacPherson, m. (1) Harvey MacKay.
                    D1   Dorothy MacKay, m. Melvin Deveau.
                    D2   Earl MacKay.
                    Mary Ann m. (2) [?] Ambrose.
            C7   Donalena MacPherson (Dolly), m. Claude LeRoy Wyland (Roy).
                    D1   Ruth M. Wyland, m. W. Arthur Grover.
                    D2   Leslie Wyland.
                    D3   Vivian Wyland, m. Robert Walker.
                            E1   John Walker.
                            E2   Robert Walker.
                            E3   David Walker.
                    D4   Rosamund Wyland, m. Robert Weaver.
            C8   Mary MacPherson (Mamie), m. John Cidney Rowell.
                    D1   Russell James Rowell, m. Barbara May Bowman.
                            E1   James R. Rowell, Jr.
                            E2   Bradford Vaughn Rowell.
            C9   Christina Belle MacPherson.
    B6   Neil Campbell, m. Christine MacLeod (Christy).
            C1   Janetta Campbell, m. William C. Mayne.
                    D1   Neil Campbell Mayne.
    B7   John Murdoch Campbell, m. Anne Mary MacRae.
            C1   Malcolm Campbell.
            C2   Janet Campbell, m. Clarence A. Andrew.
            C3   Donald Campbell, m. Adah Herring.
            C4   Euphemia Campbell.
            C5   Annie Laura Campbell.

B8 Christina Catherine Campbell (Christy), m. Murdoch Campbell.
    C1 Sarah Ann Campbell.
    C2 Malcolm Archibald Campbell.
    C3 Simon Alexander Campbell, m. Ruth Amelia Mellish (see B5-C3-D2, p. 22).
        D1 Malcolm James Campbell, m. (1) Mary Elizabeth Murphy.
            E1 Deborah Jean Campbell, m. Blair Joseph MacLean.
                F1 Bradley Jonathan MacLean, m. Kimberley Ann Hornmoen.
                    G1 Mary Emma Lynn MacLean.
                    G2 Malcolm Evan Jacob MacLean.
                    G3 Melanie Ella Audrey MacLean.
                F2 Monica Jill MacLean, m. Alexander Eugene Affleck.
                    G1 Percy Thorne Affleck.
                    G2 Jack Harrison Affleck.
                    G3 Carly Affleck.
            E2 Alexander James Campbell (Sandy), m. Debra Lori Jones.
                F1 Matthew Alexander Campbell.
            E3 Jill Elizabeth Campbell, m. Brian Edgar Gervais.
                F1 Mary Elizabeth Gervais.
                F2 Danielle Courtney Gervais.
        Malcolm James (D1) m. (2) Sheila Lucy Warren.
            E4 James Garnet Campbell.
        D2 Donald Murdock Campbell, m. (1) Florence Bowers.
            E1 Donald Campbell Devitt (Brent), m. Lisa Spruijt.
                F1 Alexandra Heather Devitt.
                F2 Ryan Devitt.
                F2 Jessica Julie Devitt.
            E2 Heather Lynn Campbell Devitt, m. Raymond Winters (Ray).

                F1   Kyle Ray Winters (adopted).
                F2   Kalyn Marie Winters (adopted).
          E3   Douglas Gregory Campbell Devitt.
    Donald Murdock (D2) m. (2) Elizabeth Deruiter, (3) Frances O'Hara.
    D3   Jean Florence Campbell, m. Allison Ivan MacLean.
          E1   Bonnie Ruth MacLean, m. Timothy Leslie (Tim).
          E2   Mary Beth MacLean, m. Francois Weber.
                F1   Corey Campbell Weber.
                F2   Amelia Nicolle Weber.
          E3   Scott Allison MacLean, m. Angela Bigney.
                F1   Joshua Scott MacLean.
                F2   Laura Jean MacLean.
                F3   Jessica Ruth MacLean.
                F4   Matthew James MacLean.
                F5   Justin Merle MacLean.
                F6   Emma Angela MacLean.
                F7   Mitchell Brandon MacLean.
    D4   Christine Catherine Campbell, m. Marcus Kramarczyk (Mike).
          E2   Kent Matthew Kramarczyk, m. Tracey Breton.
                F1   Dylan Reginald Simon Kramarczyk.
          E2   Ruth Ann Kramarczyk, m. David Kyle Pickersgill (Kyle).
                F1   Alexander James Pickersgill.
    C4   James Murdoch Campbell.
B9 Flora Campbell, m. Donald MacKinnon (Dan).
B10 Donald MacDonald Campbell, m. (1) Christina Mary MacRae.
    C1   Donald Campbell.
    C2   Christina Grace Campbell.
    C3   Euphemia Janetta MacKay Campbell.
    Donald m. (2) Euphemia Gillespie.
    C4   Sarah Campbell.
    C5   Ruth M. Campbell.
    C6   William Campbell.
    C7   Olive Campbell.
    C8   Marjorie Campbell, m. Carl Gryte.

        D1   Carl Campbell Gryte.
        D2   Daniel Gillespie Gryte.
        D3   Stephen Gryte.
    C9   James Campbell.
B11   Simon Alexander Campbell, m. Euphemia MacLean.
    C1   Neil Campbell, m. Naomi Lott.
        D1   James Murchison Campbell, m. Frances [?].
            E1   Merle Campbell, m. Steve Hildebrandt.
                F1   Merle Hildebrandt.
            E2   Coleen Campbell, m. Larry Varico.
                F1   Robbie Varico.
                F2   Katie Varico.
            E3   Richard Campbell.
        D2   Murray Campbell, m. Marlene [?].
            E1   Heather Campbell, m. Jeff Berry.
                F1   Raymond Berry.
                F2   Gavin Berry.
            E2   Cheryl Campbell, m. Bob Holiday.
                F1   Ryan Holiday.
                F2   Jonathan Holiday.
            E3   Daryl Campbell, m. Vicky [?].
                F1   Natasha Campbell.
            E4   Michelle Campbell.
        D3   Christine Campbell, twin to Caroline, m. David Norris.
            E1   Destanne Norris, m. Norma Brown.
                F1   Tekarra Norris.
                F2   James Norris.
                F3   Leah Norris.
            E2   Kevin Norris, m. Denise [?].
                F1   Allison Norris.
                F2   Jacklyn Norris.
                F3   Treanne Norris.
            E3   Danna Norris.
        D4   Caroline Campbell, twin to Christine, m. Ronald Stickle.
            E1   Teresa Stickle (Teri), m. John Reeve.
            F1   Tony Reeve (adopted).
            E2   Marc Stickle, m. Jill [?].
                F1   Jamie Paige Stickle.
                F2   Chet Stickle.

                    E3   Kelly Stickle, m. Lori [?].
                            F1   Roderick Stickle.
                            F2   Gabrielle Stickle (Ellie).
            D5   Maynard Campbell, m. Shannon [?].
    C2   John Campbell, m. Edna Lott.
            D1   Robert Alexander Campbell, m. (1) Marlene McGregor.
                    E1   Gordon Robert Campbell, m. Wendy [?].
                            F1   Scott John Campbell, m. Sharon Larouse.
                                    G1   Jeffery Britt Benoit Josiah Campbell.
                            F2   Nicole May Campbell.
                    E2   Clinton James Campbell, m. Cathy Koazk.
                            F1   Jason Campbell.
                            F2   Jamie Campbell.
                    E3   Mikael John Campbell.
                    Robert Alexander m. (2) Thelma Fennell.
            D2   Marjorie Elvera Campbell, m. Thomas Darwin Churchill (Darry).
                    E1   Victor Darwin Churchill, m. Heather [?].
                            F1   Scott Churchill.
                    E2   Kim Doyle Churchill, m. Tracy Moen.
                            F1   Travis Churchill.
                            F2   Jenna Churchill.
            D3   Doreen Campbell, m. Larry James Churchill.
                    E1   Kathrine Dawn Churchill.
                    E2   Karl James Churchill, m. Dianna Ford.
                    E3   Nadine Edna Churchill, m. Douglas Kelly.
                            F1   Tawny Justine Kelly.
                            F2   Kara Edna Kelly.
            D4   Ronald Donald Campbell, m. Mariel Ilona Jean Wickstrom.
                    E1   Marnie Gail Campbell, m. Pat Fagherty.
                            F1   Amanda Jean Fagherty.
                            F2   Arielle Jade Fagherty.
                    E2   Shane MacLean Campbell.
    C3   Malcolm Campbell.
    B12   Malcolm Hector Campbell.
A2 John Campbell (James), m. Euphemia Murchison.
    B1   James Campbell.

- B2 Neil Murchison Campbell, m. Euphemia MacKenzie (Effie).
  - C1 James Arthur Campbell, Sr., m. Ethel Letitia Rogers.
    - D1 James Arthur Campbell, Jr., m. Alice Ellen Fitzgerald.
      - E1 Kevin James Campbell, m. Susan Darrough.
        - F1 Michael Wyndham Darrough Campbell.
        - F2 Paul Aaron Campbell.
      - E2 Jon Brian Campbell.
      - E3 Ellen Letitia Campbell, m. Dave Birdie.
        - F1 Kaitlyn Campbell-Birdie.
        - F2 Jamie Campbell-Birdie.
      - E4 Robert Gordon Campbell, m. Lisa Wood.
        - F1 Brennan Campbell.
        - F2 Christopher Scott Campbell.
        - F3 Erin J. Campbell.
    - D2 John Gordon Campbell (Jack), m. (1) Beverly [?].
      - E1 Sally Campbell.

      John Gordon m. (2) Barbara [?].
    - D3 Donald Bruce Campbell, m. Mary Ann Lind.
      - E1 Sharon Campbell, m. (1) Richard Guthrie, (2) Michael Cain.
      - E2 Cindy Campbell, m. Ted Ackley.
      - E3 Jim Campbell, m. Sue Rambert.
      - E4 Donald Campbell, m. Jill Tyson.
  - C2 John Clarence Campbell, m. Helen Story.
    - D1 John Collins Campbell.
    - D2 Jean Campbell, m. Robert Ernest Roman.
      - E1 Shirley Jeanne Roman.
      - E2 Lolly Story Roman, m. Chris Sangster.
        - F1 Teague Colin Sangster.
      - E3 Christina Campbell Roman, m. George Lee.
  - C3 Myrtle Euphemia Campbell, m. Hubert Little.
    - D1 Alice Jean Little, m. Laurence Ainsworth.
      - E1 Timothy Ainsworth, m. Karen Leaf.
      - E2 Jean Ainsworth, m. [?] Dennis.
        - F1 Ariel Dennis.
        - F2 Rachiel Dennis.
      - E3 Lorraine Ainsworth.

      E4 Bill Ainsworth, m. Kathryn Olmstead.
         F1 Julie Ainsworth.
         F2 Sarah Ainsworth.
         F3 Isabella Ainsworth.
    D2 Eva Rose Little.
  C4 Donald Neil Campbell, m. Delphia Moore.
  C5 Glen Stuart Campbell, m. Maybelle Dalton.
  C6 Falconer Everett Campbell, Sr., m. Gladys Hawkins.
    D1 Falconer Everette Campbell, Jr. (Oscar), m. Virginia Lee Howells.
      E1 Franklin Everette Campbell, m. Margaret Ann Hoeflich.
         F1 Alexander Everette Campbell.
         F2 Katherine Taylor Campbell.
         F3 Samantha Ann Campbell.
         F4 Christina Grace Campbell.
      E2 David Stuart Campbell, m. Heather Lynn Catherwood.
         F1 Scott Daniel Campbell.
         F2 Jeffrey Stuart Campbell.
         F3 Holly Anne Campbell.
         F4 Bradley David Campbell.
      E3 Michael Phillip Campbell, m. Delia Jimenez.
         F1 Adam Frank Campbell.
         F2 Ally Virginia Campbell.
    D2 Robert Douglas Campbell, m. Margie MacKenzie.
      E1 Kenneth Campbell.
      E2 Kirk Campbell, m. Connie Borg.
         F1 Kyle Campbell.
         F2 MacKenzie Campbell.
      E3 Douglas Campbell, m. Monica Lichter.
         F1 Taylor Campbell.
         F2 Lindsay Campbell.
  C7 Walter Campbell.
B3 Euphemia Campbell, m. Peter Murchison.
  C1 John Alexander Murchison, m. [?] Davis.
    D1 George Murchison.
    D2 Neil Murchison.
    D3 Euphemia Murchison (Grace), m. George Stowe.
      E1 Janet Murchison Stowe, m. Philip Shelby.

                F1   Stewart Shelby.
         E2   Alan Walker Stowe.
C2 Sarah Murchison (Sadie), m. Angus A. MacDonald.
C3 Simon Malcolm Murchison, m. Mary Ellen Park.
    D1   Peter Murchison, m. Albina [?].
    D2   Malcolm Murchison (Mac).
         E1   Ann Murchison, m. [?] Babb.
         E2   Randy Murchison.
         E3   Donald Murchison.
         E4   Brian Murchison.
    D3   Euphemia Murchison (Phemie), m. Clifford Stevenson.
         E1   James Stevenson (Jim).
         E2   Garth Stevenson.
    D4   Nellie Murchison, m. William MacIntosh.
         E1   Barry MacIntosh.
    D5   Myrtle Murchison, m. [?].
         E1   Wilfred.
         E2   Kenneth (Ken).
         E3   Larry.
         E4   Marie Rose.
C4 John Neil Murchison, m. Elizabeth Hennebury.
    D1   Murdoch Pringle Murchison, m. Doris Emma Butts.
         E1   David Carlson Murchison (Carl).
         E2   James Pringle Murchison (Jamie).
         E3   Laurie Bruce Murchison.
         E4   Heather Anne Murchison.
    D2   Robert Murchison, m. Katherine [?] (Kay).
         E1   Irene Murchison.
         E2   Earl Murchison.
         E3   Robert Murchison.
         E4   Donna Murchison.
    D3   Carl Murchison, m. Elizabeth Hill (Libby).
         E1   Deborah Murchison.
         E2   Ross Murchison.
         E3   Leslie Murchison.
    D4   Gordon Murchison, m. Mary [?.]
    D5   Lloyd Murchison, m. Catherine Day.
         E1   Glenn Murchison.
         E2   Neil Murchison.

                    E3   Michael Murchison.
              D6   Isabell Murchison.
        C5   Murdock M. Murchison, m. Florence Gadsby.
              D1   Peter James Murchison, m. Albina [?].
              D2   Joseph Murchison.
              D3   Donald Murchison.
        C6   Donald Murchison.
        C7   James Murchison, m. Maude [?].
        C8   Joseph Murchison.
        C9   Euphemia Murchison, m. Gerard De LeMarr Hopkins.
              D1   Joan Eleanor Hopkins, m. Donald Edward Smith.
                    E1   Donald Campbell Smith, m. Debra-Jo Weber.
                    E2   Ann Brew Smith, m. Robert Merrill Woodworth.
                          F1   Caroline Campbell Woodworth.
                          F2   Neil Smith Woodworth.
              D2   Jean Louise Hopkins, m. Lawrence C. Kief.
                    E1   Kathryn Marie Kief, m. Millard Dority.
                          F1   Heather Dority.
                          F2   Deidre Dority, m. Adam Bishop.
                                G1   Greta Dority Bishop.
                    E2   Karen Murchison Kief, m. Peter Cole.
                    E3   David Lawrence Kief, m. Chris Kirk.
                          F1   Joseph Lawrence Kief.
                          F2   Amelia M. Kief.
        C10   Mary Isabella Murchison, m. Robert MacAllister.
              D1   Robert Murchison MacAllister, m. Marjorie Linley [?].
                    E1   Sandra Murchison MacAllister.
                    E2   Lynn Marie Murchison MacAllister.
                    E3   Thomas MacAllister.
B4   Christy Ann Campbell, m. Hugh Martin.
      C1   Euphemia Martin.
      C2   Flora Ann Martin, m. (1) William Gordon MacLeod.
            D1   Euphemia MacLeod, m. John P. Jordan (Jack).
                  E1   Ann Jordan, m. Alfred Anastasiou.
                        F1   Christina Anastasiou.
                        F2   Juliana Anastasiou.
                  E2   Grace Jordan, m. Robert Slawkinski.
                        F1   Sarah Slawinski.

    F2 John Slawinski.
  E3 Margaret Jordan, m. Craig Bixler.
    F1 Emily Bixler.
    F2 Jordan Bixler.
    F3 Lauren Bixler.
Flora Ann (C2) m. (2) Henry Lloyd Robbins.
D2 James Henry Lloyd Robbins, m. (1) Ruth Turner.
  E1 William Robbins (Bill), m. Christine [?].
  E2 Paula Robbins, m. Mark Swim.
  E3 Jill Robbins, m. Bill Malloy.
  E4 Jonathan Robbins, married.
  James Henry m. (2) Alice Lethbridge.
D3 Hugh Martin Robbins, m. Helen Margaret Behm.
  E1 Helen Anne Robbins, m. Harvey MacEwen.
    F1 Charles Edward MacEwen (Ted), m. Nadia Authier.
      G1 Gabrielle Rebecca MacEwen.
    F2 John Harvey MacEwen.
    F3 Margaret Roseanne MacEwen (Peggy).
    F4 Robert Hugh MacEwen.
  E2 Teryl Hugh Robbins (Terry), m. Doris Neimer.
    F1 Jennifer Marie Robbins.
    F2 Christopher Hugh Robbins.
  E3 Donald Lloyd Robbins (Donnie), m. Frances Gormley.
    F1 Sherri Lynn Robbins (child of Frances, adopted by Donald).
    F2 Joseph Lloyd Robbins (Joey), m. Esther Carroll.
      G1 Brennan Timothy Joseph Robbins (twin of Griffin).
      G2 Griffon Donald Lloyd Robbins (twin of Brennan).
    F3 Pamela Marie Robbins (Pam).
  E4 Leslie Harold Robbins (Les), m. Kathy Whatmore (née Herrington).
    F1 Hugh Martin Robbins.

      F2 Garrett William Robbins.
      F3 Marilyn Grace Robbins.
   E5 Joyce Lorraine Robbins, m. Michael Cavanagh (Mike).
      F1 Brendan Shanley Cavanagh.
      F2 Keelan Michael Cavanagh.
      F3 Connor Hugh Cavanagh.
   E6 Philip John Robbins (Phil), m. Faye MacKinnon.
      F1 Ellen Marion Robbins.
D4 Florence Ellen Robbins (Flo), m. Haywood William MacLean.
   E1 Carl Lydell MacLean.
   E2 Sterling MacLean, m. Mary Ellen [?].
      F1 Mark MacLean.
      F2 Shawn MacLean.
      F3 Marvin MacLean.
      F4 Jeff MacLean.
      F5 Jennifer MacLean.
   E3 Lester MacLean.
   E4 Darrell Lloyd MacLean.
   E5 Darlene Catherine MacLean.
   E6 Sharon Lynn MacLean.
D5 John Campbell Robbins, m. (1) Emily Mildred Martin.
   E1 Lloyd Winston Robbins.
   E2 David Martin Robbins, m. Lesley Budge.
      F1 Corrie Robbins (twin of Christopher).
      F2 Christopher Robbins (Chris, twin of Corrie).
      F3 Kirsten Robbins.
   E3 Jacqueline Goss Robbins, m. Bob Lane.
      F1 Darlene Lane, m. Steve Fournier.
         G1 Ashley Fournier.
         G2 Natalie Fournier.
         G3 Eric Fournier.
      F2 Laurie Lane.
      F3 Emily Lane.
John (D5) m. (2) Carol [?].

- D6 Alexander Robbins (Sterling), m. Sheila Mary MacKinnon.
  - E1 Paul Robbins Vaughn, m. Stacey [?].
    - F1 James Vaughn.
    - F2 Kathryn Vaughn.
    - F3 Emily Meagan Vaughn.
  - E2 Kathy Robbins, m. Michael Whiteway.
    - F1 April Whiteway.
    - F2 Sara Whiteway.
    - F3 Matthew Whiteway.
    - F4 William Whiteway (Billy).
  - E3 Robert Robbins (Robbie).
- D7 Harry Robbins (Elwood), m. Marion Euphemia MacDougall.
  - E1 Gary Elwood Robbins, m. Diana Boyer.
    - F1 Mark Robbins.
    - F2 Aaron Robbins.
  - E2 David Alan Robbins, m. Natalie [?].
  - E3 Melinda Robbins, m. Peter Wolters.
    - F1 Grant Wolters.
    - F2 Isaac Wolters.
- D8 Preston Sanford Robbins, m. Charlotte Winifred Gosse (Winnie).
  - E1 Peter Sandford Robbins, m. Faith Barbara Tiller.
    - F1 Tonia Gloria Robbins (child of Faith, adopted by Peter).
    - F2 Rebecca Charlotte Robbins.
    - F3 Meagan Patricia Robbins.
    - F4 James Sandford Robbins.
  - E2 Jeffrey David Robbins, m. Rhonda Mildred Young.
    - F1 Benjamin Mildred Young.
    - F2 Allyson Lynn Robbins.
  - E3 Karen Lynn Robbins, m. David Spowart.
- C3 John Campbell Martin.
- C4 Donald Martin, m. Emily MacKay.
  - D1 Marjorie Donalda Martin, m. James Paynter.
    - E1 Rachel Paynter.
    - E2 James Paynter (Gary), m. Velda Laird.

      F1 Pam Paynter, m. Michael James (Mike).
        G1 Harrison James.
        G2 [Daughter].
      F2 Grant Paynter.
      F3 Dawn Paynter.
      F4 Crystal Paynter.
    E3 Garth Martin Paynter, m. Margaret Elizabeth Cotton (Beth).
      F1 James Garth Paynter.
      F2 Leslie John Paynter, m. Lily Catherine Wildy.
        G1 Karla Wildy.
    E4 Daniel Norris Paynter, m. Marie DesRoches.
      F1 Rachel Paynter.
      F2 Christopher Paynter, m. Phyllis [?].
      F3 Kendall Paynter.
 C5 Emily Campbell Martin, twin to Sarah (Sadie), m. Arthur Ladner.
    D1 Hugh Ladner, m. Bea [?].
    D2 Claude W. Ladner (Cal), m. Helen Gifford.
    D3 Helen Ladner, m. [?] Nagel.
 C6 Sarah Catherine Martin (Sadie), twin to Emily.
 C7 Ernest Martin, m. Reta Florence Hicken.
    D1 Margaret Christine Martin, m. (1) Jon Miller MacDonald.
      E1 Ian MacDonald, m. Deborah Beaton (Debbie).
        F1 Joel MacDonald.
        F2 Benjamin Luke MacDonald.
      E2 Susan MacDonald, m. Joe Mouris.
        F1 Margaret Catherine Johanna Mouris.
        F2 Joanna Mouris.
      E3 Kirsten MacDonald, m. Frank Drew.
    Margaret (D1) m. (2) Ninian LeBlanc.
    D2 George Martin, m. Marjorie Volk.
      E1 David Martin.
      E2 Catherine Martin.
      E3 Karen Martin.
    D3 Muriel Martin, m. William Davis (Bill).

		E1	Bill Davis, Jr.

- E1 Bill Davis, Jr.
- E2 Anne Davis.
- E3 Carol Davis.
- E4 Wendy Davis.
- D4 John Campbell Martin.
- C8 Margaret Irene Martin, m. Fred Carroll.

B5 James Murdoch Campbell, m. Margaret Catherine MacLeod.
- C1 Euphemia Campbell, m. Edward Jackson.
- C2 John MacLeod Campbell.
- C3 Flora Campbell.
- C4 Mary Campbell, m. Martin Mathies.
- C5 Ann Campbell, m. Claude Spousa.
- C6 Gertrude Campbell, m. C.A. Weethmouth.

B6 Samuel Campbell, m. (1) Catherine MacLeod. Obituaries of of Catherine MacLeod and Samuel Campbell may be found in the appendix.
- C1 John Campbell, m. Edith Anne MacNeill.
  - D1 Samuel Ewen Campbell, m. Norma Trodden.
    - E1 John Campbell, m. Margaret Hayes.
      - F1 Samuel John Campbell.
      - F2 William Isaac Campbell.
      - F3 Simon Thomas Campbell.
      - F4 Maria Elise Campbell.
    - E2 Donald Campbell, m. Ruth Coleman.
      - F1 Andrea Rebecca Campbell.
      - F2 Ashley Elizabeth Campbell.
      - F3 Abraham Samuel Campbell.
    - E3 Douglas Campbell, m. Wendy Bogstie.
      - F1 Michael Dale Campbell.
      - F2 David James Campbell.
      - F3 Amy Pearl Campbell.
    - E4 Marilyn Jane Campbell, m. Pierre Romeo Sincennes.
      - F1 Nicholas Alexander Sincennes.
      - F2 Benjamin Samuel Sincennes.
      - F3 Emily Elizabeth Sincennes.
  - D2 Donald Campbell (Roy), m. Olive Harris (Maida).
    - E1 James Harris Campbell, m. Virginia Brown.
      - F1 Corey Jean Campbell.
      - F2 Derek Roy Campbell.

- E2 Ian Hugh Campbell, m. Marie-Claude Marchessault.
  - F1 Genevieve Marie-France Campbell.
  - F2 Julie Anne Campbell.
  - F3 Florence Campbell.
- E3 Catherine Grace Campbell (Cathy), m. Michael Ungar (Mike).
  - F1 Scott Ungar Campbell.
  - F2 Megan Marcellina Ungar Campbell (Meg).
- E4 Heather Ann Campbell, m. Joseph Driscoll (Joe).
  - F1 Vanessa Driscoll.
  - F2 Jason Driscoll.

D3 Rebecca Catherine Campbell, m. Ronald Edgar Williams.
- E1 Katherine Anne Williams (Kathy), m. (1) John Ryan McKenzie.
  - F1 Elizabeth Anne McKenzie Fleming (adopted by John, below), m. Keith Christopher Redmond.
    - G1 Grace Leslie Faith Redmond.
    - G2 Brooke Katharine Redmond (twin to Elizabeth).
    - G3 Elizabeth Florence Redmond (Beth, twin to Brooke).
    - G4 Jack Christopher Fleming Redmond (adopted).
  - F2 David Ryan McKenzie, m. Teresa Martine Bogle.
    - G1 Keira Grace McKenzie.
  - F3 Rebecca Leslie McKenzie.

  Katherine (E1) m. (2) John Cuthbertson Fleming (Jack).
  - F4 Jason William Fleming (stepson to Katherine).
- E2 Ronald Williams (Winton), m. Elaine Naugler.

The Descendants of James Campbell and Christy MacDonald

              F1   Kimberley Sandra Williams, m. Steven Ulchek.
- G1   Brody Ulchek (twin to Jared).
- G2   Jared Ulchek (twin to Brody).

              F2   Benjamin Michael Williams, m. Cindy Louise Bryant.
- G1   Kelly Victoria Elaine Williams.
- G2   Mitchell Benjamin Williams.

       E3   Julie Elizabeth Williams (Elizabeth), m. Gordon Alfred Tarras.
- F1   Jefferson James Tarras.
- F2   Andrea Leigh Tarras, m. Keegan Douglas Kermode.
  - G1   Cole David Kermode.

       E4   Andrew James Williams, m. Karen Lee Sharun.
- F1   Collin Michael Williams.
- F2   Mark David Williams.
- F3   Carlene Marie Williams.

    D4   Clarence Murdoch Campbell, m. Dot Bussey.
- E1   Evelyn Anne Campbell, m. Stephen Miller (Steve).
  - F1   Charlotte Louise Miller.
  - F2   Jack Thomas Miller.
- E2   John Campbell.

    D5   Sheldon James Campbell.

    D6   Eva Elizabeth Campbell, m. Marcel Pronovost.

C2   Euphemia Campbell (Etta), m. Allan Campbell Stewart (see A1-B4-C9, p. 18).

C3   Mary Isabel Campbell.

C4   Sadie Jeanette Campbell.

C5   Ada Ruth Campbell, m. William Benson (Bill).
- D1   Barbara Benson, m. [?] Caldwell.
  - E1   Laurel Caldwell.
  - E2   Eric Caldwell.

C6   Eva Emily Campbell, m. Samuel Watson Cantelo (Sam).
- D1   Joan Beverly Cantelo, m. Dwight Alva Kellogg.

    E1 Kim Kellogg, m. Alan Daniel Devoe.
      F1 Malcolm Devoe.
      F2 Cameron Devoe.
      F3 Bryce Devoe.
    E2 David Dwight Kellogg.
    E3 Jenny Elizabeth Kellogg.
  C7 John Donald Campbell (Wilfred), m. Mary Margaret MacLean.
    D1 Samuel Wilfred Campbell (Buddy), m. Noreen O'Laughlin.
      E1 Ronald David Campbell.
      E2 John Malcolm Campbell.
      E3 David Alan Campbell.
    D2 John Ronald Campbell.
    D3 Everett Glen Campbell, m. Evelyn Tessneer.
      E1 Wayne Alan Campbell.
    D4 Edward Watson Campbell.
    D5 Donald William Campbell, m. Esther Avallana Palerma (Tet).
      E1 Jonathan Donald Campbell.
      E2 Matthew Martin Campbell.
      E3 Jeremiah Andrew Campbell.
    D6 Cheryl Marie Campbell MacLean.
  Samuel (B6) m. (2) Isabel MacLeod.
B7 Emily Campbell.
B8 Simon Donald Campbell, m. (1) Margaret Bruce.
  C1 John Chester Campbell.
  C2 Alexander Bruce Campbell.
  C3 Euphemia Campbell, m. Gordon Morrison.
    D1 Dorothy Margaret Morrison.
  C4 James Arthur Campbell.
    D1 James Reginald Campbell.
  C5 Jessie Florence Campbell, m. Parker MacDougall.
    D1 Parker MacDougall (Donald).
  C6 Margaret Bruce Campbell, m. Archibald MacKinnon.
  Simon Donald m. (2) Mary Jane MacDonald.
A3 Margaret Campbell, m. Alexander Stewart (Sandy).
  B1 Christy Stewart, m. Angus Norman MacLeod.
  B2 Catherine Stewart, twin of Christy, m. Malcolm D. MacDonald.
  B3 Donald Stewart, m. Sarah Ann Campbell (Marion), see A1-B4, p. 18.

- B4 James Stewart, m. Euphemia Murchison.
    - C1 Donald Alexander Stewart.
    - C2 Neil Donald Stewart.
    - C3 Alexander Stewart, m. [?] Smith.
    - C4 John Stewart.
    - C5 Simon Stewart.
    - C6 Margaret Stewart, never married.
    - C7 Annie Stewart.
- B5 Neil Stewart.
- B6 Margaret Stewart.
- B7 John N. Stewart.
- B8 Donald Stewart (Dan), m. Abigail Bertha Ross.
    - C1 Roberta Lillian Stewart (Berta).
    - C2 Ross Stewart.
    - C3 Campbell Stewart.
    - C4 Ruth Stewart, m. George Kidd.
    - C5 Baden Powell Stewart.
    - C6 Maynard Stewart.
    - C7 Arlene Stewart.
    - C8 Donald Stewart.
        - D1 Beverly Stewart, raised by her grandmother, Abigail Bertha Ross Stewart (B8, above).
    - C9 Lawrence Stewart.
- B9 Alan Stewart, m. Isabel MacLeod.
    - C1 Carroll Stewart.
    - C2 MacLeod Stewart.
- B10 Emily Stewart, m. Harry Maynard.
    - C1 Margaret Maynard.
    - C2 Eva Maynard.
    - C3 Catherine Maynard.

A4 Sarah Campbell (Marion), m. Samuel Martin.
- B1 Margaret Martin, m. John Martin.
    - C1 Margaret Martin.
- B2 Hugh Martin, m. Emma Balzer.
    - C1 Sarah Margaret Martin, m. Ludwig Larsen.
        - D1 Eric Larsen, m. Helen Healy.
            - E1 Christine Larsen, m. Jeffry Eisenbooth.
            - E2 Christopher Larsen, m. Randine Jaastad.
                - F1 Todd Ludwig Larsen.
                - F2 Andrew Thomas.
                - F3 Heide Marie Larsen.

      F4 Erika Larsen.
    E3 Amy Lyn Larsen.
    E4 Anders Thomas Larsen.
  D2 Malcolm Larsen.
  D3 Edward Larsen, m. Marion Ivy.
  D4 John Larsen.
  D5 Robert Larsen.
C2 Neil Martin.
C3 Catherine Martin, m. William Bishop.
  D1 David Bishop, m. May Barber.
    E1 Becky Lyn Bishop.
  D2 Janice Bishop, m. [?] Quigley.
    E1 John Henry Quigley, m. Margy [?.]
      F1 Michael Quigley, m. Joan [?].
      F2 Catherine Quigley.
      F3 [Third child].
  D3 Esther Bishop, m. Sol Draznin.
    E1 Martin Draznin, m. [?].
      F1 Charlie Draznin.
    E2 Debra Draznin, m. Ken Texara.
      F1 Ben Texara.
      F2 Jake Texara.
    E3 James Draznin, m. Lorely French.
      F1 Leif James Draznin.
    E4 Katherine Draznin.
C4 May Bertha Martin, m. James A. Burner.
  D1 May Margaret Burner, m. (1) George Bradley.
    E1 James Michael Bradley, m. Sylvia [?].
      F1 Alesia Bradley.
      F2 James Bradley, Jr. (Rusty), m. Brenda [?].
        G1 Allison Bradley.
        G2 Joshua Bradley.
        G3 Carolyn Joyce Bradley.
      F3 Todd Bradley, m. Andrea [?].
        G1 Amanda Bradley.
    E2 Barbara Jean Bradley, m. (1) Robert Furst.
      F1 James Furst, m. (1) Carol McGrew.
        G1 Natalie Furst.
      James m. (2) Shelley Feinburg.
        G2 Sarah Jane Furst.

James (F1) m. (3) Kim [?].
           G3   George Bradley Furst.
           G4   James Kadden Furst.
        Barbara (E2) m. (2) Gildo Ferraro.
   E3   Dennis Patrick Bradley, m. (1) Nancy [?].
        F1   Hugh Bradley.
        F2   Hal Bradley.
        Dennis m. (2) Nancy [?].
   E4   Sharon Ann Bradley, m. Thayne MacDonald.
        F1   Douglas MacDonald.
   E5   Richard Allen Bradley, m. Georgiann [?].
   May Margaret (D1) m. (2) Joseph Phillip.
   E6   Kathy Phillip, m. Douglas Trudeau.
        F1   Justin Trudeau.
   May Margaret m. (3) Henry Culpepper.
D2   James Burner, m. Margaret Booth.
D3   Hugh Burner, m. Marie [?].
   E1   Hugh Burner.
D4   Richard Burner, m. Pat [?].
C5 John Arthur Martin, m. (1) Ella Hoffman.
   D1   Hugh Martin, m. Doris Martin (Barbara).
        E1   Douglas Martin, m. Carol Traxler.
             F1   Kevin Martin (adopted).
             F2   Ryan Martin.
        E2   Denis Martin, m. Deborah Miller.
        E3   Bruce Martin, m. Kathy McKenna.
   D2   Lois Martin, m. Samuel McCully.
        E1   Karen McCully, m. Se June Hong.
             F1   Kessely Hong, m. Ted Hong.
                  G1   Gabriel Hong.
                  G2   Caleb Hong.
        E2   Samuel McCully, m. (1) Genie Lambourn.
             F1   Samuel McCully.
             F2   Lucas McCully.
             Samuel m. (2) Cindy [?].
        E3   Alan McCully, m. [?].
             F1   MacKenzie McCully, m. James Pryer.
             F2   Megan McCully, m. Brett Benson.
                  G1   Braun Benson.

                    F3   Charles McCully.
               E4   Susan McCully, m. Timothy Rychel.
                    F1   Katherine Rychel.
                    F2   Madeline Rychel.
          John Arthur (C5) m. (2) Christine Brezenski.
B3   John Samuel Martin, m. Harriet MacKenzie (Hattie).
     C1   Sarah Margaret Martin.
     C2   Mary Emily Martin, m. Alexander MacLeod.
          D1   Jessie MacLeod, m. M. Arthur MacLeod.
               E1   David MacLeod.
               E2   Donald MacLeod.
               E3   Roger MacLeod.
          D2   John MacLeod.
     C3   Annie Campbell Martin, m. (1) William Albert Jenkins, (2) Ewen Gillis.
     C4   Samuel Martin, m. Mary Martin MacLeod.
          D1   Sarah Martin (Sadie), m. Al Coventry.
               E1   John Coventry.
          D2   MacLeod Martin (Mac), m. Alfreda Rogers.
               E1   John Martin, m. Geraldine [?].
                    F1   Cheryl Martin.
                    F2   Heather Martin.
                    F3   Daniel Martin.
               E2   Elaine Martin, m. Earl Zimmerman.
                    F1   Patricia Zimmerman.
                    F2   Daryl Zimmerman.
               E3   Marabel Martin, m. Greg Hetherington.
                    F1   Lisa Hetherington.
                    F2   Gerald Hetherington.
          D3   William Alexander Martin (Billy).
          D4   Doris Martin, m. Harold Crossman.
               E1   Samuel Crossman.
               E2   Michael Crossman.
               E3   Cindy Crossman.
          D5   Evelyn Martin, m. (1) John Dunlop, (2) John Greenshields.
               E1   Wayne Greenshields.
               E2   Wanda Greenshields.
               E3   John Greenshields.
               E4   Donna Greenshields.
          D6   Annie Mae Martin, m. Everett James MacDougall.

- E1 William Everett Noel MacDougall, m. (1) Margaret Isbel MacInnis.
  - F1 Everett Noel Gregory MacDougall.
  - F2 Deneen MacDougall, m. Bruce Ferguson.
    - G1 Megan Ferguson.

  William m. (2) Margaret MacKenzie.
- E2 [Infant son].
- E3 [Infant daughter].
- E4 [Infant].

D7 Leida Jane Martin, m. Clifford Hayden Lea.
- E1 Paul Dingwell Lea, m. Carol [?].
  - F1 John Lea.
  - F2 Paul Lea.
- E2 Glenda Ferne Lea, m. Robert Steeves.
  - F1 Roberta Steeves.
  - F2 Shane Steeves (twin).
  - F3 [Twin brother to Shane].
  - F4 Lorne Steeves.
  - F5 Regan Steeves.
  - F6 Monty Steeves.
- E3 Mary Jane Lea, m. Fred Grant.
- E4 Dorothy Lea, m. Gary Fisher.

D8 Lloyd Martin, m. Lucinda MacInnis (Dickie).
- E1 Barry Malcolm Martin, m. Sharleen Lamb.
  - F1 William Barry Martin (Billy).
  - F2 Mary Bethany Martin.
- E2 Clayton Lloyd Martin, m. Janet LaFerte.
  - F1 Jennifer Lynn Martin.
- E3 Debra Anne Martin, m. Charles Thomas.
  - F1 Michael Charles Thomas.
  - F2 Laurie Anne Thomas, m. Ryan Brehaut.
    - G1 Noah Thomas Brehaut.
- E4 Donald Irwin Martin, m. Lorie Volker.
  - F1 Vanessa Lorraine Volker.

D9 Donald Martin, m. (1) Viola [?].
- E1 Leslie Martin.
- E2 Cheryl Martin.
- E3 [Daughter].

Donald (D9) m. (2) Ila [?].
- D10 Donna Mary Martin, m. Erroll Lloyd Green.
  - E1 Lorna Green.
  - E2 Heather Green.
  - E3 Wendy Green.
- C5 John W. Martin.
- C6 Hugh James Martin, m. Bessie Goss MacPhee.
  - D1 Annie Martin (Joyce), m. Perley Sterling Drake.
    - E1 Gary Francis Drake.
    - E2 William Drake (Allison), m. Ardyth Sherwood.
      - F1 Rodney Trevor Drake, m. Karen [?].
        - G1 Ethan Drake.
      - F2 Adenara Gail Drake.
      - F3 Gregory Tyler Drake.
    - E3 John Drake (Melvin), m. Katherine Jean Cummings (Jean).
      - F1 Shelly Marie Drake.
      - F2 Ryan Sterling Drake, m. Marin MacCallum.
        - G1 Aiden John Drake.
      - F3 Courtney Jean Drake, m. Clinton Myers.
        - G1 Cameron John Myers.
    - E4 Derrell Hugh Drake, m. Mary Snow.
    - E5 Florence Darlene Drake, m. Robert Hennessey.
      - F1 Connor Robert Hennessy.
      - F2 Daniel Drake Hennessy.
      - F3 Catherine Hennessy.
    - E6 Sheila Drake (Gwen), m. John Chow.
      - F1 Sarah Elizabeth Chow.
      - F2 Laura Christina Chow.
    - E7 Cindy Dianne Drake, m. Michael Gaudet.
  - D2 Emily Mildred Martin, m. John Campbell Robbins (see A2-B4-C2-D5, p. 34).
  - D3 John Douglas Martin (Doug), m. Annabella D. Youngston (Ann).
    - E1 Deborah Ann Martin (Debbie), m. Douglas Wright.

- F1 Michael Douglas Wright.
- F2 Amanda Christine Wright.
- E2 William Hugh Martin (Billy), m. Kathy Lily.
  - F1 Jesse William Martin.
  - F2 Molly Heather Martin Bauer.
- E3 Troy Douglas Martin, m. Susie Seara.
  - F1 Hunter Joseph Martin.
  - F2 Kendra Diane Martin.
- D4 Mary Noreen Martin (Molly), m. Donald William Drake.
  - E1 Barbara Dianne Drake.
  - E2 Paul Douglas Drake, m. Vivian Eileen Oakes.
    - F1 Austin Donald Drake (twin of Ian).
    - F2 Ian Frederick Drake (twin of Austin).
    - F3 Vivian Lynn Drake (Lynn).
  - E3 Larry Wade Drake, m. Karen Louise Gregor.
    - F1 Nicholas Larry Drake.
    - F2 Jill Caroline Drake.
  - E4 Leslie Randall Drake, m. Dorothy Christina Shaw.
    - F1 Adam Randall Drake.
    - F2 Patrick Donald Drake.
    - F3 Sarah Christina Drake.
- D5 Robert Winston Martin, m. Joan Catherine Correy.
  - E1 Joanne Lynn Martin, m. Michael Grier.
    - F1 Sydney Grier.
    - F2 Wesley Grier.
  - E2 Holly Alana Martin, m. Maurat Beshtoev.
    - F1 Olivia Beshtoev.
- D6 Edith Dianne Martin.
- C7 James Boyce Martin, m. Katherine Bruce (Katie).
  - D1 Loren Boyce Martin, m. Margaret Casey.
    - E1 Arlene Martin, m. Anthony Taylor.
  - D2 Emily Christine Martin, m. Joseph Harold White.
    - E1 Loren Harold White (Hal), m. Ann Denise Rhodenhizer.

F1 Shawn Martin White.
F2 Derek Stephen White.
E2 Patricia Catherine White (Patsy), m. (1) Anthony Ronald Brown.
F1 Jennifer Catherine Brown.
Patricia m. (2) Joseph Gerard Hebert Lelievre.
F2 Kim James Lelievre.
E3 Emily White (Gail).
D3 Alexander MacLeod Martin (Buster).
D4 Marilyn Anne Martin, m. (1) William Roy Murnaghan (Bill).
E1 Sheryl Lee Murnaghan (Sherry).
E2 Jorel James Roy Murnaghan.
Marilyn m. (2) Gary Kenneth Milne.
B4 Christy Ann Martin, m. George Wood.
C1 Emma Martin, m. Boyce MacKie.
D1 Dorothy MacKie.
D2 Harold H. Mackie, m. (1) Rhena Louise Cameron.
E1 Carolyn MacKie (Joyce).
Harold m. (2) Marion Emily Martin.
D3 Jean MacKie.
D4 Wilbur MacKie.
B5 Catherine Martin, m. Kenneth MacLean.
C1 Margaret B. MacLean.
C2 Samuel Martin MacLean.
C3 Sarah Janette MacLean, m. Alexander Matheson.
D1 Catherine Matheson.
D2 Florence Matheson.
D3 Ruth Matheson.
C4 Angus William MacLean.
C5 Margaret MacLean (Ella), m. Thomas Richards MacLean.
D1 Catherine MacLean (Jean), m. George Pickard (Keith).
E1 George Thomas Pickard.
E2 Ellen Carolyn Pickard, m. John Barry Cudmore.
F1 Carrie Jeanne Cudmore.
F2 Heather Ruth Cudmore.
F3 Andrew Keith Cudmore.
F4 Peter Clayton Cudmore.

- E3 Barbara Jean Pickard, m. Blair Robert MacDonald.
  - F1 Catherine Pauline MacDonald.
  - F2 Alexander Blair Ronald MacDonald.
  - F3 Keith Thomas MacDonald.
- E4 Deborah Lynn Pickard.
- E5 Doris Ruth Pickard.

D2 Anna Elizabeth MacLean, m. John Allan Shaw.
- E1 Ian Ernest Shaw, m. Catherine MacEachern.
  - F1 Jonathan Alexander Shaw.
- E2 Paul Thomas Shaw, m. Elizabeth Pendergast (Liz).
  - F1 Madeline Donalda Anne Shaw.
- E3 Margaret Elizabeth Shaw (Beth), m. Paul MacDonald.
  - F1 Sarah Anne MacDonald.
  - F2 Mary Catherine MacDonald (Kate).
  - F3 Grace Elizabeth MacDonald.

D3 Ruth Agnes MacLean, m. Weston George MacLeod.
- E1 Cheryl Ann MacLeod, m. David French.
  - F1 Tamara Ann French (Tammy).
  - F2 Mark David French.
  - F3 Laura Ruth French.
- E2 Roberta Ruth MacLeod, m. (1) Sandy Briant.
  - F1 MacLean Alexander Briant.
  - F2 Heather Rose Briant.

  Roberta Ruth m. (2) Robert Brignell.
  - F3 Jonathan Charles Thomas Brignell.
  - F4 Robert Charles Thomas Brignell.
- E3 Katherine Ella MacLeod, m. John Payne.
  - F1 Jeffrey William Payne.
  - F2 Nathan Miller Payne.
- E4 Heather May MacLeod, m. Mark Gauvin.
  - F1 Adrienne Weston Gauvin (Scott).
  - F2 Charles Eric Gauvin (Eric).
  - F3 Danielle Heather Gauvin.

        E5   Pauline Jessica MacLeod, m. Rick Farley.
              F1   Connor Weston MacLeod Farley.
              F2   Neala Siobhan Farley.
        E6   Joan Agnes MacLeod, m. Peter Follows.
              F1   Benjamin Peter Follows.
              F2   Dalton Thomas Follows.
        E7   Dianna Jean MacLeod, m. Tara McMahon.
              F1   Jessica Lane Diana McMahon.
              F2   Kyle Weston John McMahon.
    D4   James Kenneth MacLean, m. (1) Kay [?], (2) Mary Elaine James.
        E1   Michael MacLean.
    D5   Arthur Martin MacLean.
    D6   Wallace Henry MacLean, m. Helen Ann Bryan.
        E1   Roderick Thomas MacLean, m. Pamela Dianne Bonnett.
              F1   Sarah Jean MacLean.
              F2   Steven Richard MacLean.
        E2   Charles Bryan MacLean, m. Carol Shore.
              F1   Evan MacLean.
C6   Flora Catherine MacLean, m. George Harrison Rice.
    D1   Elmer Rice, m. Pearle Rowe.
        E1   Barry Rice.
        E2   Allan Rice.
        E3   Marilyn Rice, m. Allan MacLaughlan.
    D2   Wilber Rice.
    D3   Eleanor Rice.
    D4   Wilmot Rice.
    D5   Shirley Rice, m. Richard Holmes.
        E1   Richard Holmes (Paul).
        E2   Shirlene Marilyn Holmes.
        E3   Ronald George Holmes.
        E4   Donald Carlyle Holmes (Carl).
        E5   John Allison Holmes.
        E6   Glen Holmes.
C7   Annie Euphemia MacLean, m. O.R. John Ellis (Jack).
    D1   Gordon Ellis.
    D2   June Ellis.
C8   Donald MacLeod MacLean, m. Annie Beers.
    D1   Robert MacLean.
    D2   Ann MacLean, m. [?] Dillmar.

C9 Malcolm MacLean (Mac), m. Wilhelmina MacMillan.
    D1 Hugh MacMillan MacLean, m. Ada Duncan.
        E1 Susan MacLean.
        E2 Donald MacLean.
    D2 Earl MacLean (Woodrow), m. Irene Douglas Hill.
    D3 Herbert Vickerson MacLean (Vic).
    D4 Rena Myrtle MacLean, m. (1) Forrest Lea.
        E1 George Garth Lea.
    Rena m. (2) Wallace William MacPherson.
        E2 Betty Helena MacPherson.
    D5 Ernest Clinton MacLean, m. Lavenia [?].
C10 Ruth MacLean.
C11 Edwin MacLean (Clarence), m. Edith Marguerite Elizabeth Lane.
    D1 Ruth Laura MacLean, m. Ernest Disney Taylor.
        E1 Malcolm Taylor.
        E2 Bonita Ruth Taylor, m. (1) James MacDonald, (2) Richard Collins.
        E3 Linda Taylor.
        E4 Richard Taylor.
        E5 Karen Leigh Taylor, m. Robert MacLeod.
    D2 George Lane MacLean, m. Mildred Christine MacDonald.
    D3 Edwin Kenneth MacLean.
    D4 Reginald MacLean (Blair).
    D5 Clarence MacLean (Roger), m. Julie [?].
        E1 David Clarence MacLean.
    D6 Glen MacLean, m. Elaine [?].
B6 James Campbell Martin, m. Norma A. Livock.
B7 James Martin, member of a set of triplets.
B8 Emily Martin, triplet of James and Marjorie, m. Fred Beers.
    C1 James Albert Beers Martin. He lived with his uncle, the Rev. James Martin, and changed his name from Beers to Martin. He m. Elsa Heden.
        D1 Linda Martin, m. Donald Simmons.
        D2 June Martin, m. Roger Zaklukieweiz.
            E1 Kirsten Zaklukieweiz.
            E2 Wendy Zaklukieweiz.
            E3 Stephanie Zaklukieweiz.
            E4 Amanda Zaklukieweiz.
        D3 Bruce Martin.

        C2   George Beers.
        C3   Wilbur Beers.
B9   Marjorie Martin, triplet of James and Emily, m. (1) Alexander MacKay.
        C1   Christie Ann MacKay, m. Hugh Barclay.
        C2   Sarah E. MacKay (Sadie), m. Bruce Champion.
        C3   William MacKay, m. Marjorie Stanhope Cortney.
               D1   Paul Arthur MacKay.
               D2   George MacKay.
        C4   Hugh Samuel MacKay, m. Pearle MacKay.
               D1   Ralph MacKay (Scottie), m. Marianne [?].
               D2   Clive Milton MacKay, m. Jean Coffin.
                      E1   Deborah MacKay, m. Bernard O'Rourke.
                             F1   Matthew MacKay O'Rourke.
                             F2   Sarah Jean O'Rourke.
                      E2   Clive MacKay, m. Elizabeth Soper.
                             F1   Aaron Mark MacKay.
                             F2   Brendan Matthew MacKay.
        C5   George MacKay.
        C6   Ruth MacKay, m. Furley Belcher.
        C7   Robert MacKay, m. May Lockart.
               D1   Robert MacKay, m. Hilda Auld.
        C8   Emily MacKay, m. (1) Donald Martin (see A2-B4-C4, p. 35, for children).
        Emily m. (2) Daniel MacDonald.
               D1   Eileen MacDonald, m. (1) Russell MacLean.
                      E1   James MacLean.
                      E2   Laura MacLean.
                      E3   Wanda MacLean, m. Fred Livingstone.
                      E4   Garfield MacLean.
               Eileen m. (2) Arthur MacDonald.
               D2   Donald MacDonald, m. Marie Landry.
                      E1   Ronald MacDonald, m. Rita [?].
                             F1   Rhonda MacDonald.
                             F2   Rae Ann MacDonald.
                             F3   Roma MacDonald.
                      E2   Faye MacDonald.
                      E3   Jerry MacDonald.
                      E4   Mitchell MacDonald.
        Emily (C8) m. (3) Gavin Burgoyne.
        C9   Ernest MacKay, m. Charlotte Forsee.

                D1   Glen MacKay.
        C10   Glen MacKay, m. Evelyn [MacKay].
        C11   James A. MacKay, m. Muriel McNaught.
        Marjorie (B9) m. (2) Lauchlin MacKay.
B10   Sarah Martin, m. John Gunn MacKenzie.
        C1   Charlotte MacKenzie.
        C2   Margaret E. MacKenzie, m. Angus Green.
        C3   Barbara Etta MacKenzie.
        C4   Sarah A. MacKenzie, m. Walter Naylor.
        C5   George Clifton MacLenzie.
        C6   Roberta M. MacKenzie.
        C7   Samuel Martin MacKenzie.
        C8   Euphemia Catherine MacKenzie (Phemie).
        C9   Gladys MacKenzie.
        C10   Norma Adelaide MacKenzie, m. George Wesley Paynter.
                D1   Muriel Paynter, m. Norman MacRae.
                        E1   Adelaide MacRae, m. (1) Allen Clark.
                                F1   Gail Clark, m. Randy MacCaull.
                                        G1   George MacCaull.
                                        G2   William MacCaull.
                                        G3   Donovan MacCaull.
                                F2   Clair Clark, m. Rachael Reeves.
                                        G1   Matthew Clark.
                        Adelaide (E1) m. (2) Elmer MacAusland.
                                F3   Laura MacAusland.
                                        G1   Kale MacAusland.
                                        G2   Tyler MacAusland.
                                        G3   Logan MacAusland.
                        E2   Ann MacRae, m. Jack Mackie.
                                F1   Jason Mackie, m. Colleen Belanger.
                                F2   James Mackie.
                        E3   Austin MacRae, m. Paula Benett.
                                F1   Michelle MacRae.
                                F2   Anthony MacRae.
                                F3   Andrew MacRae.
                        E4   George MacRae.
                        E5   Marie MacRae, m. Ronald Ramsay.
                                F1   Natashia Ramsay.
                                F2   Nathan Ramsay.
                        E6   Cindy MacRae, m. Roger Moore.
                                F1   Jenna Moore.

              F2   Marcus Moore.
- D2   Gladys Paynter, m. Albert Stavert.
  - E1   Wendell Stavert, m. Linda Sharpe.
    - F1   Christopher Stavert, m. Tanya Gallant.
    - F2   Davis Stavart.
  - E2   Reta Stavert, m. Ivan Bernard.
    - F1   Kimberley Bernard, m. Karl Jollimore.
      - G1   Baylee Jollimore.
      - G2   Logan Jollimore.
  - E3   Willa Stavert, m. Floyd Costain.
    - F1   Duane Costain, m. Karen [?].
      - G1   Kayla Costain.
      - G2   Adam Costain.
      - G3   Jessica Costain.
      - G4   Maranda Costain.
  - E4   Jean Stavert, m. Garth MacKenzie.
    - F1   Mitchell MacKenzie.
    - F2   Tyler MacKenzie.
  - E5   Lowell Stavert, m. Wendy Whitehead.
  - E6   Gary Stavert, m. (1) Shelly Betts.
    - F1   Shanae Stavert.

    Gary m. (2) Sandra MacArthur.
  - E7   Sharon Stavert, m. Paul Gallant.
    - F1   Richard Gallant.
- D3   Herbert Paynter, m. Margaret Somers.
  - E1   Brian Paynter, m. Ellen Blackett.
    - F1   Ashley Paynter.
    - F2   Allyson Paynter.
  - E2   Dawson Paynter, m. Christine Carr.
    - F1   Daniel Paynter.
    - F2   William Paynter.
    - F3   Johnathan Paynter.
  - E3   Stephen Paynter.
  - E4   Norma Paynter, m. Kenneth MacLeod.
    - F1   Devin MacLeod.
  - E5   Martin Paynter, m. Kathie Brown.
    - F1   Kyle Paynter.
    - F2   Ryan Paynter.
  - E6   Tracy Paynter, m. Dennis Phillips.

            F1   Megan Phillips.
            F2   John Phillips.
      D4   Douglas Paynter, m. (1) Betty Burgess.
            E1   Ronald Paynter.
            Douglas m. (2) Mollie Samways.
            E2   Glen Paynter, m. Sheryl [?].
                  F1   Kaylynn Paynter.
                  F2   Bradley Paynter.
            E3   Merle Paynter, m. Paula [?].
      D5   Joan Paynter, m. Wesley Cole.
            E1   Connie Cole, m. David Reeves.
                  F1   Ryan Reeves.
                  F2   Jeremy Reeves.
                  F3   Richard Reeves.
            E2   Linda Cole, m. Robert Crozier.
                  F1   Robbie Crozier.
                  F2   Christopher Crozier.
                  F3   Linden Crozier.
            E3   Barbara Cole, m. Dennis Dunn.
                  F1   Jason Dunn.
                  F2   Rachael Dunn.
            E4   Stephen Cole, m. (1) Mary Andrews, (2) Sheryl Gill.
      D6   Brenda Paynter, m. Hugh Baglole.
            E1   Rodney Baglole.
            E2   April Baglole.
   C11 James Andrew MacKenzie, m. (1) Vera Paynter, (2) Edna MacInnis.
B11 John Donald Martin, m. Mary Ella MacKenzie.
   C1   Etta Martin.
   C2   Harold Neil Martin.
   C3   Catherine Grace Martin.
   C4   Catherine Martin (Muriel), m. Willard Campbell MacLeod (see A1-B3-C2-D2, p. 17).
      D1   Mary MacLeod (Elva), m. Donald Glen Nicholson.
            E1   Donald Gordon Nicholson (Gordon), m. Judith Elizabeth Carver (see A1-B5-C3-D4-E5, p. 24).E2 Douglas Nicholson.
            E3   Lea Nicholson.

- D2 Donald Malcolm MacLeod, m. Lorna May MacDonald.
  - E1 Jeffrey MacLeod, m. Carla Brecken.
  - E2 Donald Andrew MacLeod, m. Priscilla [?].
    - F1 Jonathan MacLeod.
    - F2 Kaylee MacLeod.
  - E3 John MacLeod, m. Nicola Claire Mather.
    - F1 Kate MacLeod.
    - F2 Colin MacLeod.
- D3 Angus Keith MacLeod, m. Catherine Elizabeth Brehaut (Kay).
  - E1 Richard Keith MacLeod, m. Pam Kays.
  - E2 Janice Helen MacLeod, m. (1) David Patterson, (2) Charles Gillis.
    - F1 Amanda Beth Gillis.
- D4 Robert Martin MacLeod (Bobbie), m. (1) Sarah Stewart (Sally).
  - E1 Randy MacLeod.
  - E2 Robin MacLeod.
  - E3 Nancy MacLeod.
  - E4 Mary Louise MacLeod.

  Robert m. (2) Edith MacLeod (Clara).
- D5 Florence Eleanor MacLeod, m. Munroe Kenneth Wheeler.
  - E1 Susan Wheeler, m. Mackie Dixon.
    - F1 Kelcie Jeanette Dixon.
    - F2 Melinda Dixon.
    - F3 John Dixon.
  - E2 Stephen Wheeler, m. Darla [?].
  - E3 Wendy Wheeler, m. James Sharkey.
  - E4 Paul Wheeler, m. Charlotte [?].
  - E5 Leslie Wheeler, m. Terri Anne [?].
- D6 Harold Walton MacLeod, m. Heather Ann Gillis.
  - E1 Gwendolyn MacLeod.
  - E2 Kevin MacLeod.

C5 Marion Emily Martin, m. Harold H. MacKie.
- D1 Jessie Emma MacKie (Bonnie), m. Fred Burke.
  - E1 Will Burke.
  - E2 Robert Burke (Bob), m. Rosanne [?].
  - E3 Allison Burke.

             E4   Colin Burke.
       C6   Samuel Hugh Martin, m. Mary Annie Bozan.
             D1   Brenda Martin, m. William Irwin (Bill).
                   E1   Jackie.
                   E2   Billy-Jo.
                   E3   Travis.
                   E4   Bobby-Sue.
                   E5   Jason.
                   E6   Adam.
             D2   Ronald Martin, m. Wanda Smith.
                   E1   Julie.
                   E2   Erwin.
             D3   John Donald Martin.
       C7   Lloyd George Martin, m. Daisy Johnston Bowles.
 B12   Malcolm Campbell Martin, m. Ella May Parks.
       C1   June Martin.
       C2   Margaret Cecelia Martin.
       C3   Eleanor Katherine Martin.
 B13   Samuel Angus Martin, m. Nettie Fielding.
       C1   Wallace James Martin.
       C2   Jean Martin, m. Ernest Yeo.
       C3   Margaret Martin.
       C4   Malcolm Martin.
A5 Donald Campbell, m. Christy MacLeod.
 B1   James Campbell.
 B2   Archibald Campbell.
 B3   John Campbell.
 B4   Sarah Campbell (Marion), m. Robert James Stewart.
       C1   Ira Alexander Stewart, m. Margaret May Grant.
             D1   Robert Alexander Stewart.
             D2   Elizabeth May Stewart (Bessie), m. William Sinclair MacLean.
                   E1   William MacLean (Sinclair), m. April MacLean.
             D2   Edith Joyce Stewart, m. John Ralph Stewart.
                   E1   Gail Charlene Stewart, m. James Joseph Isaac.
                         F1   Allison Margaret Isaac, m. Ross Potter.
                   E2   Deborah Ann Stewart, m. Gerald Ralph Ward.

D4 Sterling James Stewart, m. (1) Ruth Constance Namee.
    E1 Lesley Margaret Stewart, m. Michael Hanley.
        F1 Jason Michael Hanley, m. Arin Tomson.
        F2 Robyne Lynn Hanley, m. Bradley Kirk.
            G1 Hunter Stewart Kirk.
    E2 Jeffrey Grant Stewart, m. Ann Elizabeth McKee.
        F1 Sara Elizabeth Stewart, m. Liam Breedon.
            G1 Bailey Breedon.
        F2 Katherine Ellen Stewart.
        F3 Michael Jeffrey Stewart.
        F4 James Alexander Stewart.
    E3 Barbara Alexander Stewart, m. Frank Gratton.
        F1 Benjamin Raymond Gratton.
        F2 Patrick James Gratton.
        F3 Carolyn Rose Gratton.
    E4 Kimberly Ruth Stewart, m. John Pollock.
        F1 Joshua Hart Pollock.
        F2 Ian Pollock.

Sterling James (D4) m. (2) Jessie Mary Furey Adam.

D5 Jean Shirley Stewart, m. Harold Gordon MacKay.
    E1 Brian Gordon MacKay.
    E2 Dana Harold MacKay.
    E3 Kenneth Ira MacKay, m. Linda Laybolt.
    E4 Lois Leanne MacKay.
    E5 John Scott MacKay.

D6 Hazel Irene Stewart, m. William Philip Merkel.
    E1 Bonnie Eve Merkel, m. Jeffrey Sexton.
    E2 Laurel Jean Merkel.
    E3 William Stewart Merkel.

C2 Lulu Christina Stewart, m. Harris Penna Moore.
    D1 Mabel Moore, m. (1) Robert Chisholm.
        E1 Judy Chisholm, m. Wayne Myers.
            F1 Joanne Myers, m. Roland Proulx.

       G1 Jonathan Proulx.
    Mabel (D1) m. (2) Clyde York.
  D2 H. June Moore, m. Myron MacDonald Weeks.
    E1 David Kevin Weeks, m. Joan Butcher.
      F1 Will David Weeks.
    E2 Nancy Jean Weeks, m. David McGrath.
      F1 Laura Helen McGrath.
      F2 Steven Joseph McGrath (twin of Kelly).
      F3 Kelly Erin McGrath (twin of Steven).
    E3 Paul Wayne Weeks, m. Frances O'Conner.
      F1 Chantal Marie Weeks.
    E4 Beryl June Weeks, m. Donald Moses.
    E5 John Earle Weeks.
    E6 Douglas Steven Weeks.
    E7 Gordon Weeks (Blair), m. Shelley Musika.
    E8 Wendy Faye Weeks, m. Andrew Oakley.
      F1 Megan Sarah Weeks.
 C3 John James Stewart (J.J.), m. Hazel Glen Brehaut.
  D1 Hazel Stewart (Ruth), m. Carmen Douglas Carle.
    E1 Heather Carle, m. William Hayward.
      F1 James Hayward.
      F2 Erin Hayward.
      F3 Lauren Hayward.
    E2 Lynn Carle, m. Robert Poirier.
      F1 Alyson Poirier.
      F2 Andrew Poirier.
    E3 Beth Carle, m. Roy Piercey.
  D2 Mary Stewart (Fay), m. Robert Marshall.
    E1 Robert Marshall, m. Frances Fraser.
      F1 Jocelyn Marshall.
      F2 Matthew Marshall.
    E2 Andrew Marshall.
    E3 John Marshall, m. Sherry MacRae.
      F1 Emilyne Marshall.
      F2 Barett Jay Marshall.
B5 Donald Campbell (Dan).
B6 Malcolm Campbell.
B7 Christy Ann Campbell, m. Uriah Crossland.
 C1 Ernest Crossland.

           C2   Ada Crossland.
- B8 Jessie Campbell.
- B9 Angus MacLeod Campbell, m. Ina Wilcox.
  - C1 Inez MacLeod Campbell.
  - C2 Angus MacLeod Campbell.
  - C3 Donald Wilcox Campbell.
  - C4 Ray Wilkinson Campbell.
- B10 Margaret Ann Campbell.

A6 Ann Campbell, m. Donald Murchison.
- B1 Euphemia Murchison.
- B2 Margaret Murchison, m. Alexander MacLeod.
  - C1 Donald M. MacLeod.
  - C2 Malcolm Murchison MacLeod, m. Elizabeth MacPherson.
    - D1 Walter A. MacLeod, m. Elma Lois Bowles.
    - D2 Malcolm MacLeod.
    - D3 Ann MacLeod.
    - D4 Ruth MacLeod.
    - D5 Alice MacLeod.
    - D6 Bruce MacLeod.
  - C3 Angus Murchison MacLeod.
- B3 Mary Murchison, m. Allan Matheson.
  - C1 Catherine Matheson (Katie), m. Charles Douglas John MacLeod.
    - D1 John MacLeod (foster son).
  - C2 Donald J. Matheson.
  - C3 Annie Matheson, m. John Alex MacDonald.
    - D1 Douglas Matheson MacDonald.
    - D2 Hugh Wallace MacDonald.
    - D3 Mary Nichol MacDonald.
    - D4 Janet Murchison MacDonald.
    - D5 Kenneth Gordon MacDonald.
  - C4 James Craig Matheson, m. Jessie MacPherson.
  - C5 Alexander Matheson.
  - C6 Christine Anne Matheson, m. William Neil Ross.
    - D1 Mary Isabel Ross, m. Donald A. Morrison.
      - E1 Neil Ross Morrison.
      - E2 Donna Morrison, m. James Knox.
    - D2 Eleanor Ross, m. Donald Alexander MacPherson.
      - E1 Sandra Elinor MacPherson, m. (1) David Benjamin Acorn.

                    F1   Julie Lynn Acorn, m. Randy Mahar.
                        G1   Logan Alexander Mahar.
                  Sandra (E1) m. (2) Scott John MacPhail.
                    F2   Gregory Scott MacPhail.
               E2   Bonnie Lynn MacPherson.
               E3   Kathy Ann MacPherson.
          D3   Alexander Ross, m. Marion MacDonald.
               E1   Judy Ross.
               E2   Craig Ross.
               E3   Mary Ross.
               E4   Lorna Ross.
          D4   Eliot Ross.
          D5   Ann Ross.
          D6   Peggy Ross m. Clarence Criss.
     C7   Margaret Mary Matheson, m. William Alexander MacQueen.
          D1   Mary C. MacQueen.
          D2   Barcley MacQueen.
          D3   Katherine MacQueen, m. Carleton MacLeod.
B4   Neil Murchison, m. Flora Murchison.
     C1   Annie Campbell Murchison, m. Alfred D. Swogger.
          D1   Flora Elizabeth Swogger.
          D2   Malcolm M. Swogger.
          D3   Alfred Dallas Swogger, m. Joyce Wiley.
     C2   Katie MacDonald Murchison.
B5   James Murchison.
B6   Christianna Murchison (Christy), m. Robert Stewart.
B7   James Campbell Murchison.
B8   Ann Murchison, m. Hugh A. Gillis.
     C1   Edward Gillis.
B9   Peter Simon Murchison, m. Lucille Trainor.
     C1   John Malcolm Murchison.
     C2   Peter Simon Murchison.
     C3   Charles Murchison.
     C4   Louise Murchison, m. Floyd Warner.
     C5   Samuel Murchison.
     C6   Muriel Murchison.
B10 Donald Murchison, m. Mary Ann MacDonald.
     C1   Donald Murchison.
     C2   Mary Murchison, m. L.L. Schaffner.
     C3   John Ronald Murchison.

                C4   Margaret Murchison.
        B11   James Donald Murchison, m. Janet Euphemia Stewart.
                C1   Annie Campbell Murchison, m. Kenneth John MacRae.
                        D1   Janet Catherine MacRae, m. Winston Smith.
                                E1   Cynthia Anne Smith, m. (1) Peter Cyr.
                                        F1   Shawn Colin Peter Cyr, m. Tracy Collins.
                                                G1   Riley Robert Neil Shawn Cyr.
                                        F2   Sharilyn Anne Cyr.
                                        Cynthia Anne m. (2) Andrew Windsor.
                                        F3   Tobias Franklin Windsor.
                                E2   Catherine Jane Smith, m. Frank Gendron.
                                        F1   Jason Matthew Gendron.
                                        F2   Michael Stephen Gendron.
                                        F3   Sarah Elizabeth Gendron.
                                E3   Winston Kenneth Smith (Kenneth), m. (1) Sherri Wade.
                                        F1   Wade Winston Smith.
                                        F2   Jessi-Lynn Elizabeth Smith.
                                        Winston (E3) m. (2) Patti Mailman.
                                        F3   Peter Winston Smith (Lucas).
                                E4   Malcolm Smith (Irwin).
                                E5   Mary-Lynn Smith, m. David Smith.
                                        F1   Alexander Daniel Pierre Smith (Pierre).
                                E6   Susan Gail Smith, m. Glen Hancock.
                                        F1   Chelsea Lynn Hancock.
                                        F2   Jonathan Glen Hancock.
                        D2   Judith Ann MacRae, m. Gordon Richard Hickman.
                                E1   Joanne Catherine Hickman, m. Peter Boyd.
                                        F1   Megan Anne Boyd.
                                        F2   Benjamin Joseph Boyd.
                                E2   James Gordon MacRae Hickman.
                                E3   Nancy Suzanne Hickman.
                C2   Leonard [Carr] Murchison, m. Margaret Estelle MacLean (Peggy).
        B12   Samuel Alexander Murchison, m. Catherine Florence MacLeod (Cassie).

- C1 Annie Catherine Murchison.
- C2 Dorothy Murchison, m. (1) Mario Buzzi.
  - D1 Susan Buzzi, m. Paul Vickers.

  Dorothy m. (2) Donald Black.
- C3 Edna Florence Murchison, m. John Einer Andre.
  - D1 John Murchison Andre, m. (1) Barbara J. Sorensen.
    - E1 Jon Christian Andre, m. Christine Daniels.
    - E2 Heather Marie Andre, m. (1) Ron Ornenstien, (2) Stephen Breslin. Heather has four children: Adam, Courtney, Nicole and Tyler.

    John m. (2) Linda Schmidtke, (3) Lisa Coolidge.
- C4 Muriel Murchison, m. [?] Gilligan.
  - D1 Catherine Gilligan, m. [?] Nutter.
  - D2 Edward Gilligan (Ned).
- C5 John Neil Murchison.
- B13 John Malcolm Murchison.
- B14 John Neil Murchison.
- B15 Margaret Ann Murchison.
- B16 Harriet Elizabeth Murchison, m. Charles Smith.
  - C1 David Smith.
  - C2 Donald M. Smith.
  - C3 John Neil Smith.

A7 Christy Campbell, m. Joseph Beers.
- B1 Moses Beers.
- B2 Christena Ann Beers (Christy), m. (1) John Vere Wheeler.
  - C1 George Herbert Wheeler.
  - C2 Beatrice Wheeler, m. William Millar.
    - D1 William M. Millar, m. Virginia [?].
  - C3 Lucy May Wheeler, m. Thomas DeNike.
    - D1 James DeNike.
  - C4 John Vere Wheeler, m. Bessie May Marks.
    - D1 John William Vere Wheeler, m. Elizabeth Johnson.
    - D2 Gerard Heath Wheeler, m. Verlie Pauline White.
    - D3 Mary Evelyn Wheeler, m. Roy Cornish.
    - D4 Beatrice Ann Wheeler.

  Christena m. (2) Neil MacLeod.
- B3 Benjamin Beers.

B4   James Campbell Beers, m. Annie Jardine.
    C1   Christina Beers.
    C2   Hannah Myrtle Beers, m. Farrell B. Richards.
        D1   Donald Richards.
    C3   Clara Martha Beers, m. Harold Trolander.
    C4   James Milton Beers, m. Marcella R. Fritz.
        D1   James Beers.
        D2   Caralou Beers, m. Norman Erickson.
    C5   Dorothy Christina Beers, m. Herman King.
    C6   Jennie Belle Beers, m. (1) [?] Hinckley.
        D1   James Hinckley.
        D2   Joan Hinckley.
        D3   Lianne Hinckley.
        D4   Barbara Hinckley.
    Jennie Belle m. (2) [?] Carter, (3) [?] Klingenberg.
    C7   Joseph Christopher Beers, m. [?].
        D1   Margaret Ann Beers.
    C8   Harold Benjamin Beers, m. (1) Helen M., (2) Helen Thomas.

A1. The Descendants of Malcolm Campbell and Janet Murchison

Malcolm Campbell, b. September 10, 1821, in Skye, Scotland, d. December 9, 1906, in Uigg, PEI, buried in Orwell Head Cemetery. His obituary from *The Guardian*, January 9, 1907, reads:

> The death of Malcolm Campbell of Uigg has removed from that district another of the small surviving circle of its pioneers. These were men of noble mould, distinguished by warmth of heart, integrity, and faith in God. Theirs was the task of turning the forest primeval into fruitful fields. The arduous toil this entailed they cheerfully underwent and successfully discharged. Productive farms and comfortable homes bear witness to their industry, while their moral worth has left its impress upon their children. Mr. Campbell was born in Skye, Inverness Shire, Scotland, and was seven years old when his parents with their children emigrated about eighty years ago to Prince Edward Island. He was brought to a saving knowledge of the Truth under the ministry of that eminent servant of God, the late Rev. Donald MacDonald by whom he was ordained an elder in the Church of Scotland, and very highly esteemed. The church in which he was an office bearer for many years will miss him much; for though of late he was not able through the infirmities of age to take an active part in the service of the House of God which he once took, yet his presence was always regarded as a source of strength.
>
> He died peacefully hymning the Redeemer's praise. He married Janette Murchison, of Point Prim, in whom he found a true helpmate, who brightened life's pilgrimage by her hopeful Christian spirit and womanly grace, and soothed life's close by her devoted attention and strong faith in the happy reunion of death-divided friends in the better land where parting is unknown. A family of twelve children blessed their union. These are: James of Milwaukee, Wisc.; Donald of Uigg; Capt. Neil M. of Melbourne, Australia; John M. of Stanford, Mont., U.S.; Rev. D.M. of Lemberg, Sask.; Simon A. of Okanogan, B.C.; and Malcolm H. on the homestead; Mrs. M. McKinnon of Dundas; Mrs. D. Stewart of Point Prim (deceased); Mrs. N. McPherson of Uigg; Mrs. M. Campbell of Brookline (deceased); Mrs. D. McKinnon of Dundas. Besides his wife and ten children, there survive him forty-five grandchildren and a number of great grandchildren.

Malcolm took part in the Belfast Riot of January 26, 1847. According to Malcolm Macqueen in his *Skye Pioneers*: "Political passions were greatly aroused between the Scottish and Irish settlers over the election of rival candidates. After the melee was over, the Scots remained masters of the field. Many on both sides received wounds from which they never recovered ... Malcolm Campbell, of Uigg, also bore traces of his part in the fray. His stories of the battle, coupled with a ready display of his cranial scars, lent such romance to his presence that he continued to be an ever increasing source of wonder and delight to succeeding generations of schoolboy worshippers." (pp.181-182, 2018 edition).

Janet Murchison (Jessie), b. August 24, 1825, in Point Prim, PEI, baptized September 14, 1825, in Belfast, m. March 19, 1846, in the Church of Scotland by Rev. Donald MacDonald, d. February 23, 1911, in Uigg, buried in Orwell Head Cemetery. Her obituary from *The Examiner*, February 28, 1911, reads:

> There passed peacefully to rest at Kinross, PEI, on Thursday the 23rd of February, after a brief illness, Janet Murchison, relict of the late Malcolm Campbell, aged 85 years. The deceased was of a peaceful and quiet disposition and was much beloved by all who knew her. In early youth she had made profession of faith under the ministry of the late Rev. Donald MacDonald, and throughout a life of consistent devotion to truth, she bore undoubted testimony of the comforting and enlightening power of the Holy Spirit.

Malcolm and Janet had the following children:

B1   James Campbell, b. 1847, Uigg, d. in Michigan. He m. Harriet Elizabeth Gilmour, b. PEI, d. in Michigan. James was baptized in the Church of Scotland, Orwell Head, but not recorded, as the records do not go further back than 1853.
       C1   Malcolm Neil Campbell, b. March 26, 1874, Uigg, baptized July 27, 1874, Orwell Head. He was a minister. He m. Ida Frohmander.
           D1   Maynard V. Campbell, m. Vera Howard. Maynard was a minister.
                E1   Malcolm Campbell.
           D2   Myrna Campbell, m. Eric Beavon. Eric was a minister.
                E1   Harold Beavon.
                E2   Fred Beavon.
                E3   Chester Beavon.

- E4 Everyl Armson Beavon, m. Evelyn Wismer.
  - F1 Frederick John Malcolm Beavon, m. Spoar [?], b. in Thailand.
    - G1 Cindy Beavon. Graduate of Brown University, RI, 2007.
  - F2 Donald Neil Beavon, m. Sheila Murphy.
    - G1 Brianne Beavon.
    - G2 Samantha Beavon.
    - G3 Terra Beavon.
    - G4 Anapuma Beavon.
  - F3 Trudy Lee Ann Beavon, m. Nils Lee.
    - G1 Justin Ryan Lee. Graduate of Walla Walla College, 2006. Living in Portland, OR, 2007.
    - G2 Erin Lee (twin of Erica). Graduate of Walla Walla College, 2006. Living in Portland, OR, 2007.
    - G3 Erica Lee (twin of Erin). Graduate of Walla Walla College, 2006. Living in Portland, OR, 2007.
- D3 Laura Campbell.

C2 Laura Elizabeth Campbell, b. July 4, 1877, Uigg, baptized August 17, 1877, Orwell Head m. Warren Smith.
- D1 James Smith, m. Irene Lois Kitchcock. They had no children.
- D2 Warren Smith.
- D3 Dorothy Smith, m. [?] Gould.
- D4 Donald Smith.
- D5 Robert Smith.

C3 Chester Gilmore Campbell, b. in the USA, m. Margaret Ann Downey.
- D1 Marian Elinor Campbell, m. Edwin Cone.
  - E1 Donald Campbell Cone, m. Virginia [?].
    - F1 Kevin Cone.
    - F2 Bryan Cone.
  - E2 Bruce Eldridge Cone, m. Beverly [?].
    - F1 Cindy Cone.
    - F2 Ronda Cone.
    - F3 Sean Cone.
  - E3 Gratia Cone, m. Kenneth Hersey.
    - F1 Melissa Hersey.

      F2 David Hersey.
      F3 Allyson Hersey.
    E4 Edwin A. Cone, m. Julie [?].
      F1 Jennifer Cone.
      F2 Daniel Cone.
    E5 Ann Elizabeth Cone, m. David Vining.
      F1 Jessica Vining.
      F2 Jacqueline Vining.
  D2 Margaret Campbell, m. [?] Garland.
  D3 Janet Irene Campbell.
  D4 Ruth Campbell.
C4 Janet Campbell, b. in the USA, m. William Frohmander.
  D1 Kathryn Frohmander.
  D2 Ruth Frohmander.
  D3 Malcolm Frohmander.
  D4 William Frohmander.
C5 Albert Campbell, b. in the USA, d. in Long Beach, CA. He m. Mildred Shaw.
  D1 Marjorie Campbell.
C6 Herbert Campbell, b. in the USA, m. Catherine Hastings.
  D1 George Campbell.
  D2 Katherine Louise Campbell, m. [?] Koch.
  D3 Laura Campbell.
  D4 Melvin Campbell.
  D5 Latba Campbell.
  D6 Janet Campbell, m. [?] Kirk.
  D7 Norman Campbell.
C7 Irene Harriet Campbell, b. April 14, 1889, in the USA, d. September 7, 1977. She m. Ernest Uriah Ayars, b. November 1, 1880, in the USA, d. June 26, 1957.
  D1 Dorothy Carolyn Ayars, b. April 2, 1918, USA, m. Kenneth Harvey Emerson, b. April 4, 1918, USA. They were married on June 19, 1938.
    E1 Anita Inez Emerson, b. July 11, 1941, in the USA. She m. Robert Stanley Folkenberg, b. January 1, 1941, USA. They were married July 29, 1962.
      F1 Robert Stanley Folkenberg, b. August 12, 1964, m. Audrey Ann Gibson, b. October 29, 1964, USA. They were married June 12, 1988.

G1 Robert Stanley Folkenberg, b. June 16, 1992, USA.

G2 Randall Thomas Folkenberg, b. December 17, 1993.

G3 Katelyn Ann Folkenberg, b. June 17, 1997, USA.

F2 Kathi Lynne Folkenberg, b. December 13, 1967, USA, m. David Arnold Jensen, b. November 7, 1967, USA.

G1 Michael Allan Jensen, b. December 29, 1995, USA.

E2 Robert James Emerson, b. May 17, 1943, in the USA. He m. (1) Mary Catherine Konevich, b. October 24, 1954, (2) Linda Kaye Knolls, b. August 1, 1945.

F1 Traci Lynn Emerson, b. January 2, 1967, m. (1) Mark Edward Berault.

G1 Joshua Alan Berault, b. October 9, 1987.

G2 Brittney Lynn Berault, b. February 16, 1990.

Traci Lynn m. (2) Aaron Stanford.

G3 Megan Ashley Stanford, b. March 4, 1997.

F2 Robert Kenneth Emerson, b. August 4, 1970. Robert James (E2) m. (3) Peggy Neal, b. December 23, 1941.

E3 Richard Kenneth Emerson, b. May 11, 1948, in the USA. He m. (1) Sharon Paige, (2) Sandra Charlene Clayton, b. April 28, 1954.

F1 Ariel Elizabeth Rebecca Emerson, b. November 27, 1979.

F2 Alison Hilary Kaitlyn Emerson, b. December 16, 1990.

D2 Ernest James Ayars, b. May 24, 1925, USA, m. Carleen Louise Siems.

E1 Karen Ayars.

D3 Mildred Ayars, b. December 27, 1928, in the USA.

B2 Euphemia Campbell (Effie), b. April 26, 1849, Uigg, d. October 1, 1922, Forest Hill, PEI, buried Dundas. The 1901 census gives her year of birth as 1850. She m. Murdoch MacKinnon, b. 1838, Scotland, son of Murdoch MacKinnon and Catherine MacDonald, d. October 24, 1930, age 94, Forest Hill, PEI. Euphemia and Murdoch were married November 1, 1881, in the residence of the bride's father in Uigg by the Rev. John Goodwill. Murdoch MacKinnon emigrated to PEI in 1841. His first wife was Christy MacKay, who died at age 39, while Euphemia was his second wife. Murdoch's son Donald (Dan) by his first wife was married to Euphemia's sister Flora (see B9, below).

C1   Neil Campbell Garrett, b. June 26, 1911, Cable Head, baptized October 24, 1911, Dundas Presbyterian Church, d. March 16, 2001, buried, Dundas Church Cemetery. He m. Florence Melva Acorn, b. January 21, 1925, Dundas, daughter of Robert Acorn and Margaret Ann Swallow, baptized June 30, 1925, Dundas. Neil and Florence were married on September 23, 1944, in Dundas by the Rev. W.I. Green.

   D1   Katherine Margaret Garrett, b. December 25, 1944, Cable Head, baptized in Dundas. She m. Waldo Keith MacLeod, b. ca. 1949, Pictou, son of Waldo Eliot MacLeod and Margaret Rose MacKenzie.

      E1   Kelli Margaret MacLeod, b. December 9, 1969, baptized in Dundas.

      E2   Karla MacLeod.

   D2   Marjorie Faye Garrett, b. June 21, 1946, Forest Hill, baptized, Dundas, d. June 4, 2008, age 61, buried, Dundas Cemetery. She m. Kenneth MacDonald, son of Murdoch J. MacDonald and Janette Hamilton MacKinnon.

   D3   Arthur Daniel Garrett, b. May 10, 1948, Forest Hill, baptized, Dundas. He m. Sheila Marlene MacKenzie, b. ca. 1956, Montague, daughter of Wallace Murray MacKenzie and Mildred Catherine Garrett. They were married on November 21, 1970, in Dundas by the Rev. W. Bruce Clark. Witnesses were Jackie Garrett and Shirley MacKenzie.

   D4   John Caleb Garrett, b. June 21, 1950, Forest Hill, baptized, Dundas. He m. Shirley Dianne MacKenzie, b. ca. 1948, Montague, daughter of Wallace Murray MacKenzie and Mildred Catherine Garrett. They were married on August 21, 1971, in Dundas by the Rev. W. Bruce Clark. Witnesses were Arthur Garrett and Sheila Garrett.

   D5   Ada Garrett (Valerie), b. ca. 1956. She m. David Wallace Garrett, b. ca. 1956, son of Everett W. Garrett and Georgina May MacKenzie. They were married on December

11, 1972, in Dundas by the Rev. W. Bruce Clark. Witnesses were Henry Garrett and Marjorie MacDonald.

B3 Donald Campbell, b. February 22, 1850, Uigg, d. August 3, 1938, Kinross, buried Orwell Head. Donald was a farmer, shoemaker and tanner. He m. Flora MacLeod, b. May 17, 1855, Murray Harbour Road, baptized July 23, 1855, Orwell Head Church of Scotland, d. February 22, 1941, Uigg, in the residence of her daughter Edith, buried Orwell Head. Donald and Flora were married on August 3, 1875, at the residence of James Campbell by the Rev. John Goodwill.

    C1   Hector Campbell, b. May 23, 1876, Uigg, baptized July 17, 1876, m. (1) May Ferguson, (2) Laura Clark.

    C2   Mary C. Campbell, b. December 9, 1878, Uigg, baptized June 22, 1879, Orwell Head, d. 1974, Kinross, buried, Orwell Corner Cemetery. She was a teacher. She m. Angus Alexander MacLeod, b. November 30, 1872, Kinross, son of Lauchlin MacLeod and Margaret MacLeod, d. 1932, buried, Orwell Corner Cemetery. He was a farmer. Mary and Angus were married on October 26, 1904, in Orwell Head by the Rev. A.J. MacNeill. Attendants were Malcolm R. MacLeod and Hector Campbell.

        D1   Walter MacLeod (Gordon), b. July 31, 1905, Kinross, baptized December 19, 1905, Orwell Head, d. before 2002 in Arlington, MA. He m. Mabel MacLeod, d. in Arlington, MA.

            E1   Wayne MacLeod.

            E2   Elaine MacLeod.

        D2   Willard Campbell MacLeod, b. June 30, 1908, m. Catherine Martin (Muriel), see A4-B11-C4, p. 155.

        D3   Angus MacLeod (Allistair), b. April 25, 1912, Kinross, son of Angus Alexander MacLeod and Mary Campbell, baptized July 25, 1915, Orwell Presbyterian Church, d. March 3, 1967, Halifax, buried, Orwell Corner Cemetery. He was a lawyer. He m. Constance Belya.

            E1*   David MacLeod, a teacher.

            E2   Ian MacLeod.

        D4   Donald MacLeod (Everett), b. April 25, 1916, Kinross, son of Angus Alexander MacLeod and Mary Campbell, baptized April 19, 1916, Orwell Presbyterian Church, d. October 19, 2002, buried, Orwell Corner Cemetery. He m. Susan Alma Reid, b. February 28, 1920, d. August 3, 2002, buried, Orwell Corner Cemetery. The name on her headstone reads: Alma Susan Lyle. Donald was a pilot

in the RCAF during WWII and a teacher in both PEI and BC. He resided in BC for a number of years, then moved back to PEI, where he died in his 87th year.
- E1 Pat MacLeod, a medical doctor in BC, m. Muriel [?].
- E2 Madeline MacLeod, living in BC in 2002.
- E3 Douglas MacLeod, living in BC in 2002, m. Barbara [?].
- E4 Ross MacLeod, living in BC in 2002, m. Valerie [?].

D5 William MacLeod (Sinclair), b. September 4, 1921, Kinross, baptized March 1, 1923, Orwell Presbyterian Church, d. March 5, 2005, age 83, Halifax, buried, Orwell Corner Cemetery. He m. Elsie MacGregor.
- E1 Mary MacLeod, m. Gordon [?].
- E2 Lee MacLeod, m. Cathy [?].
- E3 Bruce MacLeod, m. Cheryl [?].
- E4 Karen MacLeod, m. Allen [?].

C3 Janette Campbell (Jessie), b. September 14, 1880, Uigg, baptized February 27, 1881, Orwell Head, d. in MA. She m. William P. Dempsey, a policeman residing in Lincoln, MA.
- D1 William Dempsey, b. in MA.
- D2 Malcolm Dempsey, b. in MA.
- D3 Frances Dempsey, b. in MA.
- D4 Florence Dempsey, b. in MA.

C4 William Malcolm Campbell, b. November 14, 1882, Uigg, baptized September 23, 1883, Orwell Head, d. May 13, 1957, buried, Orwell Head.

C5 Euphemia Campbell, b. November 28, 1885, Uigg, baptized Orwell Head, m. Owen Crouse.
- D1 Walter Crouse (also known as Walton Crouse), marine engineer born in MA.
- D2 John Everett Crouse, b. in MA.
- D3 Florence Crouse, b. in MA.

C6 Stella Dyan Campbell, b. April 28, 1889, Uigg, baptized October 23, 1889, Orwell Head, d. 1983, buried, Orwell Head. The name on her headstone is: Stella Campbell Archambaut. She m. William Cummings.
- D1 Douglas Lee Cummings, b. October 29, 1916, MA, baptized September 13, 1920, Kinross.
- D2 Beatrice Cummings, b. April 15, 1918, in Lynn, MA,

baptized September 13, 1920, Kinross, m. Clayton Stephens.

C7 Ann Evaline Campbell, b. December 3, 1890, Uigg, baptized October 19, 1891, Orwell Head, d. in the USA. She m. Albert Murphy, who died in the USA.

    D1 Albert Murphy, b. in MA.

C8* Christina Laura Campbell, b. January 1, 1893, Uigg, baptized Orwell Head Church of Scotland, d. October 8, 1922, age 29, Grandview, buried Orwell Head. She m. Alexander Martin, b. August 27, 1891, Grandview, baptized November 1, 1891, Orwell Head, d. 1978, Grandview, buried Orwell Head. Alexander was a merchant.

C9 Edith Rachel Campbell, b. November 15, 1898, Uigg, d. 1990, buried, Orwell Head. She m. Samuel Hume, b. 1891, Wood Islands, son of John S. Hume and Mary Lamont, baptized, Belle River, d. May 2, 1967, Uigg, buried, Orwell Head. He was a farmer. Edith and Samuel were married on June 4, 1919, at 80 Longworth Avenue, Charlottetown, by the Rev. Ewen MacDougall. The bondsman was William Campbell.

    D1* Donald William Hume, b. 1921, Uigg, d. July 6, 1944, in a plane crash in Goose Bay, Labrador, buried, Goose Bay. He was a navigator in the RCAF. He m. Margaret Shaw, b. 1918, Uigg, daughter of John Ernest Shaw and Margaret MacLeod (Murdina). They were married on June 6, 1943, in Chatham, NB, by the Rev. F.E. MacPherson. Witnesses were LAC B.G. Hamilton and Goldie MacInnis.

        E1* John William Hume, b. May 1944, d. June 2009, buried, June 26, 2009, Saint Andrew's United Church Cemetery, Vernon Bridge. He m. Linda Bieren.

            F1 Cathy Lynn Hume, b. June 19, 1966, baptized May 28, 1967, Vernon River, m. Sheldon Stewart.

                G1 Alyssa Jane Stewart, b. November 1994.

                G2 Braeden John Stewart, b. 1997.

            F2 Donald William Hume, m. Kelly Smyth.

                G1 Ethan William Hume, b. 1997.

                G2 Kieren Blaine Hume, b. 1999.

B4 Sarah Ann Campbell (Marion), b. January 10, 1853, Uigg, baptized February 4, 1853, Orwell Head, d. Mount Buchanan, December 16,

1896, age 43 years and 11 months after a painful illness of six months (*Patriot* newspaper), buried Orwell Head. Her headstone reads: Sarah Ann Campbell, wife of Donald Stewart, died December 16, 1896, along with the names of their children. She m. Donald Stewart, b. November 15, 1847, Murray Harbour Road, son of Alexander "Sandy" Stewart and Margaret Campbell. He was a tailor and farmer. Sarah Ann and Donald married on March 21, 1871, in Orwell Head.

C1*   James Alex Stewart, b. January 3, 1872, Murray Harbour Road, baptized March 31, 1872, Church of Scotland, d. October 14, 1940 at the home of Mr. and Mrs. Behm, Grandview, buried, Polly Cemetery. He was a farmer who at one time ranched in Montana. He m. Mary Lamont (Masie), b. in Mount Buchanan.

    D1   Mabel F. Stewart, b. November 190[?] and d. April 15 190[?] in Stanford, Montana, age 6 months. (Information from a newspaper clipping.)

    D2   Sadie Stewart, m. [?] MacKinnon.

C2   John Goodwill Stewart, b. July 11, 1875, Murray Harbour Road, baptized August 3, 1875, Orwell Head Church, d. before the 1881 census, buried Orwell Head.

C3   Janet Euphemia Stewart, b. April 13, 1877, m. James Donald Murchison (see A6.B11, p. 170).

C4*   Margaret Priscilla Stewart, b. April 26, 1880, Murray Harbour Road, baptized June 12, 1880, Orwell Head Church of Scotland, d. November 23, 1970, Mount Buchanan, buried Polly Cemetery. She m. Nelson Cantelo, b. August 8, 1878, Point Prim, d. July 11, 1970, Mount Buchanan, buried Polly Cemetery. Margaret and Nelson were married on July 28, 1909, by the Rev. Dan MacLean. Their marriage licence was issued July 28, 1909, and lists the bondsman as Donald MacKinnon and witnesses as Donald MacKinnon and Isabelle MacLeod.

C5   Malcolm Campbell Stewart, b. October 24, 1882, Murray Harbour Road, baptized June 24, 1883, Orwell Head Church. He m. Lillian Burt Main. He was residing in Florida around 1950.

C6   Euphemia Margaret Stewart (Effie), b. September 25, 1884, Murray Harbour Road, baptized May 17, 1885, Orwell Head Church of Scotland, m. William McInnis.

    D1   Arthur McInnis.

C7   Roderick MacLean Stewart, b. December 11, 1886, Murray Harbour Road, baptized March 11, 1887, Orwell Head Church of Scotland.

C8   Malcolm Hector Murchison Stewart, b. February 28, 1889,

Mount Buchanan, baptized May 12, 1889, Belfast, resided in MA and had a son and daughter. He m. Catherine MacPherson.

C9 Allan Campbell Stewart, b. May 12, 1891, Mount Buchanan, baptized September 24, 1891, Orwell Head Church of Scotland, d. April 11, 1949, Vancouver. He m. Euphemia Campbell (Etta), b. October 7, 1894, Uigg, daughter of Samuel Campbell and Catherine MacLeod, baptized November 23, 1894, Orwell Head Church of Scotland, d. February 19, 1981, Vancouver. Allan and Euphemia were married on August 29, 1910, in Charlottetown by the Rev. T.F. Fullerton. The bondsman was C.W. Harris.

    D1 Hazel Mae Stewart, b. December 15, 1910, Quincy, MA, baptized December 25, 1911, Orwell Head Church of Scotland, d. December 6, 1999, Ventura, CA. She m. Norman MacLeod, b. February 26, 1905, Glasgow, Scotland, son of Norman MacLeod and Annie MacRae, d. June 20, 1972, Fullerton, CA.

        E1 Anne Bernice MacLeod, b. December 15, 1934, Victoria, BC. She m. John Milton Andres, b. February 4, 1927, Santa Ana, CA. They were married December 29, 1956, in Riverside, CA.

            F1 Jamie Stewart Andres, b. October 7, 1957, Inglewood, CA. She m. Michael Eric Larsen, b. November 2, 1960, Oakland, CA. They were married May 24, 1986, Palos Verdes, CA.

                G1 Declan Phillip Andres-Larsen, b. November 18, 1989, Santa Cruz, CA.

            F2 Paul MacLeod Andres, b. March 6, 1959, Inglewood, CA. He m. Jeni Ann Reiz, b. February 4, 1956, Pasadena, CA. They were married March 25, 1989, Altadena, CA.

                G1 Clara Jane Andres, b. December 29, 1989, Pasadena, CA.

                G2 Charles Alexander Andres (Alex), b. August 31, 1991, Pasadena, CA.

            F3 David Allan Andres, b. September 14, 1960, Torrance, CA. He m. Susan Faye Meyer, b. February 1, 1968, Duarte,

CA. They were married June 29, 1996, Altadena, CA.
- G1 Emma Anne Andres, b. September 12, 1998, Glendale, CA.
- G2 Adam John Andres, b. February 29, 2001, Glendale, CA.
- G3 Grau Alice Andres.

F4 Phillip Campbell Andres, b. September 27, 1962, Torrance, CA. He m. Caroline Gray Schless, b. July 30, 1962, Wayne, IL. They were married July 19, 1997, Wayne, IL.
- G1 Margaret Gray Andres, b. April 21, 2000, Los Angeles, CA.
- G2 Catherine Jean Andres, b. February 24, 2002, Los Angeles, CA.

E2 Norman Stewart MacLeod, b. May 19, 1936, Victoria, BC. He m. Caroline Ruth Lee, b. February 7, 1936, in Texas. They were married November 25, 1959, in Riverside, CA.

F1 Norman Scott MacLeod, b. November 15, 1960, Riverside, CA. He m. Gabrielle Isabella Marent, b. February 14, 1960, Palo Alto, CA. They were married June 23, 1984, Los Altos, CA.
- G1 Norman Conner MacLeod, b. September 25, 1989, Oakland, CA.
- G2 Caitlin Marie MacLeod, b. July 3, 1992, Walnut Creek, CA.

F2 Shawn Allen MacLeod, b. August 24, 1963, Riverside, CA. He m. Alicia Golleher, b. January 21, 1962, Los Angeles, CA. They were married February 7, 1986, Vancouver, WA.
- G1 Callie Leah MacLeod, b. June 26, 1987.
- G2 Caitlin Ayn MacLeod, b. May 16, 1990.
- G3 Carrick Ian MacLeod, b. February 8, 1995.

F3 Leah Alyse MacLeod, b. June 27, 1969,

Santa Barbara, CA. She m. Robert Albert Irwin, b. March 14, 1967, Oregon. They were married March 21, 1998, San Jose del Cabo, Mexico.

  G1 Ceylor Alyse Irwin, b. March 9, 2006, Mount Hood, OR.

E3 Allan Kenneth MacLeod, b. September 13, 1937, Victoria, BC. He m. (1) Valeria Mavis Lygon, b. October 27, 1936, in Melbourne, Australia. They were married December 1, 1958, in Vancouver.

 F1 Laurie Ann MacLeod, b. January 19, 1961, Whittier, CA. She m. Alex Ramirez, b. February 20, 1960, Gallup, NM, d. December 18, 2003, Porterville, CA. They were married March 22, 1980, Bakersfield, CA.

  G1 Jenna Brianne Ramirez, b. September 10, 1980, Sonora, CA. She m. Ron Hulsey, baptized August 16, 1974, West Plains, MS. They were married on March 20, 1999, in Porterville, CA.

   H1 Lauryn Marie Hulsey, b. November 19, 2003.

  G2 Brandon David Ramirez, b. August 2, 1982, Kern County, CA.

  G3 Tara Karissa Ramirez, b. February 26, 1984, Ventura, CA.

  G4 Jacob Allen Ramirez, b. February 27, 1986, Gallup, NM.

  G5 Danielle Alyssa Ramirez, b. August 7, 1988, Gallup, NM.

  G6 Levi Samuel Ramirez, b. May 12, 1990, Tulare, CA.

 F2 Kerry Lynn MacLeod, b. April 15, 1965, Whittier, CA, and worked in Bakersfield, CA. She m. (1) Kelly Michael Reaves, b. October 1, 1958, Wasco, CA. They were married in 1984.

  G1 Joshua Reaves, b. September 25, 1983, Bakersfield, CA, m. Angela

Bishop, b. April 14, 1982, also in Bakersfield. They were married in 2001.

G2 Brittany Leeanne Reaves, b. May 7, 1985, Bakersfield, CA.

Kerry Lynn (F2) m. (2) Rick Lutrell, b. April 14, 1958, Bakersfield, CA, and (3) Mark Evans, b. July 3, 1961, Salinas, CA.

Allan Kenneth (E3) m. (2) Carolyn Rummens, b. October 8, 1933, in Oklahoma. They were married in January 1972 in Bakersfield, CA. He m. (3) Linda [?], b. December 9, 1937. They were married in June 1997 in Bakersfield, CA. He m. (4) Lynn [?] and m. (5) Linda Marie Templeton, b. September 1, 1955, in Pennsylvania. They were married on May 14, 1999, in Lakeworth, FL.

E4 Mary Ferguson MacLeod, b. December 9, 1942, Mineola, NY. She m. Paul Michael Saint, b. April 13, 1940, in New Jersey. They were married September 28, 1968, in Fullerton, CA.

F1 Matthew Paul Saint, b. October 5, 1972, Ventura, CA.

F2 Andrew Michael Saint, b. March 27, 1974, Ventura, CA. He m. Christy Breanna Pierce James, b. March 11, 1977, Woodland Hills, CA. (Pierce is her birth name, James is her stepfather's name.) Andrew and Christy were married June 2, 2001, in Camarillo, CA.

G1 Aiden James Saint, b. April 14, 2003, Thousand Oaks, CA.

G2 Gavin MacLeod Saint, b. June 27, 2005, Thousand Oaks, CA.

G3 Bryson Saint, b. 2007, Thousand Oaks, CA.

E5 Donald Campbell MacLeod, b. December 9, 1942, Mineola, NY. He m. (1) Victoria Qualls in 1963. He m. (2) Nancy DeVore, b. March 7, 1942, Los Angeles, CA. They were married on November 2, 1967, in Reno, NV.

F1 Julie Anne MacLeod, b. August 27, 1968,

in Orange County, CA.
- F2 David Campbell MacLeod, b. January 31, 1970, Orange County, CA, m. Erin C. Wilkinson, b. ca. 1966 in Connecticut. They were married November 26, 1994, in Hollywood, CA.
  - G1 Dawson Lauder MacLeod, b. January 1, 1997, Culver City, CA.
  - G2 Cameron Donald MacLeod, b. August 31, 1998, Culver City, CA.
  - G3 Lauren Ellie MacLeod, b. January 10, 2001, Culver City, CA.

Donald m. (3) Wiescia Salanardi in November 1988 in Palos Verdes, CA, and (4) Katherine Heaston in June 1990 in Palos Verdes, CA.

D2* Edison Campbell Stewart (Cam), b. March 1, 1915, Vancouver, BC, d. November 14, 2008, Comox, BC. He was superintendent of schools in BC. He m. Mary Elizabeth Sandall (Betty), b. September 10, 1917, NL, daughter of LeRoy Holden Sandall and Ethel Foster Crawford, d. 2001, Comox, BC. She was a teacher and served in the instructor branch of the RCN during WWII. They were married on April 2, 1942. Edison's obituary from the *Vancouver Sun* may be found in the appendix.
- E1* Maryl Elaine Stewart, b. February 20, 1944.
- E2 John Sandall Stewart (Sandy), b. May 23, 1946, in British Columbia. He m. Edith Morrison, b. July 9, 1946. They were married July 19, 1969.
  - F1 Angus John Stewart, b. April 30, 1976, m. Danita Aspin, b. March 10, 1972, Berwyn, AB. They were married in July 2001 in Sooke, BC.
    - G1 Charlie Angus Stewart, b. October 23, 2004, Victoria, BC.
    - G2 Laney Rose Stewart, b. March 10, 2007, Victoria, BC.
  - F2 Eric Donald Stewart, b. April 27, 1979.
- E3 Donald Campbell Stewart, b. October 29, 1950, in British Columbia. He m. Elizabeth Gough Azmier, b. November 21, 1945, in Ottawa. They were married in BC on February 23, 1973.

F1 Benjamin Campbell Stewart, b. May 4, 1975, Sooke, BC, d. March 4, 1999, in a skiing accident in the mountains of eastern British Columbia.

F2 Morgan Allen Stewart, b. June 15, 1978, Sooke, BC. She m. Andrew Mears, b. August 4, 1977. They were married July 9, 2005, in Victoria, BC.

E4 David Allan Stewart, b. June 13, 1952, Peace River, AB. He m. Diane Lynn Piper, b. May 4, 1953, Peace River, AB. They were married November 30, 1972, in Terrace, BC.

F1 Catherine Melissa Stewart (Cathy), b. April 22, 1973, Terrace, BC, m. Eric Terrance Nordgren, b. May 7, 1975, Kamloops, BC. They were married August 12, 1995, Kamloops, BC.

G1 Flynn Eric Nordgren, b. February 7, 2003, Calgary, AB.

G2 Anika Nordgren, b. 2005, Calgary, AB.

F2 Shawna Lee Stewart, b. January 29, 1975, Victoria, BC, m. Dale Philip Melvin, b. May 17, 1975, Tors Cove, NL. They were married July 22, 2000, in Kamloops, BC.

G1 Isabelle Anne Melvin, b. July 10, 2001, Calgary, AB.

G2 Olivia Melvin.

E5 Elizabeth Anne Stewart (Anne), b. March 21, 1955, in British Columbia. She m. Bob Baden and was married to him briefly. She decided to have a child a few years later. The father's name is Alexander, born in Glasgow, Scotland.

F1 David Alexander Stewart, b. May 1, 1989, in British Columbia.

E6 Robert Clifford Stewart (Cliff), May 8, 1961, Courtney, BC. He m. Ann Michele Smyth, b. August 23, 1964, Vancouver, BC. They were married June 26, 1999, in West Vancouver, BC.

F1 Georgia Mary Stewart, b. January 17, 2006, North Vancouver, BC.

The Descendants of James Campbell and Christy MacDonald 81

D3 Donald Arthur Stewart, b. September 19, 1917, Vancouver, BC, d. February 1996 in Vancouver. He was a mechanical engineer who served on convoy duty in the Atlantic with the RCN during WWII. He m. Winifred Georgina Anne Robertson (Win), b. November 14, 1917, Vancouver, d. 1998, Vancouver. They were married on August 8, 1942 and later divorced.

    E1 Allan Robertson Stewart, b. October 19, 1944, Vancouver. He m. Sharon Barrie Harmer, b. September 20, 1944. They were married on April 18, 1970, and later divorced.

    E2 Robert Livingstone Stewart, b. July 30, 1946, Vancouver, BC. He m. Audrey Cecilia Thornton, b. May 16, 1948, Vancouver, BC. They were married April 26, 1968, in Vancouver.

        F1 Aaron Michael Stewart, b. June 24, 1971, Vancouver, d. (murdered) March 26, 1995, Burnaby, BC.

        F2 Todd Donald Stewart, b. July 29, 1975, Vancouver, BC. He m. Elysia Dhyana Meen on March 10, 2008, in Grand Cayman Island.

    E3 Georgina Anne Campbell Stewart, b. March 28, 1949, Vancouver, BC. She m. Michael Angelo Manuel Manchon, b. March 3, 1950, in London, England. They were married on August 21, 1971, in Vancouver.

        F1 Alexander Stewart Manchon, b. September 30, 1975, in London, England.

        F2 Nicholas Velandi Manchon, b. May 3, 1978, Murrayville, BC. He m. Andrea Kathleen Freer, b. July 17, 1974, New Westminster, BC. They were married in New Westminster.

        F3 Melissa Maria Manchon, b. April 4, 1980, Murrayville, BC.

D4 Allan Stewart (John), b. May 12, 1919, Vancouver, BC, d. April 1, 1992, Richmond, BC. He was an electrical engineer who served in the RCN during WWII. He m. Margaret Esplin (Jean), b. January 29, 1924, Vancouver, daughter of James Esplin and Roberta Stewart. They were married on March 4, 1944, in Vancouver.

E1 James Allan Stewart (Jim), b. May 28, 1946, Richmond, BC, d. January 18, 1982, in a small plane crash with his brother-in-law in the mountains of eastern British Columbia. He m. Sharrin Catherine Beruschi, b. June 13, 1947. They were married on April 11, 1970, in British Columbia.

    F1 Abigail Jean Stewart, b. July 8, 1971, in British Columbia. She m. Brent Petterson in Kelowna, BC.

        G1 Matthew James Petterson, b. August 26, 1998.

    F2 Catherine Marie Stewart, b. March 17, 1974, in British Columbia, m. [?] Murphy.

        G1 Olivia Anne Murphy, b. February 2005 in British Columbia.

E2 John Alexander Stewart, b. January 10, 1948, Richmond, BC. He m. (1) Randise Gail McLaughlin (Randy), b. in British Columbia, on July 27, 1974, and divorced in 1984.

    F1 Jesse Alexander James Stewart, b. September 29, 1975, Richmond, BC, m. Lora Lau.

        G1 Emily Stewart, b. January 9, 2008, in British Columbia.

    F2 Colin John Stewart, b. July 12, 1977, Richmond, BC.

John m. (2) Jean Garrie, b. March 26 [year unknown].

    F3 Hayley Stewart, b. September 17, 1987, Richmond, BC.

    F4 Benjamin Stewart, b. November 29, 1989, Richmond, BC

E3 Kenneth Esplin Stewart, b. April 2, 1949, Richmond, BC. He m. Donna Jean Belden, b. February 8, 1949, Richmond, BC. They were married November 7, 1970, in Richmond.

    F1 Ian James Stewart, b. May 14, 1974, m. Nicole Brassard, b. in Alberta. They were married January 2, 1999, Hinton, AB.

        G1 Nathan James Stewart, b. July 6,

2004, Nelson, BC.
G2   Logan James Stewart, b. September 6, 2005, Vernon, BC.
F2   Amy Leanne Stewart, b. March 12, 1976. She m. (1) Patrick Novak ca. 2002 and divorced, then m. (2) Jay Thorbourn.
E4   Roberta Jean Stewart, b. July 4, 1951, Richmond, BC. She m. Hatto Heinrich Horn, b. in Nieder-Olm, Germany.
E5   Daniel Maynard Ross Stewart, b. October 19, 1956, Richmond, BC. He m. (1) Darcy [?], b. 1960. They were married ca. 1984 and divorced.
F1   Travis Stewart, b. August 1, 1981, in British Columbia.
F2   Ashley Stewart, b. June 20, 1986, Richmond, BC.
F3   Kayla Stewart, b. May 26, 1989, Richmond, BC.
Daniel m. (2) Kristine Findlay, b. 1970 in Alberta.
F4   Claudia Piper Stewart, b. 2007 in British Columbia.
F5   Henry Daniel Stewart, b. 2007 in British Columbia.
Daniel has a son with a First Nation woman to whom he was not married. She would have lost her treaty rights if she had married Daniel.
E6   Heather Ruth Stewart, b. October 24, 1959, Richmond, BC. She m. Glen Arthur Lynskey, b. November 13, 1950, Toronto, ON. They were married in 1987 in Whistler, BC.
F1   Torin Stewart Lynskey, b. July 2, 1991, Whistler, BC.
F2   William John Lynskey, b. April 6, 1996, Whistler, BC.
C10   Christy Ann Stewart, b. December 1, 1893, Mount Buchanan, baptized July 3, 1894, Orwell Head, m. William Ross.
C11   Donald or Daniel Stewart, b. January 24, 1896, Mount Buchanan, no date given for baptism. He m. Ida Louise Keith, b. August 18, 1900, Montague, daughter of Henry Levi Keith and his wife, baptized May 7, 1909, Montague Methodist Church.
D1   Bernard Stewart.

          D2   Richard Stewart (Dickie).
          D3   Donald Stewart (Donnie).
B5   Margaret Campbell, b. December 4, 1854, baptized March 23, 1855, Orwell Head, d. 1912, Uigg, buried, Orwell Head. She m. (1) Malcolm Archibald MacPherson, b. June 9, 1851. Grandview, baptized August 1852, Valleyfield, d. February 16, 1876, Uigg, buried, Valleyfield. Malcolm was a farmer.
     C1* Malcolm James MacPherson, b. February 19, 1875, Grandview, baptized May 30, 1875, Orwell Head Church of Scotland, d. February 24, 1935, Port Elgin, NB, buried, Orwell Head. He was a minister. Malcolm lived with his Campbell grandparents after his father's death. He m. Ella Mabel Stavert on June 30, 1903, by the Rev. D.B. MacLeod. Ella was b. 1875, Kelvin Grove, daughter of William Stavert (mother's name unknown), d. May 11, 1959, Charlottetown, buried, Orwell Head.
Margaret m. (2) Neil MacPherson, b. July 22, 1836, China Point, baptized March 23, 1837, Belfast, d. June 23, 1911, Uigg, buried, Orwell Head. Neil was also a farmer.
     C2   Daniel MacPherson, b. December 25, 1878, Scentia, baptized July 1879, Orwell Head, d. October 6, 1886.
     C3   Janet Florence MacPherson (Jenny), b. June 26, 1880, Scentia, d. July 28, 1974, Charlottetown, buried, Union Road Cemetery. She m. John Thomas Mellish, b. May 9, 1879, Union Road, son of John Henry Mellish and Amelia MacLaren, d. March 23, 1945. He was a farmer. Janet and John were married on December 19, 1906, by the Rev. W. Dobson in First Methodist (Trinity) Church in Charlottetown. The bondsman was John T. Mellish.
          D1   Clarence William Mellish, b. April 21, 1910, Union Road, baptized May 21, 1911, Montague Methodist Church, d. November 22, 1964, in the Prince Edward Island Hospital, buried, Union Road Cemetery. He was never married. He was a carpenter and mechanic and served with the RCAF in WWII.
          D2   Ruth Amelia Mellish, b. September 24, 1911, m. Simon Alexander Campbell (see B8.C3, p. 89).
          D3   Margaret Florence Mellish, b. May 18, 1913, Union Road, baptized February 4, 1914, Montague Methodist Church, d. October 4, 1969, age 56, buried, Gladstone Cemetery. She was a teacher. She m. Robert Alexander Munn (Bob), b. June 28, 1907, Murray River, son of

Alexander Munn and Kate MacLean, baptized July 25, 1908, Murray Harbour Presbyterian Circuit, d. December 31, 1981, buried, Gladstone Cemetery. He was a carpenter. Margaret and Robert were married January 2, 1935, at the Baptist parsonage in Charlottetown by the Rev. A.C. Vincent.

    E1   Merrill Munn, b. July 15, 1938, Murray River. He was a fisherman and carpenter. He m. Georgina Penny, b. April 19, 1945, Murray Harbour, daughter of Bert Penny and Lena MacKenzie. She was a nurse.

        F1   Lisa Margaret Munn, b. June 7, 1965.

        F2   Penny Michelle Munn, b. October 18, 1972. She is a teacher and nurse.

        F3   Lincoln Merrill Munn, b. April 20, 1976. He is a fisherman.

    E2   Boyd Munn, March 26, 1950, Murray River. He is a carpenter and contractor. He m. Leona Anstie, daughter of Harry Anstie and Elizabeth Hopkins.

        F1   Robert Fitzpatrick, b. October 18, 1972.

        F2   Ronald Boyd Munn (Ronnie), b. November 6, 1978, in Montague.

        F3   Lindsay Margaret Munn, b. December 2, 1982, in Montague.

    E3   Blair Douglas Munn, b. February 1, 1957, Murray River. He was a carpenter.

D4   Elsie May Mellish, b. September 8, 1919, Union Road, d. December 15, 2005, buried, Union Cemetery. She was a teacher. She m. Charles Frederick Carver (Fred), b. October 12, 1922, Alliston, son of John Carver and Mary Hannah MacDonald, d. May 21, 1996, buried, Union Road. He was a farmer and trucker. Elsie and Charles were married December 20, 1941, by the Rev. Richardson.

    E1   Evelyn Joyce Carver, instructor at Dalhousie University, m. Richard Black

    E2   Margaret Jean Carver, b. May 2, 1946. She was a nurse. She m. (1) Elmer Gillis, b. in Belle River, son of Duncan Gillis and Evaline Smith, d. 1997.

        F1   Terry Lynn Gillis, b. December 9, 1965, m. Jim Renn.

       G1 Shannon Renn, b. April 24, 1997.
    F2 Kevin Frederick Gillis, b. May 29, 1971.
Margaret (E2) m. (2) Douglas Kitchen, a farmer.
 E3 Mary Jeanette Carver, b. June 25, 1947, m. Basil Higginbotham, a fisherman.
    F1 Cindy Lynn Higginbotham, b. March 14, 1968, m. Donald MacMillan, son of Sinclair MacMillan and Jean MacWilliams.
       G1 Tiffany MacMillan, b. April 17, 1997.
    F2 Patricia Ann Higginbotham, b. December 23, 1969, m. Robert Carver, son of Otis Carver and Florence Marie Campbell. They were married August 4, 2000.
       G1 Samantha Marie Carver, b. September 4, 2002.
    F3 Michael Higginbotham, b. September 8, 1971, m. Christa MacSwain, daughter of Lynn MacSwain and Darlene Campbell.
       G1 Mary Hannah Higginbotham, b. March 21, 1996.
       G2 Hope Higginbotham, b. October 1997.
    F4 Marilyn Higginbotham, b. October 12, 1972, m. Wade MacLean.
       G1 Topanga Sea MacLean, b. June 6, 2000.
 E4 Muriel May Carver, b. August 17, 1948. She worked in a PEI government office. She m. David Augustine Power, b. April 17, 1947, Greenfield, son of Emmett Power and Mary Kelly, d. November 29, 1997, at his home in Greenfield, buried, Saint Mary's Parish Cemetery.
    F1 Adam David Power, b. April 8, 1975, a mechanic. He m. Tracy Landry on April 26, 2003.
    F2 Kelly Rose May Power, b. March 13, 1979. She was an office worker living in Ottawa in 1997. She m. Troy Griese on September 2, 2002.

      G1 Kirsten Rose May Griese, b. February 11, 2005, Ottawa.
  E5 Judith Elizabeth Carver, b. September 10, 1951. She m. Donald Gordon Nicholson (Gordon), b. November 25, 1953, in Toronto, son of Donald Glen Nicholson and Mary Elva MacLeod, baptized July 12, 1954, Orwell Head. He was a feed mill operator.
    F1 Mary Christine Nicholson, b. November 19, 1979.
    F2 Raymond Donovan Nicholson, b. September 14, 1985.
    F3 Donald Matthew Nicholson, b. October 1987.
C4 Sarah Catherine MacPherson, b. July 8, 1882, Uigg, baptized November 12, 1882, Orwell Head, d. August 29, 1908, age 26, buried, Orwell Head. She has no headstone.
  D1 Chester MacPherson, b. December 14, 1907, Uigg, baptized August 12, 1911, Orwell Head, d. in Ottawa, buried, Orwell Head Cemetery. There is no tombstone. Chester was raised by his mother's sister, Euphemia. He was a teacher and accountant. He m. Rosalie Favell, b. in England and d. in Ottawa.
    E1 Joyce MacPherson, b. July 1932, m. James Wilson (Jim).
    E2 Gloria June MacPherson, b. June 2, 1936, Ottawa, d. January 29, 2002, Maple Ridge, BC, buried, Maple Ridge Cemetery. She m. Peter S. Boyle.
      F1 Debbie Boyle, b. ca. 1958. She was a veterinarian. She m. John Quon.
        G1 Brian Quon, b. 1985.
        G2 Lori Ann Quon, b. 1987.
        G3 Jacquelin Quon, b. 1992.
      F2 Diane Boyle, b. ca. 1960, m. Randy Alex.
        G1 Ricky Alex, b. 1992.
        G2 Shaun Alex, b. 1996.
        G3 Breeanna Alex.
C5 Euphemia MacPherson (Phemie), b. August 20, 1885, The Point (Orwell area), baptized January 19, 1886, Vernon River Bible Christian Church, d. April 17, 1967, Beach Grove Home, buried, Uigg Baptist Cemetery. She m. Adrian Hiram Reynolds,

b. September 14, 1888, Cape Breton, d. July 21, 1969, Beach Grove Home, buried, Uigg Baptist Cemetery. He was a farmer and station agent. Euphemia and Adrian were married on December 12, 1912, by the Rev. Jacob Heaney in First Methodist (Trinity) Church. The bondsman was C.W. Patterson.

    D1   Arthur Stroud Reynolds, b. May 24, 1959, Uigg, baptized August 6, 1917, Vernon River, d. 1997 in Ottawa. He m. Elizabeth Weir (Betty), d. Ottawa. They had no children.

C6   Mary Ann MacPherson, b. September 7, 1887, Uigg, baptized January 7, 1888, Orwell Head, d. in MA. She m. (1) Harvey MacKay, b. and d. in MA.

    D1   Dorothy MacKay, m. Melvin Deveau. Both b. and d. in MA.

    D2   Earl MacKay, b. ca. 1914 in MA. The 1930 census gives his age as 16.

May Ann m. (2) [?] Ambrose

C7*   Donalena MacPherson (Dolly), b. November 27, 1889, Uigg, baptized January 7, 1890, Vernon River, d. in Ipswich, MA. She m. Claude LeRoy Wyland (Roy), b. ca. 1881 in Canada, son of H. Wyland and his wife, d. in Ipswich, MA. They were married on December 26, 1910, in Ipswich by the Rev. F. Ward and the Rev. H.B. Smith. The bride's sister Mary was a witness.

    D1   Ruth M. Wyland, b. ca. 1912 in MA, m. W. Arthur Grover.

    D2   Leslie Wyland, b. ca. 1917 in MA.

    D3   Vivan Wyland, b. ca. 1919 in MA, m. Robert Walker.

        E1   John Walker.

        E2   Robert Walker.

        E3   David Walker, buried, Ipswich, 1996.

    D4   Rosamund Wyland, m. Robert Weaver.

C8   Mary MacPherson (Mamie), b. December 13, 1891, m. John Cidney Rowell.

    D1   Russell James Rowell, b. July 16, 1920, Boston, MA. He was a medical doctor. He m. Barbara May Bowman, b. April 23, 1921, in Boston. They were married May 28, 1944, in Beverly, MA.

        E1   James R. Rowell, Jr., b. June 20, 1948, Beverly, MA, deceased.

        E2   Bradford Vaughn Rowell, b. December 17, 1955, in Beverly, MA.

C9   Christina Belle MacPherson, b. August 7, 1894, Uigg, baptized April 8, 1898, Orwell Head, d. September 25, 1913, age 19,

Uigg, buried, Orwell Head (no headstone).

B6 Neil Campbell, b. January 12, 1857, Uigg, baptized March 29, 1857, Orwell Head, d. January 7, 1911, age 54, Oakland, CA. Neil was a ship captain. He m. Christine MacLeod (Christy), b. June 22, 1857, Kinross, baptized July 13, 1857, Orwell Head Church of Scotland, d. in California.
    C1   Janetta Campbell, m. William C. Mayne.
           D1   Neil Campbell Mayne.

B7 John Murdoch Campbell, b. October 10, 1858, Uigg, baptized November 13, 1858, Orwell Head, d. in Montana. He m. Anne Mary MacRae on February 27, 1884, in the manse in Kinross by the Rev. Don Goodwill. Anne Mary was b. September 4, 1861, Point Prim, baptized in Belfast, d. in Eureka, Montana.
    C1   Malcolm Campbell.
    C2   Janet Campbell, m. Clarence A. Andrew.
    C3   Donald Campbell, m. Adah Herring.
    C4   Euphemia Campbell.
    C5   Annie Laura Campbell. She was a teacher.

B8 Christina Catherine Campbell (Christy), b. October 7, 1860, Uigg, baptized March 3, 1861, in the Church of Scotland by the Rev. Donald MacDonald, d. September 24, 1892, age 32, Brooklyn, buried, Valleyfield Cemetery. She was a teacher. She m. Murdoch Campbell, January 19, 1887, in the City Hotel by the Rev. John M. MacLeod. Murdoch was b. ca. 1849 in Kendrum, Kilmuir Parish, Skye, d. of heart failure, January 23, 1911, age 62, Brooklyn, buried, Valleyfield Cemetery. He was a farmer, storekeeper and secretary.
    C1   Sarah Ann Campbell, b. November 13, 1887, Brooklyn, baptized September 7, 1890, Caledonia Church, d. March 7, 1896, age 8 years and 4 months, buried in Valleyfield.
    C2   Malcolm Archibald Campbell, b. March 7, 1889, Brooklyn, baptized September 7, 1890, Caledonia Church, d. of a stroke July 9, 1939, San Francisco, CA, buried Cypress Lawn Cemetery, San Francisco. He never married.
    C3   Simon Alexander Campbell, b. December 19, 1890, m. Ruth Amelia Mellish (see B5.C3.D2, p. 84).
           D1   Malcolm James Campbell, b. January 24, 1934, Brooklyn, baptized April 18, 1935, Caledonia Presbyterian Church. He was in the RCAF and also a commissionaire. He m. (1) Mary Elizabeth Murphy, b. January 10, 1936, Vernon Bridge, daughter of Charles Murphy and Edna Fraser, d. December 20, 1966, Vernon Bridge, buried, Saint

Joachim's Cemetery. She was a stenographer.

- E1 Deborah Jean Campbell, b. May 3, 1955, in Newfoundland. She is a financial clerk. She m. Blair Joseph MacLean, b. September 21, 1954, in Summerside, son of Jack MacLean and Joyce Thompson. He is a financial supervisor at the tax centre.
    - F1 Bradley Jonathan MacLean, b. October 21, 1974. He is a hydro consultant. He m. Kimberley Ann Hornmoen, b. April 24, 1975, Chester, NS. She is a nurse (BScN). They were married September 23, 2000, in Chester, NS.
        - G1 Mary Emma Lynn MacLean, b. August 28, 2003.
        - G2 Malcolm Evan Jacob MacLean, b. May 13, 2005.
        - G3 Melanie Ella Audrey MacLean, b. January 31, 2008, Halifax.
    - F2 Monica Jill MacLean, b. September 24, 1976. She is an accountant. She m. Alexander Eugene Affleck, a farmer, b. January 1, 1974. They were married July 1, 2002, in Bedeque United Church.
        - G1 Percy Thorne Affleck, b. May 29, 2004, Summerside.
        - G2 Jack Harrison Affleck, b. March 3, 2006, Prince County Hospital, Summerside.
        - G3 Carly Affleck.
- E2 Alexander James Campbell (Sandy), b. December 25, 1959, in Toronto. He is an accountant and CEO for West Jet. He m. Debra Lori Jones, b. September 13, 1955, in Alberta, daughter of Alfred and Alveda Jones. She was a laboratory technician and instructor at Holland College in 2007.
    - F1 Matthew Alexander Campbell, b. April 25, 1985, Lethbridge, AB.
- E3 Jill Elizabeth Campbell, b. November 11, 1962, Calgary, AB. She is a legal clerk. She m. Brian Edgar Gervais, an accountant, b. January 5, 1964,

in Fort MacLeod, AB, son of Raymond and Clara Gervais.

    F1   Mary Elizabeth Gervais, b. October 17, 1997, Brooks, AB.

    F2   Danielle Courtney Gervais, b. January 14, 2001, Brooks, AB.

Malcolm James (D1) m. (2) Sheila Lucy Warren, b. October 9, 1938, Summerside, daughter of Garnet and Melvina Warren. She was an Island Telephone employee.

    E4   James Garnet Campbell, b. September 11, 1972.

D2   Donald Murdock Campbell, b. May 18, 1935, Brooklyn, baptized August 18, 1935, Caledonia Presbyterian Church. He was a systems engineer. He m. (1) Florence Bowers, b. in Halifax. She was a nurse. The couple divorced.

    E1   Donald Campbell Devitt (Brent), b. February 7, 1960, Kingston, ON. He was a businessman. He m. Lisa Spruijt, b. February 3, 1962. They were married December 18, 1984.

        F1   Alexandra Heather Devitt, b. May 26, 1990, Vancouver, BC.

        F2   Ryan Devitt, b. May 6, 1994, Vancouver, BC.

        F2   Jessica Julie Devitt, b. November 18, 1995, Vancouver, BC.

    E2   Heather Lynn Campbell Devitt, b. December 5, 1960, Whitehorse. She m. Raymond Winters (Ray), b. May 26, 1961, in British Columbia. His parents had emigrated from Holland. He was a police sergeant and dog trainer. They were married September 24, 1982.

        F1   Kyle Ray Winters, b. March 7, 1992, Richmond, BC, adopted.

        F2   Kalyn Marie Winters, b. May 23, 1995, Nelson, BC, adopted.

    E3   Douglas Gregory Campbell Devitt, b. February 18, 1963, Vancouver.

Donald Murdock (D2) m. (2) Elizabeth Deruiter, b. in Holland. She was a model. The couple divorced. He m. (3) Frances O'Hara, b. in Saint John, NB.

D3   Jean Florence Campbell, b. March 26, 1937, Brooklyn.

She was a dental hygienist and RN. She m. Allison Ivan MacLean, b. December 26, 1934, Wheatley River, son of John A. MacLean and Edna Mae Smith. He was a mechanic. They were married on September 17, 1961, in the Caledonia Presbyterian Church.

E1 Bonnie Ruth MacLean, b. April 15, 1963, baptized in Hunter River Presbyterian Church. She is a Department of Veteran Affairs employee. She m. Timothy Leslie (Tim), b. February 23, 1961. His business is sales of motorcycle equipment. They were married on June 23, 2001, in Stanley Bridge.

E2 Mary Beth MacLean, b. June 18, 1966, baptized, Hunter River Presbyterian Church. She is an economist with the Department of Veterans Affairs. She m. Francois Weber, b. November 12, 1966, North Bay, ON, son of Otto Weber and Carmen Gaudette. He is a teacher and entertainer. Mary Beth and Francois were married on October 3, 1992, in North Bay, ON.

    F1 Corey Campbell Weber, b. April 20, 1994, Ottawa, baptized, Spring Park United Church.

    F2 Amelia Nicolle Weber, b. April 22, 1999, baptized, Spring Park United Church.

E3 Scott Allison MacLean, b. July 26, 1967. He m. Angela Bigney, b. September 17, 1966, daughter of Merle Bigney and Ruth MacLennan. They were married September 22, 1989, Charlottetown Bible Chapel. Scott is a home inspector and Angela is an architectural technician.

    F1 Joshua Scott MacLean, b. August 30, 1990, Queen Elizabeth Hospital.

    F2 Laura Jean MacLean, b. October 10, 1992, Queen Elizabeth Hospital, baptized, Charlottetown Bible Chapel.

    F2 Jessica Ruth MacLean, b. November 14, 1995, Queen Elizabeth Hospital, baptized, Charlottetown Bible Chapel.

    F4 Matthew James MacLean, b. June 12, 1999, Queen Elizabeth Hospital, baptized, Charlottetown Bible Chapel.

F5 Justin Merle MacLean, b. December 2, 2002, Queen Elizabeth Hospital, baptized Charlottetown Bible Chapel.

F6 Emma Angela MacLean, b. November 15, 2005, Queen Elizabeth Hospital, baptized Charlottetown Bible Chapel.

F7 Mitchell Brandon MacLean, b. October 24, 2007, Queen Elizabeth Hospital.

D4 Christine Catherine Campbell, b. August 1, 1938, Brooklyn, baptized October 10, 1953, Caledonia Presbyterian Church. She is an x-ray technician. She m. Marcus Kramarczyk (Mike), b. November 6, 1934, Larder Lake, ON, son of Stan and Maria Kramarczyk, who emigrated from Poland. He is a mine ventilation technician. Christine and Marcus were married in June 1962 in Eliot Lake, ON.

E2 Kent Matthew Kramarczyk, b. June 4, 1963, Elliot Lake, ON. He works in the Canadian Tire office. He m. Tracey Breton, a bank employee, on June 4, 1963. They are divorced.

F1 Dylan Reginald Simon Kramarczyk, b. November 9, 1992.

E2 Ruth Ann Kramarczyk, b. July 6, 1966, Elliot Lake, ON. She is an office worker. She m. David Kyle Pickersgill (Kyle), b. January 19, 1968, in Ontario, son of Jim Pickersgill and Patricia. They were married September 19, 1992.

F1 Alexander James Pickersgill, b. January 23, 1995, London, ON.

C4 James Murdoch Campbell, b. August 29, 1892, Brooklyn, baptized September 29, 1892, Brooklyn, d. of a heart attack February 27, 1958, Winnipeg, buried, Brookside Cemetery, Winnipeg. James was raised by his mother's parents, Malcolm and Janet Campbell (Jessie), Uigg. He was with the 5th Siege Battery in WWI and worked as a logger in BC. He never married.

B9 Flora Campbell, b. January 8, 1863, baptized February 26, 1863, in Orwell Head. She m. Donald MacKinnon (Dan), October 31, 1894, in her parents' home by her brother the Rev. D.M. Campbell. Dan was b. June 17, 1869, in Forest Hill and was a farmer. He d. February 3, 1948, in Forest Hill, aged 79 years, 6 months and 29 days, buried in Dundas. Flora died September 17, 1955, in Sunset Lodge, Charlottetown, buried in Dundas.

B10* Donald MacDonald Campbell, b. November 22, 1864, Uigg, baptized January 12, 1865, Orwell Head, d. in Saskatoon. He was a minister. He m. (1) Christina Mary MacRae, b. May 20, 1864, Point Prim, daughter of Donald MacRae and Euphemia Murchison, baptized Belfast, d. December 11, 1896, age 32, buried Belfast. Donald and Christina were m. May 8, 1888, Orwell Head, by the Rev. D.B. MacLeod.

    C1   Donald Campbell, b. March 2, 1889, Uigg, baptized March 3, 1889, Orwell Head, d. March 10, 1889.

    C2   Christina Grace Campbell, b. September 18, 1892, Orwell.

    C3   Euphemia Janetta MacKay Campbell, b. December 5, 1896, Orwell, baptized August 26, 1897 in the residence of Donald Cambridge by the Rev. D. MacLean.

Donald m. (2) Euphemia Gillespie, b. December 20, 1873, Carleton Point, daughter of James Gillespie and Sarah Jane Campbell, baptized March 15, 1874, Church of Scotland, d. 1953 in Saskatoon.

    C4   Sarah Campbell
    C5   Ruth M. Campbell, a teacher residing in Saskatoon.
    C6   William Campbell.
    C7   Olive Campbell.
    C8   Marjorie Campbell, m. Carl Gryte.
        D1   Carl Campbell Gryte.
        D2   Daniel Gillespie Gryte.
        D3   Stephen Gryte.
    C9   James Campbell, a medical specialist, Saskatoon.

Further information about the Rev. Donald MacDonald Campbell may be found in the appendix.

B11* Simon Alexander Campbell, b. October 8, 1866, Uigg, baptized July 11, 1867, Orwell Head, d. May 24, 1951, Silver Creek, BC. He was in the lumber business. He m. Euphemia MacLean, b. September 27, 1870, Point Prim, d. February 21, 1937, Silver Creek, BC.

    C1   Neil Campbell, b. October 15, 1903, m. Naomi Lott.
        D1   James Murchison Campbell, d. October 23, 2005. He was a minister with the Seventh Day Adventist Church. He m. Frances [?].
            E1   Merle Campbell, m. Steve Hildebrandt.
                F1   Merle Hildebrand.
            E2   Coleen Campbell, m. Larry Varico.
                F1   Robbie Varico.
                F2   Katie Varico.

The Descendants of James Campbell and Christy MacDonald

            E3   Richard Campbell.
- D2 Murray Campbell, m. Marlene [?].
  - E1 Heather Campbell, m. Jeff Berry.
    - F1 Raymond Berry.
    - F2 Gavin Berry.
  - E2 Cheryl Campbell, m. Bob Holiday.
    - F1 Ryan Holiday.
    - F2 Jonathan Holiday.
  - E3 Daryl Campbell, m. Vicky [?].
    - F1 Natasha Campbell.
  - E4 Michelle Campbell.
- D3 Christine Campbell, twin to Caroline, b. April 9, 1937, in BC, d. February 15, 2005. She m. David Norris.
  - E1 Destanne Norris, m. Norma Brown.
    - F1 Tekarra Norris.
    - F2 James Norris.
    - F3 Leah Norris.
  - E2 Kevin Norris, m. Denise [?].
    - F1 Allison Norris.
    - F2 Jacklyn Norris.
    - F3 Treanne Norris.
  - E3 Danna Norris.
- D4 Caroline Campbell, twin to Christine, b. April 9, 1937, in BC, m. Ronald Stickle.
  - E1 Teresa Stickle (Teri), m. John Reeve.
    - F1 Tony Reeve (adopted).
  - E2 Marc Stickle, m. Jill [?].
    - F1 Jamie Paige Stickle.
    - F2 Chet Stickle.
  - E3 Kelly Stickle, m. Lori [?].
    - F1 Roderick Stickle, b. 1989.
    - F2 Gabrielle Stickle (Ellie), b. 1991.
- D5 Maynard Campbell, m. Shannon [?].

C2 John Campbell, b. November 15, 1907, d. 1997 in BC. He m. Edna Lott, b. June 25, 1918, Salmon Arm, BC. They were married in BC on April 13, 1934.
- D1 Robert Alexander Campbell, b. October 12, 1934, BC, d. August 24, 2001, in BC. He m. (1) Marlene McGregor in 1955. She died ca. 1980.
  - E1 Gordon Robert Campbell, b. May 15, 1956, m. Wendy [?], b. July 1, 1963.

      F1 Scott John Campbell, b. January 4, 1985, m. Sharon Larouse in British Columbia.
        G1 Jeffery Britt Benoit Josiah Campbell, b. August 1, 2000.
      F2 Nicole May Campbell, b. August 23, 1986.
   E2 Clinton James Campbell, b. 1958, d. 1989. He m. Cathy Koazk, ca. 1981.
      F1 Jason Campbell, b. 1983.
      F2 Jamie Campbell, b. 1985.
   E3 Mikael John Campbell, b. 1960.

Robert Alexander (D1) m. (2) Thelma Fennell, d. July 20, 1991.

D2 Marjorie Elvera Campbell, b. March 9, 1937, BC. She m. Thomas Darwin Churchill (Darry), b. October 8, 1935. They were married in 1958 and celebrated their 50th wedding anniversary on August 28, 2008.
   E1 Victor Darwin Churchill, b. March 7, 1959. He was a millwright. He m. Heather [?].
      F1 Scott Churchill.
   E2 Kim Doyle Churchill, b. January 11, 1963. He was a mechanic. He m. Tracy Moen.
      F1 Travis Churchill.
      F2 Jenna Churchill.

D3 Doreen Campbell, b. March 19, 1939, m. Larry James Churchill, b. September 11, 1934.
   E1 Kathrine Dawn Churchill, b. December 1, 1956.
   E2 Karl James Churchill, b. May 24, 1960. He m. Dianna Ford.
   E3 Nadine Edna Churchill, b. July 28, 1956, m. Douglas Kelly, b. April 7, 1964. They were married October 6, 1984.
      F1 Tawny Justine Kelly.
      F2 Kara Edna Kelly.

D4 Ronald Donald Campbell, b. May 5, 1945, BC, d. February 8, 2007, in Fort Saint John. He m. Mariel Ilona Jean Wickstrom, b. July 7, 1944, SK. They were married in BC.
   E1 Marnie Gail Campbell, b. September 13, 1965, m. Pat Fagherty, b. July 13, 1963. They were married August 13, 1989, and have divorced.
      F1 Amanda Jean Fagherty, b. February 9,

       1992.
    F2 Arielle Jade Fagherty, b. September 17, 1995.
  E2 Shane MacLean Campbell, b. May 12, 1968.
 C3 Malcolm Campbell, d. ca. 1974, Vancouver, BC, never married.

B12 Malcolm Hector Campbell, b. March 26, 1870, in Uigg, PEI, baptized March 29, 1870, in Orwell Head. He was a chauffeur in Boston and later had a general store in Uigg. Malcolm d. August 19, 1932, in Forest Hills, of cancer, and was buried in Orwell Head cemetery. The funeral was at the home of his brother-in-law in Orwell, who was a partner in the firm of Campbell & MacDonald, the general store in Uigg. Malcolm m. Mary Ann MacDonald, b. May 18, 1873, in Orwell, baptized August 31, 1873, in the Church of Scotland, Orwell Head, d. January 28, 1955. Her siblings were Daniel, Murdoch, John Finlay (partner in the store) and Mary Christy. Malcolm and Mary Ann had no children.

A2. The Descendants of John Campbell and Euphemia Murchison

John Campbell (James), b. May 24, 1823, in Skye, emigrated in 1829. He was a farmer. He d. May 5, 1907, in Uigg and was buried in Orwell Head.

John m. Euphemia Murchison, b. February 28, 1830, at Point Prim, d. December 12, 1844, in Uigg, buried in Orwell Head. John and Euphemia were married on February 20, 1850, by the Rev. Donald MacDonald.

The following obituary was obtained from a newspaper clipping:

Mr. John Campbell died at Uigg, Sabbath evening, May 5th, and was buried on May 7th, in Orwell Head churchyard. Death came to him at the ripe age of eighty-three years. He was perceptibly ailing for the last few years; but for a week the end appeared near at hand.

His father, James Campbell, with his family, emigrated from Skye, Scotland, in the year 1829, and settled in Uigg, PEI. John, the second of the family, was then about five years of age.

While in his teens, he experienced a saving change under the preaching of the late Rev. Donald MacDonald. From that day onwards, his was a devoted, but unobtrusive, Christian life. This soon marked him as suitable for the duties of the eldership, to which he was ordained among the first group of elders to Orwell Head Church. He proved himself eminently fitted for the office, and was a pillar of strength in the congregation, till laid aside by failing health.

He found a true helpmeet and life companion in Euphemia Murchison of Point Prim. She died 22 years ago, leaving him a family of seven: four boys—Simon, who stayed with him in the home; Samuel, who also has his home in Uigg; Neil, the eldest, in Oregon; James M., in Montana—and three daughters: Mrs. Hugh Martin, Orwell Head; Mrs. Peter Murchison, Dundee; and Miss Emily, who is in Boston.

A large number of friends and some acquaintances gathered at the home in Uigg to show their sympathy with the bereaved family and their respect for the departed. The funeral service was conducted by Messrs. J. MacNeill, late pastor of the congregation, who is presently under call to Murray Harbour South; and John Gillis, who is visiting friends in the district; and H. Michael, the pastor of the congregation.

Mr. Campbell will be much missed by a wide circle of friends by whom he was respected as a man of sterling qualities. He was recognized by his acquaintances as a man of strong and steadfast convictions, but withal, charitable towards those who differed from him. Though of a quiet manner, he was always forward with a good cause. His was a long, consistent Christian life, and his end was peace. His death has made a blank in a district, and especially in Orwell Head congregation, which cannot easily be filled.

Death Notice from the *Daily Examiner,* December 29, 1844:

Died at Uigg on the 12th of December, Euphemia, daughter of Neil Murchison, and beloved wife of John Campbell, in the 54th year of her life, leaving an affectionate husband and seven children (four sons and three daughters), with a large circle of relations and friends to mourn their loss. Her end was peace. "Blessed are the dead which die in the Lord from henceforth; yea, saith the spirit, that they may rest from their labours and their works do follow them—Rev. XIV.13." She was a sister of Malcolm Campbell's wife Janet and a sister of Ann Campbell's husband Donald Murchison.

John and his brother Malcolm were obviously very close to one another: initially, they farmed the old homestead together, but gradually acquired their own farms and continued to work closely together. It is said that they shook hands on their first meeting each day. While Malcolm bought and moved to his own farm nearby, sometime after 1861, John acquired the back 50 acres of an adjacent farm from his neighbour Kelly in 1872, probably with the prospect in mind that his son Neil would be staying on the farm with him. When Neil decided against farming and moved to North Dakota, the land was sold to Neil's brother Samuel, who bought the front 50 acres of Kelly's farm as well, giving him a total of 100 acres. Samuel farmed and raised his family on the property until he turned it over to his son John in 1927. John, in turn, worked the farm and raised his family there until 1949, when he sold it to a neighbour's son, Hugh Robbins, who was a great-great grandson of James Campbell.

In John's will (#18-486, November 1897), he leaves his son James Murdoch $50, his daughter Emily $40, and the farm to Simon D.

The descendants of John and Euphemia are:

B1 James Campbell, b. December 21, 1853, in Uigg, baptized February 12, 1854, in Orwell Head, d. October 30, 1859, aged 5 years and 10 months, buried in Uigg Pioneer Cemetery.

B2* Neil Murchison Campbell, b. November 29, 1855, Uigg, baptized March 2, 1856, Church of Scotland, Orwell Head, by the Rev. Donald MacDonald, d. May 2, 1911, Woodburn, Oregon. He m. Euphemia MacKenzie (Effie), b. April 26, 1864, Uigg, daughter of James MacKenzie and Ann Martin, baptized June 19, 1864, Church of Scotland, Orwell Head, by the Rev. Donald MacDonald, d. 1935 in Los Angeles, California. Articles about Neil M. Campbell and Euphemia MacKenzie may be found in the appendix.

    C1 James Arthur Campbell, Sr., b. October 7, 1882, North Dakota, d. Stockton, California. He was a dentist. He m. Ethel Letitia Rogers, d. 1987, California.

        D1 James Arthur Campbell, Jr., b. September 20, 1920, Hanford, CA, d. March 17, 1990, San Leandro, CA. He was a professor of cranial facial radiology who owned a string of dental radiology offices. He m. Alice Ellen Fitzgerald, b. June 13, 1913, San Francisco, daughter of Earle Fitzgerald and Henrietta Hoffman, d. December 22, 1996, San Leandro, CA. She was an artist. James and Alice were married in 1946.

            E1 Kevin James Campbell, b. October 29, 1948, San Francisco, CA, d. May 1991 on a golf course in Monterey county, CA. He was a dentist and writer. He m. Susan Darrough in 1974.

                F1 Michael Wyndham Darrough Campbell, b. 1976, Chico, CA.

                F2 Paul Aaron Campbell, b. 1980, Berkeley, CA.

            E2 Jon Brian Campbell, b. September 5, 1951, Oakland, CA, d. January 30, 2003, Washburn, WI. He was the owner of a comic book store and screen writer.

            E3 Ellen Letitia Campbell, b. June 7, 1956, San Francisco, CA. She worked in catering and as an art docent. She m. Dave Birdie in August 1989 in San Francisco, CA, and later divorced.

                F1 Kaitlyn Campbell-Birdie, b. February 2, 1991, Greenbrae, CA.

                F2 Jamie Campbell-Birdie, b. December 27,

1993, Greenbrae, CA.
- E4 Robert Gordon Campbell, b. October 9, 1958, San Francisco, CA, d. December 2005, San Luis Obispo, CA. He was a dentist and associate pastor. He m. Lisa Wood, b. October 9, 1958, Glendale, CA. She was a sign language counsellor. They were married in 1980 in the Redwood City Covenant Church.
  - F1 Brennan Campbell, b. 1988.
  - F2 Christopher Scott Campbell, b. 1990.
  - F3 Erin J. Campbell, b. October 1996.
- D2 John Gordon Campbell (Jack), b. ca. 1923, Hanford, CA, d. ca. 1993. He m. (1) Beverly [?]
  - E1 Sally Campbell, b. ca. 1955, adopted child of John and Beverly.

John Gordon m. (2) Barbara [?]

- D3 Donald Bruce Campbell, b. ca. 1926, Hanford, CA, d. October 22, 1985. He m. Mary Ann Lind, b. Oakland, CA.
  - E1 Sharon Campbell, b. October 10, 1946, Oakland, CA. She m. (1) Richard Guthrie, b. May 6, 1943, Philadelphia, d. February 2000, Sacramento, CA. They were married May 31, 1963 in Reno, NV. She m. (2) Michael Cain, b. August 10, 1941, Oakland, CA. He was a fireman in Oakland. They were married May 30, 1976, in Reno, NV.
  - E2 Cindy Campbell, m. Ted Ackley.
  - E3 Jim Campbell, b. May 9, 1952, Oakland, CA. He was a carpenter. He m. Sue Rambert, b. November 23, 1953, Chicago, IL. She was a nurse. They were married September 1, 1979, in Marin County, CA.
  - E4 Donald Campbell, b. October 13, 1958, Oakland, CA, m. Jill Tyson.

C2 John Clarence Campbell, b. October 9, 1890, Pingree, North Dakota, d. June 6, 1976, California. He was dentist in San Francisco. He m. Helen Story, b. April 1, 1902, d. May 5, 2001, Santa Barbara, California.
- D1 John Collins Campbell, b. February 2, 1928, San Bernadino, California. He was a dentist (orthodontist).
- D2 Jean Campbell, b. November 19, 1933, San Francisco. She m. Robert Ernest Roman, b. March 25, 1923, Portland,

OR, d. June 2002, Santa Barbara, CA.
- E1 Shirley Jeanne Roman, b. February 8, 1965, San Jose, CA.
- E2 Lolly Story Roman, b. February 12, 1967, San Jose, CA, m. Chris Sangster.
  - F1 Teague Colin Sangster, b. 2003.
- E3 Christina Campbell Roman, b. June 29, 1969, San Jose, CA, m. George Lee.

C3 Myrtle Euphemia Campbell, b. October 21, 1894, North Dakota. She m. Hubert Little, b. March 11, 1894, d. September 8, 1962. He was a peach farmer.
- D1 Alice Jean Little, b. February 21, 1923. She m. Laurence Ainsworth, b. ca. 1920, d. 1955, Sacramento, CA. He was a banker.
  - E1 Timothy Ainsworth, b. ca. 1952, m. Karen Leaf.
  - E2 Jean Ainsworth, b. ca. 1955, m. [?] Dennis.
    - F1 Ariel Dennis, b. 1996.
    - F2 Rachiel Dennis, b. 1998.
  - E3 Lorraine Ainsworth, b. ca. 1958.
  - E4 Bill Ainsworth, b. ca. 1960, m. Kathryn Olmstead.
    - F1 Julie Ainsworth.
    - F2 Sarah Ainsworth.
    - F3 Isabella Ainsworth.
- D2 Eva Rose Little, b. 1930, d. 1945 after falling off a hay wagon.

C4 Donald Neil Campbell, b. July 24, 1895, in North Dakota, d. February 25, 1988. He was a field auditor for the state of Oregon. He m. Delphia Moore, b. 1888, Oregon, d. 1975, Glendale, California.

C5 Glen Stuart Campbell, b. 1902, Pingree, North Dakota, d. 1996, California. Glen was a M.D. and EENT specialist in Washington. He m. Maybelle Dalton, d. 1999, Moro Bay, California.

C6 Falconer Everett Campbell, Sr., b. August 7, 1901, Pingree, North Dakota, d. December 31, 1966, Glendale, California. He was a dentist. He m. Gladys Hawkins, b. October 21, 1904, Marion, Kansas, daughter of William Hawkins and Sarah Auxier, d. July 4, 2000, Pasadena, California. Falconer and Gladys were married on June 19, 1930, in Riverside, California.
- D1 Falconer Everette Campbell, Jr. (Oscar), b. February 22, 1932, Los Angeles. He was a dental surgeon. He m. Virginia Lee Howells, b. October 16, 1933, Pasadena,

CA. They were married August 3, 1957.

- E1 Franklin Everette Campbell, b. October 16, 1958, m. Margaret Ann Hoeflich, b. December 13, 1960, Eugene, OR.
  - F1 Alexander Everette Campbell, b. November 8, 1991.
  - F2 Katherine Taylor Campbell, b. March 4, 1994.
  - F3 Samantha Ann Campbell, b. July 9, 1996.
  - F4 Christina Grace Campbell, b. June 23, 1998.
- E2 David Stuart Campbell, b. November 9, 1959, Seattle, WA. He was a dentist. He m. Heather Lynn Catherwood, b. October 10, 1967, Pasadena, CA, daughter of Daniel Catherwood and Sandra. They were married July 28, 1990, in Pasadena, CA.
  - F1 Scott Daniel Campbell, b. January 11, 1992, Arcadia, CA.
  - F2 Jeffrey Stuart Campbell, b. June 18, 1993, Arcadia, CA.
  - F3 Holly Anne Campbell, b. December 1, 1997, Arcadia, CA.
  - F4 Bradley David Campbell, b. November 10, 1999, Arcadia, CA.
- E3 Michael Phillip Campbell, b. May 2, 1962. He m. Delia Jimenez, b. October 26, 1961, a graduate of the University of Southern California. They were married January 21, 1995, Carmel, CA.
  - F1 Adam Frank Campbell, b. February 3, 1997.
  - F2 Ally Virginia Campbell, b. February 22, 2000.

D2 Robert Douglas Campbell, b. October 5, 1934, m. Margie MacKenzie
- E1 Kenneth Campbell, b. 1958, d. ca. 1964.
- E2 Kirk Campbell, b. September 23, 1959, m. Connie Borg, b. July 7, 1961. They were married August 27, 1988, in San Marino, CA.
  - F1 Kyle Campbell, b. October 4, 1989.
  - F2 MacKenzie Campbell, b. May 27, 1994.

    E3 Douglas Campbell, b. January 25, 1961, m. Monica Lichter, b. October 30, 1962. They were married October 29, 1994.
      F1 Taylor Campbell, b. January 6, 1996.
      F2 Lindsay Campbell, b. August 2, 1998.
  C7 Walter Campbell, b. ca. 1901, d. 1994. He was handicapped.

B3* Euphemia Campbell, b. November 17, 1857, Uigg, baptized February 14, 1858, Orwell Head, d. February 6, 1928, age 70, at the home of her daughter, Mrs. Angus MacDonald, in Somerville, Massachussets. She m. Peter Murchison, b. November 20, 1850, son of John Peter Murchison and Marion (Sarah) Murchison, baptized February 14, 1858, Orwell Head, d. suddenly in Dundee, age 63, buried Orwell Head. Euphemia and Peter were m. November 23, 1876, in Orwell Head by the Rev. John Goodwill.
  C1 John Alexander Murchison, b. September 22, 1879, Dundee, baptized December 28, 1879, Orwell Head, d. in Sydney, NS. He m. [?] Davis.
    D1 George Murchison. He was in Grade 3 in Uigg School in March 1922.
    D2 Neil Murchison. Killed by a car in or near Van Kleek Hill, Ontario.
    D3 Euphemia Murchison (Grace), b. February 15, 1916. Both her parents died in Sudney, NS, and she was raised by her Aunt Sadie in the USA. She m. George Stowe, b. March 26, 1918.
      E1 Janet Murchison Stowe, b. September 14, 1944, m. Philip Shelby.
        F1 Stewart Shelby.
      E2 Alan Walker Stowe.
  C2 Sarah Murchison (Sadie), b. April 19, 1884, Dundee, baptized July 10, 1884, Orwell Head, resided in Somerville, Massachusetts, in 1927. She m. Angus A. MacDonald.
  C3 Simon Malcolm Murchison, b. March 21, 1886, Dundee, d. September 28, 1958, Maizond, Saskatchewan. He m. Mary Ellen Park, b. June 28, 1887, Watson's Corner, Ontario, d. May 16, 1970, Gravelbourg, Saskatchewan.
    D1 Peter Murchison, m. Albina [?]. They had no children.
    D2 Malcolm Murchison (Mac), d. 1955.
      E1 Ann Murchison, m. [?] Babb.
      E2 Randy Murchison.
      E3 Donald Murchison.

	E4	Brian Murchison.
D3		Euphemia Murchison (Phemie), m. Clifford Stevenson.
	E1	James Stevenson (Jim).
	E2	Garth Stevenson.
D4		Nellie Murchison, m. William MacIntosh.
	E1	Barry MacIntosh.
D5		Myrtle Murchison, m. [?].
	E1	Wilfred.
	E2	Kenneth (Ken).
	E3	Larry.
	E4	Marie Rose, married, name of husband unknown.

C4* John Neil Murchison, b. December 8, 1881, Dundee, baptized June 29, 1882, Orwell Head, d. February 21, 1937, in Sydney, NS, after living in Sydney for about 30 years. He is buried in Hardwood Hill Cemetery, Sydney. He m. Elizabeth Hennebury, b. in Newfoundland, d. 1973. John worked for the Dominion Steel and Coal Company in Sydney. An obituary of John Neil may be found in the appendix.

	D1		Murdoch Pringle Murchison, b. 1916, Sydney, NS, d. 1979. He m. Doris Emma Butts.
		E1	David Carlson Murchison (Carl), b. 1944, d. 1994.
		E2	James Pringle Murchison (Jamie), b. 1947.
		E3	Laurie Bruce Murchison, b. 1949.
		E4	Heather Anne Murchison, b. 1957.
	D2		Robert Murchison, m. Katherine [?] (Kay). Robert is deceased.
		E1	Irene Murchison.
		E2	Earl Murchison.
		E3	Robert Murchison.
		E4	Donna Murchison.
	D3		Carl Murchison, m. Elizabeth Hill (Libby). Carl is deceased.
		E1	Deborah Murchison.
		E2	Ross Murchison.
		E3	Leslie Murchison.
	D4		Gordon Murchison, m. Mary [?].
	D5		Lloyd Murchison, m. Catherine Day. Lloyd is deceased.
		E1	Glenn Murchison.
		E2	Neil Murchison.
		E3	Michael Murchison.
	D6		Isabell Murchison.

- C5 Murdock M. Murchison, b. January 17, 1888, Dundee, baptized July 4, 1888, Orwell Head, d. 1954, Brittania Beach, BC. He m. Florence Gadsby in 1914. She was b. 1887, d. 1969, Brittania Beach, BC.
    - D1 Peter James Murchison, b. May 13, 1915, Kinross, baptized March 9, 1918, m. Albina [?]. They had no children.
    - D2 Joseph Murchison.
    - D3 Donald Murchison.
- C6 Donald Murchison, b. March 18, 1890, Dundee, baptized July 14, 1890, Orwell Head, resided in Vancouver in 1913, d. between 1913 and 1928.
- C7 James Murchison, b. September 21, 1891, Dundee, baptized January 11, 1892, Orwell Head, d. May 1, 1971, probably in Maizond, Saskatchewan. He m. Maude [?].
- C8 Joseph Murchison, b. December 9, 1893, Dundee, baptized November 25, 1894, Orwell Head, d. in British Columbia, probably Vancouver.
- C9 Euphemia Murchison, b. January 26, 1896, Dundee, d. March 16, 1968, Bar Harbor, Maine. She was a nurse. She m. Gerard De LeMarr Hopkins, b. May 2, 1899, Sullivan, Maine, son of Sontiene L. Hopkins (b. 1868) and Lillian A. Watson (1881-1948), baptized June 6, 1930, in the Bar Harbor Congregational Church by J. Homer Nelson, d. July 24, 1992, Bar Harbor, Maine. Euphemia and Gerard were married on May 4, 1927, in Somerville, Massachusetts, by the Rev. Robert I. Barbor, at the residence of Angus MacDonald.
    - D1 Joan Eleanor Hopkins, b. January 11, 1930, West Palm Beach, FL, baptized July 11, 1930, Bar Harbor Congregational Church by J. Homer Nelson. She m. Donald Edward Smith, b. January 2, 1928, Bar Harbor, ME, son of Clarence Kilburn Smith (1885-1968) and Mona Agnes Goss (1888-1970). Joan and Donald were married September 2, 1950 in Bar Harbor, ME.
        - E1 Donald Campbell Smith, b. March 31, 1953, Washington, DC. He m. Debra-Jo Weber, b. May 28, 1952. They were married September 27, 1975, in Chevy, Chase, MD. They had no children.
        - E2 Ann Brew Smith, b. November 26, 1956, Washington, DC. She m. Robert Merrill Woodworth, b. August 14, 1951, Bar Harbor, ME, son of Herman A. Woodworth (1912-1999) and Elizabeth Failor

(1921-2002), d. October 2004, Bar Harbor. They were married December 15, 1979, Bar Harbor, ME.
- F1 Caroline Campbell Woodworth, b. November 22, 1985, Bar Harbor, ME.
- F2 Neil Smith Woodworth, b. August 13, 1988, Bar Harbor, ME.

D2 Jean Louise Hopkins, b. December 16, 1932. She m. Lawrence C. Kief, b. February 21, 1928, d. April 11, 2003. They were married April 20, 1951, in Bar Harbor, ME.
- E1 Kathryn Marie Kief, b. October 24, 1954, m. Millard Dority, b. 1953.
  - F1 Heather Dority, b. February 23, 1971.
  - F2 Deidre Dority, b. April 19, 1978, m. Adam Bishop, b. January 26, 1977.
    - G1 Greta Dority Bishop, b. September 21, 2002.
- E2 Karen Murchison Kief, b. January 8, 1955. She m. Peter Cole, b. September 30, 1951. They were married June 20, 1981.
- E3 David Lawrence Kief, b. November 3, 1958, m. Chris Kirk, b. September 19, 1958. They were married September 11, 1993.
  - F1 Joseph Lawrence Kief.
  - F2 Amelia M. Kief, b. July 11, 1995.

C10 Mary Isabella Murchison, b. January 31, 1898, Dundee, d. in Concord, New Hampshire, where she had lived since at least 1928. She m. Robert MacAllister, d. in Concord.
- D1 Robert Murchison MacAllister, m. Marjorie Linley [?].
  - E1 Sandra Murchison MacAllister.
  - E2 Lynn Marie Murchison MacAllister.
  - E3 Thomas MacAllister.

B4* Christy Ann Campbell, b. April 9, 1860, Uigg, baptized June 10, 1860, Orwell Head, d. March 27, 1939, buried Orwell Head. She m. Hugh Martin, b. May 3, 1861, Kinross, son of Donald Martin and Flora MacDonald, baptized June 16, 1861, Orwell Head Church of Scotland, d. August 3, 1940 in his residence in Uigg, buried Orwell Head. Hugh was a farmer on Malcolm's homestead. The bondsman at Christy and Hugh's wedding was Duncan Martin and the witnesses were Samuel Campbell and Catherine MacPherson.

C1* Euphemia Martin, b. February 12, 1891, Uigg, baptized June

1891, Orwell Head, d. suddenly on October 7, 1913, in Cambridge Hospital, age 22, buried Orwell Head.

C2 Flora Ann Martin, b. December 4, 1892, Uigg, baptized January 17, 1893, Orwell Head, d. September 7, 1971, Uigg, buried, Saint Andrew's Cemetery, Vernon. She m. (1) William Gordon MacLeod, b. July 12, 1894, Vernon, son of John Martin MacLeod and Mary Margaret Jenkins, baptized November 19, 1894, Orwell Head, d. March 4, 1918, Vernon, age 24, of "rheumatism of the heart," buried, Orwell Corner Cemetery.

    D1* Euphemia MacLeod, b. June 29, 1916, Kinross, baptized September 24, 1920, Orwell Presbyterian Church, d. April 27, 2001, buried, Oak Park, IL. She m. John P. Jordan (Jack), b. in Chicago.

        E1 Ann Jordan, b. January 23, 1948, m. Alfred Anastasiou.

            F1 Christina Anastasiou.

            F2 Juliana Anastasiou.

        E2 Grace Jordan, m. Robert Slawkinski.

            F1 Sarah Slawinski.

            F2 John Slawinski.

        E3 Margaret Jordan, m. Craig Bixler.

            F1 Emily Bixler.

            F2 Jordan Bixler.

            F3 Lauren Bixler.

Flora Ann (C2) m. (2) Henry Lloyd Robbins, b. May 29, 1896, Bangor Road, Morrell, son of James Henry Lloyd Robbins and Flora E. MacPhee, baptized July 17, 1897, Saint Peter's Presbyterian Church, d. April 14, 1990, buried, Saint Andrew's Cemetery, Vernon. He was a farmer and carpenter.

    D2 James Henry Lloyd Robbins, b. October 4, 1925, MA, baptized June 14, 1928, Saint Peter's Bay United Church, d. April 24, 1887, Lockeport, NS. He was a medical doctor. He m. (1) Ruth Turner.

        E1 William Robbins (Bill), m. Christine [?].

        E2 Paula Robbins, m. Mark Swim.

        E3 Jill Robbins, m. Bill Malloy.

        E4 Jonathan Robbins, married.

    James Henry (D2) m. (2) Alice Lethbridge.

    D3* Hugh Martin Robbins, b. August 29, 1927, Morrell, baptized March 2, 1929, Saint Peter's Bay United Church, He m. Helen Margaret Behm, b. in Grandview, daughter of

Harold Behm and Sarah Ann Behaut (Sally). Helen was a teacher. Hugh and Helen were married July 5, 1950, at the home of the bride's parents by the Rev. A.C. Fraser.

- E1 Helen Anne Robbins, b. August 28, 1951, baptized June 1, 1952, Orwell Head. She m. Harvey MacEwen, b. August 28, 1948.
  - F1 Charles Edward MacEwen (Ted), b. February 27, 1976, m. Nadia Authier on October 12, 2002.
    - G1 Gabrielle Rebecca MacEwen, b. March 23, 2005.
  - F2 John Harvey MacEwen, b. April 21, 1978.
  - F3 Margaret Roseanne MacEwen (Peggy), b. January 7, 1981.
  - F4 Robert Hugh MacEwen, b. January 18, 1983.
- E2 Teryl Hugh Robbins (Terry), b. February 8, 1953, baptized October 8, 1953, Orwell Head, m. Doris Neimer.
  - F1 Jennifer Marie Robbins, b. June 5, 1981.
  - F2 Christopher Hugh Robbins, b. August 4, 1988.
- E3 Donald Lloyd Robbins (Donnie), b. January 21, 1955, baptized June 19, 1955, Orwell Head, m. Frances Gormley. They lived on the old homestead of Sam Campbell.
  - F1 Sherri Lynn Robbins (child of Frances, adopted by Donald).
  - F2 Joseph Lloyd Robbins (Joey), b. April 5, 1980, m. Esther Carroll.
    - G1 Brennan Timothy Joseph Robbins (twin of Griffin), b. July 5, 2007.
    - G2 Griffon Donald Lloyd Robbins (twin of Brennan), b. July 5, 2007.
  - F3 Pamela Marie Robbins (Pam), b. May 7, 1982.
- E4 Leslie Harold Robbins (Les), b. July 20, 1957, baptized October 5, 1958, m. Kathy Whatmore (née Herrington).
  - F1 Hugh Martin Robbins, b. November 7, 1990.

- F2 Garrett William Robbins, b. July 24, 1992.
- F3 Marilyn Grace Robbins, b. March 29, 1994.
- E5 Joyce Lorraine Robbins, b. January 13, 1962, baptized June 24, 1963, m. Michael Cavanagh (Mike) on August 27, 1988.
  - F1 Brendan Shanley Cavanagh, b. August 10, 1989.
  - F2 Keelan Michael Cavanagh, b. October 11, 1991.
  - F3 Connor Hugh Cavanagh, b. August 9, 1994.
- E6 Philip John Robbins (Phil), b. February 26, 1967, baptized May 28, 1967, m. Faye MacKinnon on November 14, 2003.
  - F1 Ellen Marion Robbins, b. July 7, 2002.
- D4* Florence Ellen Robbins (Flo), b. March 2, 1929, Marie, baptized September 29, 1929, Saint Peter's Bay. She m. Haywood William MacLean, b. 1919, Montague, son of Neil Haywood MacLean and Catherine Edith MacLeod, d. April 13, 1994, age 74, Prince Edward Home, buried, Belfast Cemetery. Florence and Haywood were married July 5, 1949, at Orwell Head by the Rev. A.C. Fraser.
  - E1 Carl Lydell MacLean, b. February 28, 1952, d. 1953 in infancy, buried, Belfast Cemetery.
  - E2 Sterling MacLean, m. Mary Ellen [?].
    - F1 Mark MacLean.
    - F2 Shawn MacLean.
    - F3 Marvin MacLean.
    - F4 Jeff MacLean.
    - F5 Jennifer MacLean.
  - E3 Lester MacLean.
  - E4 Darrell Lloyd MacLean, b. and d. 1954, buried, Belfast Cemetery.
  - E5 Darlene Catherine MacLean, b. and d. 1956, buried, Belfast Cemetery.
  - E6 Sharon Lynn MacLean, b. and d. 1959, buried, Belfast Cemetery.
- D5* John Campbell Robbins, b. November 17, 1930, Uigg, baptized August 15, 1932, Orwell Head. He m. (1) Emily Mildred Martin, b. August 19, 1931, Grandview,

daughter of Hugh James Martin and Bessie Goss MacPhee, baptized August 14, 1933, Orwell Head.

- E1 Lloyd Winston Robbins, b. April 19, 1950, Toronto, baptized August 10, 1952, Orwell Head.
- E2 David Martin Robbins, b. October 14, 1953, m. Lesley Budge.
    - F1 Corrie Robbins (twin of Christopher).
    - F2 Christopher Robbins (Chris, twin of Corrie).
    - F3 Kirsten Robbins.
- E3 Jacqueline Goss Robbins, b. April 18, 1956, m. Bob Lane.
    - F1 Darlene Lane, m. Steve Fournier.
        - G1 Ashley Fournier, b. August 2002.
        - G2 Natalie Fournier, b. December 21, 2004.
        - G3 Eric Fournier, b. November 2005.
    - F2 Laurie Lane.
    - F3 Emily Lane.

John (D5) m. (2) Carol [?].

D6* Alexander Robbins (Sterling), b. October 31, 1931, Uigg, baptized August 15, 1932, Orwell Head, d. 1988, buried, Uigg Baptist Cemetery. He was a medical doctor in Lockeport, NS. He m. Sheila Mary MacKinnon, b. 1932, Uigg, daughter of William MacKinnon and Sally McConaghy, d. 1977, buried, Uigg Baptist Cemetery.

- E1 Paul Robbins Vaughn, b. in NS. He is an orthopaedic surgeon. He m. Stacey [?]. Paul was adopted by the Vaughns.
    - F1 James Vaughn.
    - F2 Kathryn Vaughn.
    - F3 Emily Meagan Vaughn.
- E2 Kathy Robbins, m. Michael Whiteway.
    - F1 April Whiteway.
    - F2 Sara Whiteway.
    - F3 Matthew Whiteway.
    - F4 William Whiteway (Billy).
- E3 Robert Robbins (Robbie)

D7 Harry Robbins (Elwood), b. March 6, 1934, Uigg, baptized August 13, 1934, Orwell Head. He m. Marion Euphemia MacDougall, b. December 12, 1935, daughter of John D. MacDougall and Rhoda Eastham. They were married September 25, 196[?] in Saint John's Presbyterian Church by the Rev. Donald Nicholson. Witnesses were Mrs. Everett MacPhee and Preston Robbins.

    E1   Gary Elwood Robbins, b. September 13, 1960, baptized June 18, 1961, Orwell Head, m. Diana Boyer.
        F1   Mark Robbins, b. October 28, 1988.
        F2   Aaron Robbins, b. February 9, 1992.
    E2   David Alan Robbins, b. October 26, 1961, baptized June 24, 1962, Orwell Head, m. Natalie [?].
    E3   Melinda Robbins, b. December 6, 1969, m. Peter Wolters.
        F1   Grant Wolters, b. September 20, 1999.
        F2   Isaac Wolters, b. May 15, 2002.

D8   Preston Sanford Robbins, b. January 21, 1937, Uigg, baptized August 8, 1952, Orwell Head. He was an officer in the RCMP. He m. Charlotte Winifred Gosse (Winnie), b. August 18, 1937, Newfoundland.

    E1   Peter Sandford Robbins, b. September 19, 1962, m. Faith Barbara Tiller.
        F1   Tonia Gloria Robbins, b. April 19, 1986, to Faith and adopted by Peter.
        F2   Rebecca Charlotte Robbins, b. August 12, 1991.
        F3   Meagan Patricia Robbins, b. September 29, 1992.
        F4   James Sandford Robbins, b. January 18, 1995.
    E2   Jeffrey David Robbins, b. December 28, 1964, m. Rhonda Mildred Young, b. May 15, 1963.
        F1   Benjamin Mildred Robbins, b. November 1994.
        F2   Allyson Lynn Robbins, b. June 9, 1999.
    E3   Karen Lynn Robbins, b. July 14, 1972. She m. David Spowart, b. December 11, 1972, son of William Spowart and Eileen Stephenson of Wellington, New Zealand. They were married April 15, 2005, in Los Angeles.

C3*   John Campbell Martin, b. January 16, 1895, Uigg, baptized July 15, 1895, Orwell Head, d. August 15, 1917, while serving in France during WWI.

C4 Donald Martin, b. March 12, 1897, Uigg, baptized April 20, 1897, Orwell Head, d. April 12, 1923, in the Boston area, buried, Orwell Head. His headstone reads: 1897-1923. He m. Emily MacKay, b. September 26, 1900, daughter of Alexander MacKay and Marjorie Martin, d. June 15, 1997, Prince County Hospital, buried, Cape Traverse United Church Cemetery. After the death of her husband in 1923, she returned from Boston to her home in Stanley Bridge. Her obituary lists 11 grandchildren, 19 great grandchildren and a number of great-great grandchildren.

    D1 Marjorie Donalda Martin, b. September 23, 1923, MA, baptized August 10, 1924, Dundas. She m. James Paynter, b. in Borden-Carlton. They were married in Stanley Bridge in 1944.

        E1 Rachel Paynter

        E2 James Paynter (Gary), b. May 14, 1949, m. Velda Laird, b. in Searletown.

            F1 Pam Paynter, m. Michael James (Mike) in Nova Scotia.

                G1 Harrison James.

                G2 [Daughter].

            F2 Grant Paynter.

            F3 Dawn Paynter.

            F4 Crystal Paynter.

        E3 Garth Martin Paynter, m. May 15, 1950, m. Margaret Elizabeth Cotton (Beth) in 1972. Garth was a carpenter and Margaret was a nurse.

            F1 James Garth Paynter, b. September 5, 1974.

            F2 Leslie John Paynter, b. December 31, 1975, m. Lily Catherine Wildy.

                G1 Karla Wildy, b. October 20, 2000.

        E4 Daniel Norris Paynter, b. October 16, 1953, m. Marie DesRoches.

            F1 Rachel Paynter. d. at nine months.

            F2 Christopher Paynter, m. Phyllis [?].

            F3 Kendall Paynter.

C5 Emily Campbell Martin twin to Sarah (Sadie), b. January 27, 1900, Uigg, baptized March 23, 1900, Orwell Head, m. Arthur Ladner. She and her twin sister Sadie both resided in Massachusetts.

- D1 Hugh Ladner, m. Bea [?]
- D2 Claude W. Ladner (Cal), b. 1929, Somerville, Massachusetts, resided in Florida, d. April 25, 2004, New Bedford, Massachusetts. He was an entertainer and hotel owner. He m. Helen Gifford, d. before 2004. Their children were:
  - E1 Willene S. Mann, New Bedford.
  - E2 Kathryn Lake, Wareham.
  - E3 Cliff Wilson, Fort Myers.
  - E4 Candace G. Steele, Tewksbury.
  - E5 Jennifer A. Rusinoski, m. Walter Mattapoisett.
- D3 Helen Ladner, m. [?] Nagel

C6 Sarah Catherine Martin (Sadie), twin to Emily, b. January 27, 1900, Uigg, baptized March 23, 1900, Orwell Head.

C7* Ernest Martin, b. April 28, 1902, Uigg, baptized May 8, 1902, Orwell Head, d. September 27, 1982, Queen Elizabeth Hospital, buried, Orwell Head. He was a farmer. He m. Reta Florence Hicken, b. 1908, Lyndale, daughter of William Adam Hicken and Johanna Stephens, d. 1994, buried, Orwell Head. Ernest and Reta were married on July 27, 1927, in the manse of the Kirk of Saint James by the Rev. W. Bruce Muir. Attendants were George Robbins, sister Ella Hicken and John E. Robbins, Morrell.
- D1 Margaret Christine Martin, b. April 26, 1928, Uigg, baptized August 15, 1932, Orwell Head. She was a nurse with a B.Sc. degree. She m. (1) Jon Miller MacDonald, b. in Charlottetown. They were married June 16, 1951, in Orwell Head Church by the Rev. A.C. Fraser.
  - E1 Ian MacDonald, m. Deborah Beaton (Debbie), daughter of Earl Beaton and Edith MacLeod.
    - F1 Joel MacDonald, b. ca. 1984.
    - F2 Benjamin Luke MacDonald, b. ca. 1987.
  - E2 Susan MacDonald, m. Joe Mouris.
    - F1 Margaret Catherine Johanna Mouris, b. ca. 1985.
    - F2 Joanna Mouris.
  - E3 Kirsten MacDonald, m. Frank Drew

  Margaret (D1) m. (2) Ninian LeBlanc
- D2 George Martin, b. Uigg. He was an engineer in Baltimore. He m. Marjorie Volk, who was an engineer with Bendix in Baltimore.
  - E1 David Martin

		E2	Catherine Martin
		E3	Karen Martin
	D3	Muriel Martin, b. 1938, m. William Davis (Bill). They were both teachers in Toronto.
		E1	Bill Davis, Jr.
		E2	Anne Davis.
		E3	Carol Davis.
		E4	Wendy Davis.
	D4	John Campbell Martin, b. August 13, 1944. He was a teacher and on the staff of the Canada Employment Agency.
C8	Margaret Irene Martin, b. September 29, 1905, Uigg, baptized January 12, 1906, Orwell Head, d. in Cambridge, Massachusetts. She m. Fred Carroll.

B5   James Murdoch Campbell, b. April 12, 1862, Uigg, baptized May 25, 1862, Orwell Head, d. June 11, 1942, in Ceres, California. James was a teacher and banker. He m. Margaret Catherine MacLeod, b. October 14, 1856, Orwell Point, daughter of John "Scentie" (pronounced "Singee") MacLeod and Mary Martin, baptized August 27, 1857, Belfast, d. after 1928 in California.

    C1   Euphemia Campbell, b. April 3, 1883, Uigg, baptized July 1, 1883, Orwell Head, m. Edward Jackson.

    C2   John MacLeod Campbell, b. August 11, 1885, d. March 1969, California.

    C3   Flora Campbell, b. June 23, 1894, d. January 1971.

    C4   Mary Campbell, d. January 1964, m. Martin Mathies.

    C5   Ann Campbell, m. Claude Spousa.

    C6   Gertrude Campbell, b. January 29, 1894, d. July 19, 1988, in Fresno, California, m. C.A. Weethmouth.

B6   Samuel Campbell, b. April 15, 1864, Uigg, baptized June 14, 1864, Orwell Head, d. May 14, 1933, age 69, in the Prince Edward Island Hospital, buried, Orwell Head. He m. (1) Catherine MacLeod, b. April 25, 1865, Kinross, daughter of John "Sandy" MacLeod and Mary MacLeod, baptized June 1, 1865, Orwell Head, d. April 6, 1907, Uigg, buried in Orwell Head. Samuel and Catherine were married February 5, 1890, in Orwell Head by the Rev. D.B. MacLeod. Attendants were Hugh Martin, John MacLeod and Emily Campbell. Obituaries of Samuel Campbell and Catherine MacLeod are in the appendix.

    C1   John Campbell, b. December 7, 1891, Uigg, baptized January 11, 1892, Orwell Head, d. May 1, 1964, Charlottetown, buried, Orwell Head. He was a farmer. He m. Edith Anne MacNeill,

b. May 1897, Little Sands, daughter of Murdoch MacNeill and Rebecca Lamont, d. March 4, 2003, in the Atlantic Baptist Nursing Home, age 105 years and 9 months, buried, Orwell Head. She was a nurse. John and Edith were married on January 15, 1929, in Charlottetown by the Rev. Ewen MacDougall.

D1* Samuel Ewen Campbell, b. November 3, 1929, Uigg. He was a locomotive engineer with the CPR. He m. Norma Trodden in Smith Falls, ON.

    E1 John Campbell, b. August 15, 1954, Smith's Falls, ON. He was a locomotive engineer for the CPR. He m. Margaret Hayes, b. in Smith's Falls, ON.

        F1 Samuel John Campbell, b. January 6, 1994.
        F2 William Isaac Campbell, b. September 2, 1996.
        F3 Simon Thomas Campbell, b. May 19, 1998.
        F4 Maria Elise Campbell, b. November 22, 2000.

    E2 Donald Campbell, b. August 1, 1955, Smith's Falls, ON, where he served on the police force. He m. Ruth Coleman, a kindergarten teacher also born in Smith's Falls.

        F1 Andrea Rebecca Campbell, b. January 23, 1981, m. Jamie Radul on August 5, 2009.
        F2 Ashley Elizabeth Campbell, b. September 19, 1983.
        F3 Abraham Samuel Campbell, b. February 3, 1987.

    E3 Douglas Campbell, b. September 19, 1957, Smith's Falls, ON. He was a photographer. He m. Wendy Bogstie, b. in Alberta.

        F1 Michael Dale Campbell, b. September 5, 1978, adopted.
        F2 David James Campbell, b. May 23, 1983.
        F3 Amy Pearl Campbell, b. May 13, 1985.

    E4 Marilyn Jane Campbell, b. February 26, 1963, Smith's Falls, ON. She m. Pierre Romeo Sincennes, b. November 1952, Hull, QC, son of Roger Sincennes and Aline Monette. Pierre was one of the vice-presidents of Loblaws. Marilyn and Pierre were married May 28, 1988, in Smith's Falls.

        F1 Nicholas Alexander Sincennes, b. November 29, 1989, Ottawa, ON.

| | F2 | Benjamin Samuel Sincennes, b. May 5, 1991, Ottawa. |
| | F3 | Emily Elizabeth Sincennes, b. October 13, 1992, Ottawa. |

D2 Donald Campbell (Roy), b. November 9, 1930. He was a university professor and former Dean of Education at the University of PEI. He m. Olive Harris (Maida), b. June 1, 1930, in Chefoo, China. She was a public health nurse. They were married on August 23, 1958.

- E1* James Harris Campbell, b. July 7, 1959, Toronto. He was an engineer in Nova Scotia. He m. Virginia Brown, b. in Nova Scotia.
  - F1 Corey Jean Campbell, b. March 2, 1990, Halifax, NS.
  - F2 Derek Roy Campbell, b. January 29, 1993, Halifax.
- E2 Ian Hugh Campbell, b. September 28, 1960, m. Marie-Claude Marchessault. Ian was a family physician in Montreal.
  - F1 Genevieve Marie-France Campbell, b. April 4, 1993, Montreal.
  - F2 Julie Anne Campbell, b. August 3, 1995, Montreal.
  - F3 Florence Campbell, b. November 30, 1998, Montreal.
- E3 Catherine Grace Campbell (Cathy), b. November 15, 1963, m. Michael Ungar (Mike)
  - F1 Scott Ungar Campbell
  - F2 Megan Marcellina Ungar Campbell (Meg)
- E4 Heather Ann Campbell, b. December 29, 1964, m. Joseph Driscoll (Joe), b. December 29, 1964, Bethel, son of Vernon and Eileen Driscoll. Joe is a maintenance supervisor for the town of Stratford.
  - F1 Vanessa Driscoll, b. January 13, 1991.
  - F2 Jason Driscoll, b. March 1, 1996.

D3* Rebecca Catherine Campbell, b. March 19, 1932, Uigg, d. March 21, 1978, Chilliwack, BC. She m. Ronald Edgar Williams, b. October 10, 1931, d. August 9, 2001.

- E1 Katherine Anne Williams (Kathy), b. October 10, 1955, in Ontario. She m. (1) John Ryan McKenzie on October 13, 1974. John is deceased.

- F1 Elizabeth Anne McKenzie Fleming (adopted by John, her mother's second husband), b. March 14, 1972, m. Keith Christopher Redmond, b. October 25, 1972.
  - G1 Grace Leslie Faith Redmond, b. August 14, 2003.
  - G2 Brooke Katharine Redmond (twin to Elizabeth), b. October 14, 2006.
  - G3 Elizabeth Florence Redmond (Beth, twin to Brooke), b. October 14, 2006.
  - G4 Jack Christopher Fleming Redmond, b. March 18, 1994 (adopted).
- F2 David Ryan McKenzie, b. December 18, 1976. He m. Teresa Martine Bogle, b. October 11, 1981, daughter of Denise Adel Bogle. They were married on June 21, 2008.
  - G1 Keira Grace McKenzie, b. January 6, 2007.
- F3 Rebecca Leslie McKenzie, b. July 16, 1978. Katherine (E1) m. (2) John Cuthbertson Fleming (Jack), b. February 16, 1950, son of William John Fleming (Jack) and Emily Theodora Fleming (Dora, née Gruber). Jack is deceased. In addition to adopting Elizabeth Ann MacKenzie, Jack also raised Jason William Fleming.
- F4 Jason William Fleming, b. October 13, 1982, stepson to Katherine.

E2 Ronald Williams (Winton), b. December 2, 1956, Toronto, ON. He operates a construction equipment business. He m. Elaine Naugler, b. May 9, 1952, Toronto, ON. She is a nurse. Ronald and Elaine married on June 30, 1982 and later divorced. Ronald adopted Elaine's children from a previous marriage.
- F1 Kimberley Sandra Williams, b. March 26, 1970, Toronto. She m. Steven Ulchek on August 17, 1996.

The Descendants of James Campbell and Christy MacDonald 119

                G1   Brody Ulchek (twin to Jared), b. October 5, 2002.

                G2   Jared Ulchek (twin to Brody), b. October 5, 2002.

        F2   Benjamin Michael Williams, b. April 21, 1974, Burns Lake, BC. He m. Cindy Louise Bryant on February 8, 1997.

                G1   Kelly Victoria Elaine Williams, b. December 11, 1994.

                G2   Mitchell Benjamin Williams, b. June 4, 1998.

    E3   Julie Elizabeth Williams (Elizabeth), b. January 14, 1960, m. Gordon Alfred Tarras, b. March 18, 1959. They were married on December 9, 1978.

        F1   Jefferson James Tarras, b. April 5, 1981.

        F2   Andrea Leigh Tarras, b. May 28, 1985, m. Keegan Douglas Kermode.

                G1   Cole David Kermode, b. February 7, 2008.

    E4   Andrew James Williams, b. June 14, 1962, in Ontario. He m. Karen Lee Sharun, b. April 16, 1964, in British Columbia.

        F1   Collin Michael Williams, b. August 1, 1990.

        F2   Mark David Williams, b. April 1, 1992.

        F3   Carlene Marie Williams, b. October 4, 1994.

D4   Clarence Murdoch Campbell, b. February 25, 1934, Uigg. He was a radiologist. He m. Dot Bussey, a nurse born in Newfoundland.

    E1   Evelyn Anne Campbell, b. June 7, 1967. She was a nurse. She m. Stephen Miller (Steve), b. in New Brunswick, an orthopaedic surgeon.

        F1   Charlotte Louise Miller, b. July 21, 1998.

        F2   Jack Thomas Miller, b. December 11, 1999.

    E2   John Campbell, b. November 26, 1970. He was an orthopaedic surgeon in Charlottetown.

D5   Sheldon James Campbell, b. April 17, 1935, Uigg, d. November 12, 2004, of cancer in Charlottetown.

D6*   Eva Elizabeth Campbell, b. November 3, 1937, Uigg, baptized December 17, 1937, Kinross Kirk. She m. Marcel Pronovost, NHL player, coach and scout.

C2   Euphemia Campbell (Etta), b. October 7, 1894, m. Allan Campbell Stewart (see A1.B4.C9, above).

C3   Mabel Isabel Campbell, b. January 14, 1896, Uigg, baptized May 7, 1896, Orwell Head. She was a nurse in New York.

C4   Sadie Jeanette Campbell, b. October 27, 1897, Uigg, baptized February 28, 1898, Orwell Head, d. April 22, 1900, Uigg, buried, Orwell Head. A death notice from a newspaper clipping reads: "At Uigg, PEI, April 22nd inst., after a short illness, of bronchial croup, Sadie Jeanette, daughter of Mr. and Mrs. Samuel Campbell, aged 2 years and six months."

C5   Ada Ruth Campbell, b. May 8, 1900, Uigg, baptized November 29, 1900, Orwell Head, d. in Braintree, Massachusetts. She m. William Benson (Bill), d. in Braintree, Massachusetts.

       D1   Barbara Benson, m. [?] Caldwell. Barbara died in Sciutate, MA.

            E1   Laurel Caldwell.

            E2   Eric Caldwell.

C6   Eva Emily Campbell, b. July 4, 1902, Uigg, baptized January 23, 1903, Orwell Head, d. in Quincy, Massachusetts, buried, Mount Wollaston Cemetery, Quincy. She worked in the first Howard Johnson's restaurant in Boston. She m. Samuel Watson Cantelo (Sam), b. July 10, 1905, Eldon, d. in Quincy, Massachusetts, buried, Mount Wollaston Cemetery, Quincy. They were married on December 17, 1926, in Pinette.

       D1*   Joan Beverly Cantelo, b. March 9, 1940, Quincy, MA. She was a teacher. She m. Dwight Alva Kellogg, b. January 12, 1940, Westfield, MA. He was in management with Bell Telephone.

            E1   Kim Kellogg, b. December 23, 1965, Syosset, NY. She is a pathologist. She m. Alan Daniel Devoe, b. February 18, 1966, Santa Monica, CA. He is an engineer. They were married May 29, 1994, in Tarrytown, NY.

                 F1   Malcolm Devoe, b. July 14, 1997, San Diego, CA.

                 F2   Cameron Devoe, b. December 25, 2000, San Diego, CA.

                 F3   Bryce Devoe, b. December 25, 2000, San Diego, CA.

            E2   David Dwight Kellogg, b. August 22, 1969, Syosset, NY. He is an engineer.

E3	Jenny Elizabeth Kellogg, b. October 16, 1982, Plainview, NY. She is a teacher.
C7	John Donald Campbell (Wilfred), b. April 7, 1904, Uigg, baptized October 7, 1904, Orwell Head, d. January 11, 1974, Berkeley, California. He m. Mary Margaret MacLean, b. December 8, 1903, Caledonia, daughter of Captain Ronald MacLean and Sarah MacPhee, baptized September 7, 1904, Valleyfield, d. October 17, 1971, Berkeley, California.
	D1 Samuel Wilfred Campbell (Buddy), b. September 10, 1927, d. November 19, 1990. He m. Noreen O'Laughlin.
	E1 Ronald David Campbell, b. June 11, 1951, Berkeley, CA.
	E2 John Malcolm Campbell, b. August 1953, Berkeley, CA.
	E3 David Alan Campbell, b. January 19, 1960, Berkeley, CA.
	D2 John Ronald Campbell, b. June 2, 1929, d. December 31, 1990.
	D3 Everett Glen Campbell, b. February 10, 1933, m. Evelyn Tessneer.
	E1 Wayne Alan Campbell, b. January 30, 1958.
	D4 Edward Watson Campbell, b. August 13, 1935, d. August 1991.
	D5 Donald William Campbell, b. January 24, 1938, m. Esther Avallana Palerma (Tet).
	E1 Jonathan Donald Campbell, b. March 17, 1982, Oakland, CA.
	E2 Matthew Martin Campbell.
	E3 Jeremiah Andrew Campbell, b. May 3, 1989, Vallejo, CA.
	D6 Cheryl Marie Campbell MacLean, b. September 4, 1948. She is a teacher residing in San Luis Obispo, California. She was married and divorced, and changed her name to MacLean. She has no children.

Samuel (B6) m. (2) Isabel MacLeod, b. September 20, 1859, Victoria Cross, daughter of Malcolm A. MacLeod and Christina Martin ("Christy"), baptized November 2, 1859, Orwell Head, d. March 31, 1927, Uigg. Samuel and Isabel were married on November 9, 1910, in the Hotel Lennox, Charlottetown, by the Rev. D.B. MacLeod. Attendants were Alex Stewart, Alex MacLeod and Celia MacMillan. Samuel and Isabel had no children but raised seven stepchildren.

B7   Emily Campbell, b. February 4, 1866, baptized March 23, 1866, in Orwell Head, d. October 18, 1926, in Boston, age 60, buried in Orwell Head. She was never married.

B8   Simon Donald Campbell, b. November 4, 1870, Uigg, baptized January 16, 1871, Orwell Head, d. March 12, 1946, in Lyndale at age 75, buried, Orwell Head. Simon farmed the old James Campbell homestead. He m. (1) Margaret Bruce, b. June 19, 1871, Valleyfield, daughter of Alexander Bruce and Jessie MacLeod, d. November 14, 1910, Uigg, buried, Orwell Head. An obituary of Margaret Bruce may be found in the appendix. Simon and Margaret were married November 30, 1897, by the Rev. D.B. MacLeod in Orwell Head. Samuel Campbell was the bondsman.

    C1   John Chester Campbell, b. October 2, 1898, Uigg, baptized February 27, 1900, Orwell Head, d. May 28, 1944, Trenton, NS. He was burned or suffocated in a fire. His obituary is presented in an appendix.

    C2*   Alexander Bruce Campbell, b. October 12, 1900, Uigg, baptized December 6, 1901, Orwell Head, d. Milwaukee, Wisconsin.

    C3   Euphemia Campbell, b. May 20, 1902, Uigg, baptized January 6, 1903, Orwell Head, d. in Arlington, Massachusetts. She m. Gordon Morrison.

        D1   Dorothy Margaret Morrison.

    C4   James Arthur Campbell, b. January 15, 1905, Uigg, baptized January 15, 1905, Orwell Head, buried in Belmont, Massachusetts.

        D1   James Reginald Campbell.

    C5   Jessie Florence Campbell, b. January 6, 1909, Uigg, baptized December 11, 1909, Orwell Head, d. in Waltham, Massachusetts. She was a nurse. She m. Parker MacDougall.

        D1   Parker MacDougall (Donald).

    C6   Margaret Bruce Campbell, b. June 25, 1910 [?], Uigg, baptized November 10, 1910, Orwell Head, d. Cambridge, Massachusetts, m. Archibald MacKinnon.

Simon Donald (B8) m. (2) Mary Jane MacDonald, b. 1868, Kinross, daughter of Allan "Hector" MacDonald and Euphemia Munroe, d. October 3, 1961, age 93, in Richard's Nursing Home, Alberry Plains, buried, Orwell Head.

A3. The Descendants of Margaret Campbell and Alexander Stewart

Margaret Campbell, b. 1826 in Skye, Scotland, emigrated in 1829 on the *Mary Kennedy*, d. February 12, 1894, buried in Orwell Head. She was living with her son Donald in 1889. She m. Alexander Stewart (Sandy), b. 1815 in Scotland, emigrated in 1840, d. March 9, 1883, age 67, buried in Orwell Head. He was a tailor on Murray Harbour Road. Margaret and Sandy were married on November 5, 1844, by the Rev. Donald MacDonald.

According to Sandy's great-great granddaughter, Anne Andres, all the children in this family were assigned Campbell as a middle name.

B1 Christy Stewart, b. August 15, 1846, on Murray Harbour Road (now Grandview), a twin of Catherine, d. June 9, 1876, on Murray Harbour Road, buried in Orwell Head. She m. Angus Norman MacLeod, b. October 16, 1829 in Lot 58 (son of Norman MacLeod and Catherine MacLennan), baptized December 17, 1829, by the Rev. John MacLennan, d. June 9, 1876, age 46, buried in Orwell Head. Christy and Angus were married on December 6, 1870, by Rev. T. Duncan, Saint James. Baptismal records show no evidence of children from this marriage. However, Angus' will suggests that he may have been married before with a child or children.

B2 Catherine Stewart, twin of Christy, b. August 15, 1846, d. May 17, 1933. She m. Malcolm D. MacDonald, b. December 27, 1849 in Murray Harbour Road, d. sometime before 1933. Catherine and Malcolm were married February 1, 1876 by the Rev. John Goodwill at the residence of Donald Murchison, Point Prim. While they had no children of their own, they raised Alan Stewart (A1.B4.C9, p. 18), son of Catherine's brother Donald and his wife Sarah.

B3 Donald Stewart, b. November 15, 1847, m. Sarah Ann Campbell (Marion), see A1.B4, p. 18.

B4 James Stewart, b. 1850, Murray Harbour Road. He m. Euphemia Murchison, b. April 14, 1852, Point Prim, daughter of Donald Murchison and Ann Campbell, baptized February 24, 1853, Orwell Head Church of Scotland. They were married August 22, 1876, at the residence of Captain Nicholson, Charlottetown, by the Rev. John Goodwill. There is an indication that the family resided in the Kinross/Orwell area at one time. The family is not found in the 1891 census. They later resided in Bath, Maine.

	C1	Donald Alexander Stewart, b. 1877, Lot 57, age 3 years in the 1881 census.
	C2	Neil Donald Stewart, b. 1879, Lot 57, age 1 year in 1881 census.
	C3	Alexander Stewart, b. 1881, Lot 57, age 4 months in 1881 census, m. [?] Smith.
	C4	John Stewart.
	C5	Simon Stewart.
	C6	Margaret Stewart, never married.
	C7	Annie Stewart.
B5		Neil Stewart, b. October 16, 1852, in Murray Harbour Road, baptized February 6, 1853, in the Church of Scotland, Orwell Head. He was a teacher and later Superintendent of Education in Vancouver, British Columbia. He died in Vancouver.
B6		Margaret Stewart, b. January 2, 1855, in Grandview, baptized February 26, 1855, in the Church of Scotland, Orwell Head.
B7		John N. Stewart, b. June 8, 1857, in Murray Harbour Road, baptized October 11, 1857, in the Church of Scotland, Orwell Head, d. 1951, buried in Crossroads Cemetery, PEI. He m. Matilda Carver (Tillie), daughter of John Carver and Elizabeth Robertson, b. 1859, d. 1944, buried in Crossroads Cemetery, PEI.
B8		Donald Stewart (Dan), b. April 5, 1860, Murray Harbour Road, d. March 13, 1927, Vancouver. He was a tailor. He m. Abigail Bertha Ross, b. July 20, 1871, in NE Margaree, Cape Breton, NS, d. June 10, 1950, North Hollywood, California. Donald and Abigail were married January 30, 1892, in Vancouver. In addition to the children below, the couple raised Beverly, the only child of their son Donald (C8, below), who was killed in an air raid in Glasgow.
	C1	Roberta Lillian Stewart (Berta).
	C2	Ross Stewart.
	C3	Campbell Stewart.
	C4	Ruth Stewart, m. George Kidd.
	C5	Baden Powell Stewart.
	C6	Maynard Stewart.
	C7	Arlene Stewart.
	C8	Donald Stewart, killed on March 13, 1941, during a bombing raid on Glasgow, Scotland, while visiting Anne Andres' grandmother. (Anne Andres is mentioned above as the great-great granddaughter of Margaret Campbell and Sandy Stewart [A3].) The grandmother and two of her daughters were also killed in the same explosion.

    D1 Beverly Stewart, raised by her grandmother, Abigail Bertha Ross Stewart.
  C9 Lawrence Stewart, d. 1993, age 92.

B9 Alan Stewart, b. May 22, 1863, Murray Harbour Road, baptized August 3, 1866, Orwell Head Church of Scotland. He was a teacher. He m. Isabel MacLeod in Vancouver.
  C1 Carroll Stewart.
  C2 MacLeod Stewart.

B10 Emily Stewart, b. July 22, 1866, d. in Vancouver, m. Harry Maynard. Emily was a teacher.
  C1 Margaret Maynard.
  C2 Eva Maynard.
  C3 Catherine Maynard.

A4. The Descendants of Sarah Campbell and Samuel Martin

Sarah Campbell (Marion), b. May 14, 1829 (probably during the Atlantic crossing, arriving May 31), baptized July 5, 1829 in Belfast, d. March 20, 1910, buried Orwell Head. She m. Samuel Martin, b. September 29, 1821, in Skye, d. March 17, 1905, in Uigg, buried Orwell Head. Sarah and Samuel were married on March 7, 1849, by the Rev. Donald MacDonald.

Her obituary in *The Examiner*, March 16, 1910, reads:

> There peacefully fell asleep in Jesus, Tuesday evening, March 8, 1910, at the residence of her son, Mr. John S. Martin, Kinross, Sarah Campbell, relict of the late Samuel Martin, Eldon, in the 81st year of her age. The deceased was a noble Christian woman, possessed of a clear intellect, a warm heart and was highly respected by all. She was the mother of a large family, whom she and her husband trained to serve God from their youth. Three of the sons, James, Malcolm and Samuel Angus are honoured ministers of the Gospel in the Presbyterian Church, U.S.A. The funeral services at the house and grave were conducted by the Rev. D.B. MacLeod. The remains were laid to rest in the family plot, Orwell Head Cemetery, where less than a year ago was consigned to the tomb the mortal remains of a beautiful, good daughter from the same home—Sarah Margaret Martin. The words of the wise man, describing the good wife and mother, apply equally to the departed: "She openeth her mouth with wisdom and in her tongue is the law of kindness. She looketh well to the ways of her household and eateth not the bread of idleness. Her children rise up and call her blessed."

> It was said that Samuel, as an older man, fell down a 60-foot well and came out of it relatively unscathed. When asked how he had been so fortunate as to escape serious injury, he replied: "When I was falling, I said, 'Lord to be under me'—and he was."

B1   Margaret Martin, b. January 2, 1850, Uigg, d. May 26, 1872, buried, Orwell Head. She m. John Martin, b. ca. 1842, Browns Creek. He was a farmer and merchant. They were married on December 20, 1870, by the Rev. T. Duncan. The bondsman was H. Martin, the witnesses Hugh Martin and Mary Martin.
        C1   Margaret Martin, b. May 16, 1872, Whim Road, baptized June 2, 1872, Orwell Head Church of Scotland.

B2   Hugh Martin, b. July 30, 1853, Uigg, baptized, Orwell Head, d. 1923, Sheboygan, Wisconsin. He m. Emma Balzer, b. 1850, daughter of John

Balzer and Catherine Kump, d. 1953.

- C1 Sarah Margaret Martin, b. 1881, d. 1958. She m. Ludwig Larsen, b. 1879, d. 1938.
  - D1 Eric Larsen, b. 1909, d. 1976. He m. Mary [?].
    - E1 Barbara Larsen, b. 1936.
  - D2 Malcolm Larsen, b. 1910, d. 1965.
  - D3 Edward Larsen, b. 1912, d. 1987. He m. Marion Ivy.
  - D4 John Larsen, b. 1918, d. 1989.
  - D5 Robert Larsen, b. 1920, d. before 2007. He m. Helen Healy.
    - E1 Christine Larsen, m. Jeffry Eisenbooth.
    - E2 Christopher Larsen, m. Randine Jaastad.
      - F1 Todd Ludwig Larsen, b. 1980.
      - F2 Andrew Thomas, b. 1983.
      - F3 Heide Marie Larsen, b. 1985.
      - F4 Erika Larsen, b. 1987.
    - E3 Amy Lyn Larsen.
    - E3 Anders Thomas Larsen.
- C2 Neil Martin, b. 1883, d. 1889.
- C3 Catherine Martin, b. 1887, d. 1986. She m. William Bishop, d. 1935.
  - D1 David Bishop, b. 1910, m. May Barber.
    - E1 Becky Lyn Bishop.
  - D2 Janice Bishop, b. 1913, m. [?] Quigley.
    - E1 John Henry Quigley, b. 1935, m. Margy [?].
      - F1 Michael Quigley, m. Joan [?]. They have four children.
      - F2 Catherine Quigley. Married with two children.
      - F3 [Third child].
  - D3 Esther Bishop, b. 1916. She m. Sol Draznin, d. 1985.
    - E1 Martin Draznin, b. 1948, married.
      - F1 Charlie Draznin, b. 1980.
        - E2 Debra Draznin, b. 1950, m. Ken Texara.
      - F1 Ben Texara, b. 1980.
      - F2 Jake Texara, b. 1986.
    - E3 James Draznin, b. 1953, m. Lorely French.
      - F1 Leif James Draznin.
    - E4 Katherine Draznin, b. 1954.
- C4 May Bertha Martin, b. 1889, d. 1980. She m. James A. Burner, b. 1887, d. 1952.

D1 May Margaret Burner, b. 1913, d. 1989. She was divorced at the time of her death. She m. (1) George Bradley, b. 1910, d. 1982. They divorced in 1945.
- E1 James Michael Bradley, b. 1932, m. Sylvia [?] and divorced.
  - F1 Alesia Bradley, b. 1955.
  - F2 James Bradley, Jr. (Rusty), b. 1956, m. Brenda [?].
    - G1 Allison Bradley, b. 1981.
    - G2 Joshua Bradley, b. 1985.
    - G3 Carolyn Joyce Bradley, b. 1987.
  - F3 Todd Bradley, b. 1957, m. Andrea [?].
    - G1 Amanda Bradley, b. 1989.
- E2 Barbara Jean Bradley, b. 1934, m. (1) Robert Furst, divorced in 1960.
  - F1 James Furst, b. 1954, m. (1) Carol McGrew, later divorced.
    - G1 Natalie Furst, b. 1977.

    James m. (2) Shelley Feinburg, later divorced.
    - G2 Sarah Jane Furst, b. 1980.

    James m. (3) Kim [?].
    - G3 George Bradley Furst, b. 1982.
    - G4 James Kadden Furst, b. 1984.

  Barbara m. (2) Gildo Ferraro. Gildo had two children from his first marriage, John, b. 1955, and Leonora, b. 1956.
- E3 Dennis Patrick Bradley, b. 1940, m. (1) Nancy [?].
  - F1 Hugh Bradley, b. 1961.
  - F2 Hal Bradley, b. 1967.

  Dennis m. (2) Linda [?].
- E4 Sharon Ann Bradley, b. 1942, m. Thayne MacDonald.
  - F1 Douglas MacDonald, b. 1961.
- E5 Richard Allen Bradley, b. 1945 m. Georgiann [?]

May Margaret (D1) m. (2) Joseph Phillip, later divorced.
- E6 Kathy Phillip, b. 1956, m. Douglas Trudeau.
  - F1 Justin Trudeau, b. 1979.

May Margaret (D1) m. (3) Henry Culpepper, d. before 2007.

D2 James Burner, b. 1917, d. 1945, m. Margaret Booth.

D3 Hugh Burner, b. 1918, m. Marie [?].
  E1 Hugh Burner, b. 1945. He was married three times. The name of his first wife was Cleva.
D4 Richard Burner, b. 1921, d. 1990, m. Pat [?].

C5 John Arthur Martin, b. 1892, d. 1972, m. and divorced (1) Ella Hoffman.
  D1 Hugh Martin, b. 1919. He m. Doris Martin (Barbara), b. March 10, 1921, d. January 1, 2009, buried, Midland, MI.
    E1 Douglas Martin, b. 1946, m. Carol Traxler.
      F1 Kevin Martin, b. 1978, adopted.
      F2 Ryan Martin, b. 1979.
    E2 Denis Martin, b. 1948, m. Deborah Miller, later divorced.
    E3 Bruce Martin, b. 1952, m. Kathy McKenna.
  D2 Lois Martin, b. 1921, m. Samuel McCully in 1944. He was a veterinarian.
    E1 Karen McCully, b. 1945, m. Se June Hong.
      F1 Kessely Hong, b. 1973, m. Ted Hong. She was a radiation oncologist at Massachusetts General Hospital in 2007.
        G1 Gabriel Hong, b. 2004.
        G2 Caleb Hong, b. 2006.
    E2 Samuel McCully, b. 1947, m. (1) Genie Lambourn, later divorced.
      F1 Samuel McCully, b. 1974.
      F2 Lucas McCully, b. 1976.
      Samuel m. (2) Cindy [?].
    E3 Alan McCully, b. 1952, married. He is a veterinarian.
      F1 MacKenzie McCully, b. 1978, m. James Pryer in June 2007.
      F2 Megan McCully, b. 1980, m. Brett Benson.
        G1 Braun Benson, b. 2004.
      F3 Charles McCully, b. ca. 1986.
    E4 Susan McCully, b. 1953, m. Timothy Rychel.
      F1 Katherine Rychel, b. 1988.
      F2 Madeline Rychel, b. ca. 1990.
  John Arthur (C5) m. (2) Christine Brezenski.

B3* John Samuel Martin, b. August 3, 1855, Kinross, baptized October 21, 1855, Orwell Head, d. June 29, 1946, at the residence of his daughter

Annie, buried, Orwell Head. John was a farmer and carpenter, but also a Member of the Legislative Assembly (Conservative) for some years and Speaker of the House. He m. Harriet MacKenzie (Hattie), b. ca. 1864, d. June 20, 1942, buried, Orwell Head.

C1 Sarah Margaret Martin, b. November 7, 1885, Kinross, d. March 8, 1909, age 23, buried, Orwell Head.

C2* Mary Emily Martin, b. June 23, 1887, Kinross, baptized November 28, 1887, Orwell Head, d. January 16, 1957, Prince Edward Island Hospital, age 69, buried in Valleyfield after a funeral at Trinity Church in Charlottetown. She was a nurse. She m. Alexander MacLeod, b. 1881, Montague, son of Angus MacLeod and Jessie MacDonald, d. August 31, 1953, Charlottetown, age 72, buried, Valleyfield. He was a businessman and teacher. Mary and Alexander were married on June 11, 1912, at the residence of John S. Martin by the Rev. Ewen MacDougall. Witnesses were William C. Jenkins and Isabel MacLeod.

    D1 Jessie MacLeod, b. October 7, 1914, Montague, d. July 18, 1986, age 72, Queen Elizabeth Hospital, buried, Valleyfield. She was a nurse. She m. M. Arthur MacLeod, b. July 7, 1913, Charlottetown, son of Murdoch "Tailor" MacLeod, d. April 7, 1966, buried, Valleyfield.

        E1 David MacLeod.
        E2 Donald MacLeod.
        E3 Roger MacLeod.

    D2 John MacLeod, b. 1918, d. January 17, 1933, in Charlottetown at age 14 from scarlet fever, buried in Valleyfield.

C3 Annie Campbell Martin, b. June 30, 1889, Kinross, baptized October 3, 1889, Orwell Head, d. August 25, 1965, in the Prince Edward Island Hospital, buried, Cherry Valley Cemetery. She m. (1) William Albert Jenkins, b. December 13, 1885, Vernon Bridge, son of William Jenkins and Margaret Dingwell, d. September 18, 1952, buried, Cherry Valley Cemetery. Annie and William were married in her parents' residence on April 15, 1909, by the Revs. D.B. MacLeod and Ewen MacDougall. The bondsman was J.D. Jenkins and witnesses were Samuel Martin and Emily Martin. Annie m. (2) Ewen Gillis, b. 1888, Orwell, son of Donald Gillis and Sarah Lamont, d. 1975, buried, Orwell Corner. They were married in Saint Peter's Manse on July 30, 1958, by the Rev. John M. Sheen. There were no children from this marriage, but Ewen had a son from his previous marriage who died young.

C4   Samuel Martin, b. August 7, 1891, Kinross, baptized December 6, 1891, Orwell Head, d. December 9, 1982, Kingston, Ontario, buried in Cataraquie Cemetery, Ontario. He was a carpenter and built many barns and houses on the Island. He m. Mary Martin MacLeod, b. January 30, 1892, Vernon, daughter of John Martin MacLeod and Mary Margaret Jenkins, baptized April 21, 1892, d. July 4, 1975. Mary was previously married to Leslie Murray and had one son, Leslie Robert Louis Murray, b. November 11, 1912. Samuel and Mary were married on July 29, 1914, by the Rev. J.C. Martin. The bondsman was Gordon MacLeod.

    D1   Sarah Martin (Sadie), b. June 22, 1915, Uigg, baptized July 10, 1915, by the Rev. J.C. Martin, d. ca. 1996. She m. Al Coventry.

        E1   John Coventry

    D2   MacLeod Martin (Mac), b. ca. 1916, d. 1982 in Burlington, ON. He m. Alfreda Rogers, b. ca. 1921.

        E1   John Martin, m. Geraldine [?].

            F1   Cheryl Martin.

            F2   Heather Martin.

            F3   Daniel Martin.

        E2   Elaine Martin, m. Earl Zimmerman.

            F1   Patricia Zimmerman.

            F2   Daryl Zimmerman.

        E3   Marabel Martin, m. Greg Hetherington.

            F1   Lisa Hetherington.

            F2   Gerald Hetherington.

    D3   William Alexander Martin (Billy), b. 1917, Vernon, d. August 4, 1967, age 50, buried, Orwell Corner Cemetery. He was unmarried.

    D4   Doris Martin, b. ca. 1918, d. 1995, Kingston, ON. She m. Harold Crossman, b. ca. 1921.

        E1   Samuel Crossman.

        E2   Michael Crossman.

        E3   Cindy Crossman.

    D5   Evelyn Martin, b. ca. 1919, d. November 2005, Sherbrooke, QC. She m. (1) Ernest John Dunlop of Montreal. They were married on September 15, 1944, in Kinross by the Rev. J.M. Fraser. She m. (2) John Greenshields.

        E1   Wayne Greenshields.

        E2   Wanda Greenshields.

- E3 John Greenshields. Died young and unmarried. He was killed in a car accident.
- E4 Donna Greenshields. Died young and unmarried. She was killed in a car accident.

D6 Annie Mae Martin, b. 1920, Kinross, raised by her uncle and aunt, Will and Annie Jenkins. She m. Everett James MacDougall, b. 1913, Glenwood, son of Edward L. MacDougall and Lena MacDonsville. They were married June 12, 1940, in Cherry Valley Church by the Rev. A.S. Weir.
- E1 William Everett Noel MacDougall, b. June 3, 1941, baptized November 20, 1941, Vernon River. He m. (1) Margaret Isbel MacInnis, b. September 13, 1935, Glen William, daughter of Colin David McInnis and Mary Isabel MacPherson. They were married on April 21, 1962, in Cherry Valley United Church by the Rev. A.S. Weir, and later divorced.
  - F1 Everett Noel Gregory MacDougall, b. October 1, 1962, Vernon, baptized May 26, 1963, Vernon River United Church.
  - F2 Deneen MacDougall, b. 1964, m. Bruce Ferguson, b. 1961.
    - G1 Megan Ferguson, b. 1992.

  William m. (2) Margaret MacKenzie.
- E2 [Infant son], b. and d. January 8, 1949, buried, Cherry Valley Cemetery.
- E3 [Infant daughter], b. November 12, d. November 13, 1950, buried, Cherry Valley Cemetery.
- E4 [Infant], b. and d. December 1942, buried, Cherry Valley Cemetery.

D7 Leida Jane Martin, b. October 17, 1921, Uigg, raised by her uncle and aunt, Dingwell and Jane Jenkins. She m. Clifford Hayden Lea, b. 1921, Vernon River, son of M.S. Lea and Marguerite VanIderstine. They were married in the bride's home in Vernon on December 12, 1940, by the Rev. A.S. Weir.
- E1 Paul Dingwell Lea, b. August 6, 1941, baptized November 12, 1943, Vernon River, m. Carol [?].
  - F1 John Lea.
  - F2 Paul Lea.

- E2 Glenda Ferne Lea, b. November 26, 1942, baptized December 12, 1943, Vernon River, m. Robert Steeves.
  - F1 Roberta Steeves.
  - F2 Shane Steeves (twin).
  - F3 [Twin brother to Shane].
  - F4 Lorne Steeves.
  - F5 Regan Steeves.
  - F6 Monty Steeves.
- E3 Mary Jane Lea, b. March 22, 1945, baptized July 27, 1945, Vernon River. She m. Fred Grant, d. 2006, Riverview. They had two children.
- E4 Dorothy Lea, b. ca. 1947, m. Gary Fisher. They had two children.

D8* Lloyd Martin, b. October 29, 1922, raised by his maternal uncle Truman and Annie Jenkins, d. February 13, 2007, age 85, in the Queen Elizabeth Hospital. He served in the military during WWII. He m. Lucinda MacInnis (Dickie), b. June 13, 1926. They were married May 5, 1949.
- E1 Barry Malcolm Martin, b. May 23, 1951, baptized August 26, 1951, m. Sharleen Lamb.
  - F1 William Barry Martin (Billy), b. April 29, 1981.
  - F2 Mary Bethany Martin, b. December 19, 1986.
- E2 Clayton Lloyd Martin, b. May 2, 1953, baptized August 16, 1953, m. Janet LaFerte.
  - F1 Jennifer Lynn Martin, b. September 21, 1988.
- E3 Debra Anne Martin, b. June 29, 1955, m. Charles Thomas on September 4, 1976.
  - F1 Michael Charles Thomas, b. July 11, 1978.
  - F2 Laurie Anne Thomas, b. October 19, 1981. She was a nurse. She m. Ryan Brehaut.
    - G1 Noah Thomas Brehaut, b. January 9, 2002.
- E4 Donald Irwin Martin, b. July 25, 1957, baptized December 15, 1957, m. Lorie Volker on September 26, 1987.
  - F1 Vanessa Lorraine Volker, b. August 31, 1991.

D9   Donald Martin, b. 1923, d. April 2, 1985, Calgary, AB. He m. (1) Viola [?].
- E1   Leslie Martin, b. ca. 1945, died young in a truck accident in Alberta. She had no children.
- E2   Cheryl Martin, b. ca. 1951, married with a daughter.
- E3   [Daughter].

Donald m. (2) Ila [?].

D10   Donna Mary Martin, b. 1935. She was the daughter of Sadie (D1) and adopted by Samuel and Mary Martin (C4). She m. Erroll Lloyd Green, b. 1932, Kingston, son of Harrison Green and Levenie Newman. They were married September 2, 1953, in Saint Andrew's United Church by the Revs. J.F. MacKay and J.M. Sheen.
- E1   Lorna Green.
- E2   Heather Green.
- E3   Wendy Green.

C5   John W. Martin, b. July 14, 1896, Kinross, d. May 23, 1919, from the effects of WWI. He belonged to the 105th Battalion of the Canadian Expeditionary Force.

C6   Hugh James Martin, b. September 1, 1898, Kinross, d. April 8, 1954, Vernon, buried, Orwell Head. He was a carpenter and farmer. He m. Bessie Goss MacPhee, b. 14 [April, 1911?], baptized April 30, 1911, Valleyfield, d. 1982, buried, Orwell Head. She was a teacher. Hugh and Bessie were married October 30, 1929, in Bellevue by the Rev. D.M. Sinclair. The bondsman was Munro Bruce.

D1*   Annie Martin (Joyce), b. June 12, 1930, baptized August 10, 1930, Orwell Head. She m. Perley Sterling Drake, d. October 8, 2001, buried, Saint Andrew's Church Cemetery. They were married on August 30, 1950, in Orwell Head.
- E1   Gary Francis Drake, b. July 13, 1951, d. October 29, 1951, buried, Cherry Valley Memorial Cemetery.
- E2   William Drake (Allison), b. July 6, 1952, baptized August 1, 1953, Vernon River. He m. Ardyth Sherwood, b. in Nova Scotia.
  - F1   Rodney Trevor Drake, b. August 12, 1977. He was a pilot. He m. Karen [?].
    - G1   Ethan Drake, b. June 24, 2003.

	F2	Adenara Gail Drake, b. July 5, 1980.
	F3	Gregory Tyler Drake, b. April 24, 1982.
E3	\multicolumn{2}{l}{John Drake (Melvin), b. February 1, 1954, Vernon, baptized May 8, 1955, Vernon River, d. before 2001. He m. Katherine Jean Cummings (Jean), b. 1955, Vernon River, daughter of John Cummings and Margaret Currie. They were married on April 21, 1973, in Saint Andrew's United Church by the Rev. John Foster.}

- E3 John Drake (Melvin), b. February 1, 1954, Vernon, baptized May 8, 1955, Vernon River, d. before 2001. He m. Katherine Jean Cummings (Jean), b. 1955, Vernon River, daughter of John Cummings and Margaret Currie. They were married on April 21, 1973, in Saint Andrew's United Church by the Rev. John Foster.
  - F1 Shelly Marie Drake, b. October 24, 1973, d. March 31, 1977, buried, Saint Andrew's United Church Cemetery.
  - F2 Ryan Sterling Drake, b. July 7, 1978, m. Marin MacCallum.
    - G1 Aiden John Drake, b. February 2, 2005.
  - F3 Courtney Jean Drake, b. April 28, 1994, m. Clinton Myers.
    - G1 Cameron John Myers, b. August 22, 2005.
- E4 Derrell Hugh Drake, b. November 11, 1955, Cherry Valley, baptized August 17, 1958, Vernon River. He m. Mary Snow. Mary had three sons from a previous marriage: Craig, Sam and Todd.
- E5 Florence Darlene Drake, b. October 24, 1959, baptized July 17, 1960, Vernon River. She m. Robert Hennessey, who is a dentist residing in Charlottetown.
  - F1 Connor Robert Hennessy, b. July 26, 1993.
  - F2 Daniel Drake Hennessy, b. 1995.
  - F3 Catherine Hennessy, b. January 17, 1997.
- E6 Sheila Drake (Gwen), b. October 17, 1962, baptized May 26, 1963, Vernon River, She m. John Chow, a doctor residing in Chilliwack, BC, in 2001.
  - F1 Sarah Elizabeth Chow, b. May 5, 1994.
  - F2 Laura Christina Chow, b. February 1997.
- E7 Cindy Dianne Drake, b. September 26, 1969. She m. Michael Gaudet, b. Metagen, NS.

D2 Emily Mildred Martin, b. August 19, 1931, m. John Campbell Robbins (see A2.B4.C2.D5, p. 110).

D3* John Douglas Martin (Doug), b. February 25, 1934, Grandview, baptized August 13, 1934, Orwell Head. He m. Annabella D. Youngston (Ann), b. June 5, 1938, Peterhead, Aberdeenshire, Scotland, daughter of Wiliam Mackie Youngston and Maude Grey Duffus. John and Annabella were married August 27, 1956.

    E1 Deborah Ann Martin (Debbie), b. November 28, 1958, Toronto, ON. She m. Douglas Wright on October 19, 1991 and divorced in July 1999.

        F1 Michael Douglas Wright, b. January 23, 1985, Mississauga, ON.

        F2 Amanda Christine Wright, b. October 31, 1992, Simcoe, ON.

    E2 William Hugh Martin (Billy), b. March 9, 1962, Toronto, ON. He m. Kathy Lily on August 9, 1991, and divorced in 1999.

        F1 Jesse William Martin, b. December 2, 1991, Mississauga, ON.

        F2 Molly Heather Martin Bauer, May 9, 2001, Brampton, ON.

    E3 Troy Douglas Martin, b. May 11, 1970, Toronto, ON. He m. Susie Seara, b. August 11, 1972. They were married on October 11, 1997, in Brampton, ON.

        F1 Hunter Joseph Martin, b. September 10, 2000, Brampton, ON.

        F2 Kendra Diane Martin, b. January 26, 2005, Brampton, ON.

D4 Mary Noreen Martin (Molly), b. February 7, 1936, baptized June 14, 1936, Orwell Head. She m. Donald William Drake, b. May 8, 1930, Vernon, son of Francis Drake and Florence Keeping and brother of Perley, the husband of Molly's sister Joyce. Molly and Donald were married October 27, 1954, in Orwell Head by the Rev. Fraser.

    E1 Barbara Dianne Drake, b. April 28, 1956, d. in infancy, May 18, 1956, buried, Cherry Valley Memorial Cemetery.

    E2 Paul Douglas Drake, b. March 25, 1958, Cherry Valley. He m. Vivian Eileen Oakes, b. June 29, 1963. They were married on November 24, 1984.

The Descendants of James Campbell and Christy MacDonald

        F1   Austin Donald Drake, b. March 25, 1986, Queen Elizabeth Hospital, Charlottetown, twin of Ian.

        F2   Ian Frederick Drake, b. March 25, 1986, Queen Elizabeth Hospital, Charlottetown, twin of Austin.

        F3   Vivian Lynn Drake (Lynn), b. June 21, 1990, Queen Elizabeth Hospital, Charlottetown.

    E3   Larry Wade Drake, b. March 20, 1961. He m. Karen Louise Gregor, b. January 14, 1963, Liverpool, NS. They were married on December 3, 1983.

        F1   Nicholas Larry Drake, b. April 26, 1988, Charlottetown.

        F2   Jill Caroline Drake, b. January 10, 1992, Charlottetown.

    E4   Leslie Randall Drake, b. October 3, 1963, Charlottetown, baptized May 10, 1969, Vernon River. He m. Dorothy Christina Shaw, b. November 20, 1965, Lorne Valley. They were married June 21, 1986.

        F1   Adam Randall Drake, b. September 20, 1989.

        F2   Patrick Donald Drake, b. May 18, 1991.

        F3   Sarah Christina Drake, b. February 2, 1994.

D5   Robert Winston Martin, b. December 16, 1941, Montague, baptized January 19, 1944, Orwell Head, worked as a mechanic and electrician. He m. Joan Catherine Correy, b. October 19, 1940. They were married in 1963.

    E1   Joanne Lynn Martin, b. October 20, 1967, Toronto, m. Michael Grier.

        F1   Sydney Grier, b. 1999.

        F2   Wesley Grier, b. 2001.

    E2   Holly Alana Martin, b. October 12, 1970, Toronto, m. Maurat Beshtoev.

        F1   Olivia Beshtoev, b. January 2006.

D6   Edith Dianne Martin, d. 1943 in infancy, buried in Orwell Head Cemetery.

C7*   James Boyce Martin, b. 1901, Kinross, d. October 2, 1953, age 53, in Bunbury, buried October 20, 1953, Orwell Head. He was a mail driver, carpenter, farmer and merchant. He m. Katherine Bruce (Katie), b. October 9, 1902, Lyndale, daughter of Daniel Roderick Bruce and Christina Margaret Gillis, baptized, Orwell Head, d. November 26, 1997, age 95, at the Dr. John Gillis Lodge, buried, Orwell Head. Katie worked as a maid for Sir Andrew MacPhail and as a housekeeper in Boston. James and Katie were married February 2, 1923, in Newton Upper Falls, Massachusetts, by the Rev. Frederick Palladino.

D1   Loren Boyce Martin, b. May 29, 1924, Boston, MA, baptized September 25, 1926, at the home of J.S. Martin, d. March 11, 2005, age 81, in the Veterans' Memorial Hospital in Halifax. He served as a radio operator with the RCAF during WWII and continued with the Air Force after the war. He m. Margaret Casey.

     E1   Arlene Martin, b. June 15, 1952, m. Anthony Taylor, living in Shubenacadie, NS.

D2   Emily Christine Martin, b. February 16, 1926, Kinross, baptized February 16, 1926, in the home of John S. Martin. She was a Licensed Nursing Assistant. She m. Joseph Harold White, b. September 15, 1923, Murray Harbour, son of James Percy White and Sarah Henrietta Beaton, d. August 9, 1993, age 69, Charlottetown, buried, Clifton Cemetery. Emily and Joseph were married December 15, 1948, in Summerside by the Rev. Kenneth C. Sullivan. James was a dispatcher for the Shell Canada plant in Charlottetown and also served in the Navy during WWII.

     E1   Loren Harold White (Hal), b. August 9, 1949, Charlottetown. He worked in the laboratory at the Prince Edward Island Hospital. He m. Ann Denise Rhodenhizer, b. March 12, 1953, daughter of Ron Rexton Rhodindizer and Hazel June Rath. She worked in the payroll office at Queen Elizabeth Hospital. Loren and Ann were married on February 3, 1973, in Charlottetown.

         F1   Shawn Martin White, b. August 9, 1973, Charlottetown. He was a computer programmer living in Ottawa in 2006.

         F2   Derek Stephen White, b. March 6, 1978, Charlottetown. He was a clerk living in Sherwood in 2006.

The Descendants of James Campbell and Christy MacDonald 139

    E2 Patricia Catherine White (Patsy), b. January 28, 1951, Charlottetown, where she was a nurse's aide. She m. (1) Anthony Ronald Brown, b. January 3, 1941, Plymouth, England. He was a retired Lieutenant Colonel in the Canadian Armed Forces. They were married June 22, 1968, in Saint John-Glenview United Church by the Rev. Ray Francis, and divorced in 1975.

      F1 Jennifer Catherine Brown, b. January 15, 1969.

    Patricia m. (2) Joseph Gerard Hebert Lelievre, b. March 15, 1947, Quebec, baptized March 17, 1947, son of John William Lelievre and Marie Eva Levesque. He was a contractor and commercial airline pilot. They were married April 2, 1980, in Sept-Isles, QC.

      F2 Kim James Lelievre, b. May 13, 1981, Sept-Isles, QC.

    E3 Emily White (Gail), b. June 13, 1952, Charlottetown.

  D3 Alexander MacLeod Martin (Buster), b. July 16, 1929, Kinross, baptized August 10, 1930, Orwell Head, d. February 28, 1932, Kinross, buried, Orwell Head.

  D4 Marilyn Anne Martin, b. May 31, 1943, baptized May 14, 1944, Orwell Head. She was a receptionist and secretary. She m. (1) William Roy Murnaghan (Bill), b. January 31, 1938. He played the guitar in a band. They were married on December 1, 1967, in Toronto, ON, and divorced in 1985.

    E1 Sheryl Lee Murnaghan (Sherry), b. July 17, 1968, Toronto, ON, where she resides.

    E2 Jorel James Roy Murnaghan, b. June 22, 1971, Toronto, ON, where he resides.

  Marilyn (D4) m. (2) Gary Kenneth Milne, b. December 22, 1937. He was a locksmith. They were married in Toronto on July 30, 1991.

B4 Christy Ann Martin, b. July 20, 1857, Murray Harbour Road, d. before 1930 in Milwaukee. She m. George Wood, who also d. in Milwaukee.

  C1 Emma Martin, b. November 17, 1879, d. June 5, 1969, age 88, LM Nursing Home, buried, People's Cemetery, Charlottetown. Her name is given as Emma MacLeod on her marriage licence.

No baptismal record can be found. She was living with her grandparents Samuel and Sarah in 1881 and 1891. She m. Boyce MacKie, b. January 25, 1869, d. January 20, 1923, age 55. Emma and Boyce were married July 12, 1900, in Charlottetown by the Rev. J.K. Fraser.

D1   Dorothy MacKie, b. May 1901.

D2   Harold H. Mackie, b. August 28, 1903, Stanley Bridge, worked as a farmer and mechanic, d. June 15, 1971, age 67, buried, People's Cemetery, Charlottetown. He m. (1) Rhena Louise Cameron, b. 1900, Charlottetown, daughter of Ewen Cameron and Jessie Walker, d. March 4, 1950, age 49, buried, People's Cemetery, Charlottetown. They were married on August 26, 1935, in Saint James Presbyterian Church, Charlottetown, by the Rev. R.M. Legate.

    E1   Carolyn MacKie (Joyce), b. February 5, 1939, d. December 5, 2003, in the Queen Elizabeth Hospital, Charlottetown. She worked as a laboratory technician and was unmarried.

Harold m. (2) Marion Emily Martin

D3   Jean MacKie, b. February 1907.

D4   Wilbur MacKie, b. May 1909.

B5   Catherine Martin, b. August 3, 1859, Kinross, baptized October 9, 1859, Orwell Head, d. August 9, 1939, age 80, Charlottetown, buried, Orwell Head. Her headstone reads: 1861-1940. Catherine was a teacher. She m. Kenneth MacLean, b. October 31, 1857, Dundas, son of Angus MacLean and Margaret MacPhee, d. September 20, 1942, buried, Orwell Head. His headstone reads: 1858-1942. Kenneth was a farmer, residing in Grandview and Alberry Plains. He was also an elder in the Orwell Head Church. Catherine and Kenneth were married on January 9, 1884, in the manse by the Rev. John Goodwill.

C1   Margaret B. MacLean, b. 1884, Albion Cross, d. 1888, buried, Orwell Head.

C2   Samuel Martin MacLean, b. July 26, 1886, Murray Harbour Road, baptized February 3, 1887, Orwell Head, d. February 2, 1906, Grandview, at age 18 of measles, buried, Orwell Head. His headstone reads: 1886-1905.

C3   Sarah Janette MacLean, b. March 15, 1888, Grandview, d. in Vancouver. She m. Alexander Matheson, b. in Grandview, d. in Vancouver. The three daughters are listed in *The Maple Leaf Magazine* of October, 1930, as unmarried.

The Descendants of James Campbell and Christy MacDonald

        D1   Catherine Matheson.
        D2   Florence Matheson.
        D3   Ruth Matheson.

C4   Angus William MacLean, b. March 15, 1890, Murray Harbour Road, baptized July 14, 1890, Orwell Head, d. June 6, 1903, after being kicked by a horse, buried, Orwell Head.

C5   Margaret MacLean (Ella), b. April 12, 1892, Grandview, baptized August 21, 1892, Orwell Head, d. March 27, 1986, Queen Elizabeth Hospital, buried, Vernon River Memorial Cemetery. She worked for the BC Telephone Company. She m. Thomas Richards MacLean, b. June 16, 1879, Alberry Plains, d. January 2, 1963, buried January 5, 1963, Vernon River Memorial Cemetery. Margaret and Thomas were married June 26, 1923, in Vernon River by the Rev. J.C. Martin. The bondsman was William MacMillan.

        D1   Catherine MacLean (Jean), b. July 28, 1924, Alberry Plains, baptized March 20, 1925, Vernon River. She m. George Pickard (Keith), son of Cyrus Pickard and his wife Vina, on August 7, 1946. George was an architect.

            E1   George Thomas Pickard, b. November 17, 1948, d. January 1, 1989.

            E2   Ellen Carolyn Pickard, b. July 3, 1951, m. John Barry Cudmore, b. August 22, 1950. They were married July 18, 1967.

                F1   Carrie Jeanne Cudmore, b. December 24, 1978.
                F2   Heather Ruth Cudmore, b. April 26, 1980.
                F3   Andrew Keith Cudmore, b. July 12, 1983.
                F4   Peter Clayton Cudmore, b. October 26, 1984.

            E3   Barbara Jean Pickard, b. April 2, 1953, m. Blair Robert MacDonald on July 25, 1978.

                F1   Catherine Pauline MacDonald, b. January 21, 1982.
                F2   Alexander Blair Ronald MacDonald, b. September 16, 1984.
                F3   Keith Thomas MacDonald, b. June 6, 1992.

            E4   Deborah Lynn Pickard, b. March 6, 1955.
            E5   Doris Ruth Pickard, b. and d. June 6, 1965.

        D2   Anna Elizabeth MacLean, b. October 4, 1925, Alberry

Plains, baptized October 4, 1925, Vernon River, d. May 26, 1998, buried, Uigg Cemetery. Anna was a nurse, PHN, VON. She m. John Allan Shaw, b. November 4, 1916, Uigg, son of John Ernest Shaw and Murdina MacLeod, baptized February 15, 1917, d. 1969. Anna and John were married August 22, 1960, in Vernon River by the Rev. N.A. Green. Witnesses were Ewen MacLeod and Jean Pickard.

- E1   Ian Ernest Shaw, b. July 22, 1961, Uigg, baptized August 27, 1961, Vernon River Church. He was a farmer. He m. Catherine MacEachern in September 1992.
  - F1   Jonathan Alexander Shaw, b. October 14, 1994.
- E2   Paul Thomas Shaw, b. May 30, 1963, Uigg, baptized August 16, 1964, Vernon River. He m. Elizabeth Pendergast (Liz) on August 19, 1994.
  - F1   Madeline Donalda Anne Shaw, b. August 25, 1997.
- E3   Margaret Elizabeth Shaw (Beth), b. February 25, 1965, Uigg, baptized October 3, 1965, Vernon River. She is a nurse. She m. Paul MacDonald on August 4, 1990.
  - F1   Sarah Anne MacDonald, b. June 27, 1993.
  - F2   Mary Catherine MacDonald (Kate), b. June 23, 1995.
  - F3   Grace Elizabeth MacDonald, b. July 17, 1997.

D3   Ruth Agnes MacLean, b. August 24, 1926, Alberry Plains, baptized October 18, 1927, Vernon River. She m. Weston George MacLeod, b. April 27, 1928, Kinross, son of Samuel MacLeod and Agnes Mae MacPherson, d. 1982 in Ontario. They were married July 28, 1948, in Vernon River by the Rev. A.D. Weir.

- E1   Cheryl Ann MacLeod, b. May 5, 1949, baptized December 9, 1949, Orwell Head. She m. David French, b. January 26, 1949. They were married in 1968.
  - F1   Tamara Ann French (Tammy), b. 1969, m. Allan Nolet on July 31, 1993.
  - F2   Mark David French, b. 1971, Ontario.

    F3 Laura Ruth French, b. 1979.
  E2 Roberta Ruth MacLeod, m. b. September 30, 1950, baptized June 1, 1952, Orwell Head. She m. (1) Sandy Briant in 1973.
    F1 MacLean Alexander Briant, b. August 1976.
    F2 Heather Rose Briant, b. 1978.
  Roberta Ruth m. (2) Robert Brignell, b. in Ontario.
    F3 Jonathan Weston Fraser Brignell, b. 1989.
    F4 Robert Charles Thomas Brignell, b. 1991.
  E3 Katherine Ella MacLeod, b. August 22, 1953, baptized June 19, 1955, Orwell Head, m. John Payne.
    F1 Jeffrey William Payne, b. 1984.
    F2 Nathan Miller Payne, b. 1986.
  E4 Heather May MacLeod, b. December 4, 1954, m. Mark Gauvin on May 14, 1977, in Ontario.
    F1 Adrienne Weston Gauvin (Scott), b. 1981.
    F2 Charles Eric Gauvin (Eric), b. 1984.
    F3 Danielle Heather Gauvin, b. 1986.
  E5 Pauline Jessica MacLeod, b. March 25, 1965, m. Rick Farley in July 1988 in Ontario.
    F1 Connor Weston MacLeod Farley, b. January 14, 1993.
    F2 Neala Siobhan Farley, b. September 1995.
  E6 Joan Agnes MacLeod, b. March 25, 1965. She m. Peter Follows, b. in England. They were married in July 1992 in Ontario.
    F1 Benjamin Peter Follows, b. August 15, 1994.
    F2 Dalton Thomas Follows, b. June 1997.
  E7 Dianna Jean MacLeod, b. 1967, m. Tara McMahon in January 1987.
    F1 Jessica Lane Diana McMahon, b. 1988, Ontario.
    F2 Kyle Weston John McMahon, b. 1990.
D4 James Kenneth MacLean, b. March 9, 1928, baptized July 16, 1930, Vernon River. He m. (1) Kay [?], (2) Mary Elaine James. James and Mary were married February 19, 1975.
  E1 Michael MacLean.
D5 Arthur Martin MacLean, b. April 17, 1929, d. June 23, 1996, buried, Vernon River Memorial Cemetery. He was

unmarried.
- D6 Wallace Henry MacLean, b. January 10, 1931, m. Helen Ann Bryan. b. in Montreal. They were married August 6, 1960, in Montreal and later divorced.
  - E1 Roderick Thomas MacLean, b. March 7, 1963, Montreal. He m. Pamela Dianne Bonnett, b. November 15, 1964, Delhi, ON. They were married July 10, 1993, in Tilsonberg, ON.
    - F1 Sarah Jean MacLean, b. December 27, 1994, Montreal.
    - F2 Steven Richard MacLean, b. November 14, 1996, Brooks, AB.
  - E2 Charles Bryan MacLean, b. August 23, 1965, Montreal, m. Carol Shore on October 4, 1997, in Ottawa.
    - F1 Evan MacLean.
- C6 Flora Catherine MacLean, b. December 13, 1893, Murray Harbour Road, baptized July 9, 1894, Orwell Head. She m. George Harrison Rice, b. Charlottetown. They were married on November 8, 1911, in the Lennox Hotel, Charlottetown, by the Rev. R.G. Straithie.
  - D1 Elmer Rice, m. Pearle Rowe.
    - E1 Barry Rice.
    - E2 Allan Rice.
    - E3 Marilyn Rice, m. Allan MacLaughlan. Marilyn died before 2005.
  - D2 Wilber Rice.
  - D3 Eleanor Rice, d. at age 13.
  - D4 Wilmot Rice, d. at age 5 from a fall.
  - D5 Shirley Rice, m. Richard Holmes. Shirley died in 2002.
    - E1 Richard Holmes (Paul), b. ca. 1933.
    - E2 Shirlene Marilyn Holmes, b. ca. 1937.
    - E3 Ronald George Holmes, b. ca. 1938.
    - E4 Donald Carlyle Holmes (Carl), b. ca. 1940. He was a registered nurse.
    - E5 John Allison Holmes, b. ca. 1942.
    - E6 Glen Holmes, b. in the 1940s.
- C7 Annie Euphemia MacLean, b. February 4, 1896, Grandview, baptized July 13, 1896, Orwell Head, d. in Vancouver. She m. O.R. John Ellis (Jack), who d. in Vancouver.
  - D1 Gordon Ellis

D2 June Ellis, married with two children.
C8 Donald MacLeod MacLean, b. March 25, 1898, Grandview, baptized July 11, 1898, Orwell Head. Donald is buried in the USA. He was a member of the 105th Battalion in WWI. He m. Annie Beers, b. 1987, Montague, daughter of Isaac Beers and Isabella Bruce, d. 1977.
D1 Robert MacLean.
D2 Ann MacLean, d. 1993. She m. [?] Dillmar.
C9 Malcolm MacLean (Mac), b. June 19, 1900, Grandview, baptized July 15, 1901, Orwell Head, d. July 8, 1992, buried, Vernon Memorial Cemetery. He was a carpenter and mill operator. He m. Wilhelmina MacMillan, b. August 25, 1897, Alberry Plains, daughter of George MacMillan and his wife Ida, d. March 16, 1986, buried, Vernon Memorial Cemetery. Wilhelmina's obituary also lists a sister, Gertrude, d. 1910, three unnamed grandchildren and three great grandchildren. Malcolm and Wilhelmina were married on December 19, 1923, in Alberry Plains by the Rev. Ernest Westmoreland.
D1 Hugh MacMillan MacLean, b. November 26, 1924, Alberry Plains, baptized March 30, 1925, Vernon River. He m. Ada Duncan in 1947.
E1 Susan MacLean.
E2 Donald MacLean, married with two children.
D2 Earl MacLean (Woodrow), b. November 25, 1925, Boston, baptized October 18, 1927, Vernon River, d. April 23, 2003, age 77, in Montague Hospital, buried, Floral Hills Memorial Gardens. He m. Irene Douglas Hill, who died before 2003.
D3 Herbert Vickerson MacLean (Vic), b. June 17, 1928, Alberry Plains, baptized February 9, 1929, Vernon River, d. April 1, 1998, buried, Vernon Memorial Cemetery.
D4 Rena Myrtle MacLean, b. May 24, 1930, Alberry Plains, baptized July 16, 1930, Vernon River, m. (1) Forrest Lea.
E1 George Garth Lea, b. August 1, 1948, Vernon River, baptized October 20, 1948, Vernon River.
Rena m. (2) Wallace William MacPherson, b. July 24, 1929, Glen Martin, son of Daniel Ronald MacPherson and Elizabeth Walker (Bessie).
E2 Betty Helena MacPherson, b. July 4, 1952, d. July 6, 1952, buried, Vernon River Memorial Cemetery.

D5 Ernest Clinton MacLean, b. October 11, 1931, Alberry Plains, baptized March 18, 1932, Vernon River, m. Lavenia [?].

C10 Ruth MacLean, b. May 23, 1902, Grandview, baptized July 14, 1902, Orwell Head, d. February 10, 1929, Alberry Plains, buried, Orwell Head.

C11 Edwin MacLean (Clarence), b. August 17, 1904, Grandview, baptized August 26, 1906, Orwell Head, d. July 2, 1940, age 36, in the Prince Edward Island Hospital following surgery, buried, Orwell Corner Cemetery. He m. Edith Marguerite Elizabeth Lane, b. December 16, 1908, Vernon River, d. May 9, 1995, buried, Orwell Corner Cemetery. Edwin and Edith were married December 28, 1929, in Saint Peter's Cathedral by the Rev. Canon Malone.

    D1 Ruth Laura MacLean, b. October 6, 1930, Alberry Plains, baptized December 30, 1931, Vernon River. She m. Ernest Disney Taylor, b. November 3, 1916, son of Samuel Taylor and Leah Maria Judson, d. October 24, 2001, age 84, in the Queen Elizabeth Hospital, buried, Saint Andrew's Cemetery, Orwell Corner. Ruth and Ernest were married in November 1947 by the Rev. T.E. MacLennan. The bondsman was Harold MacLeod. Ernest was the brother of Edison (deceased), Alvira (Kenneth) Stewart, Sylvia Lamont (deceased), John (Dedie), Ramona (John) Campbell and George.

        E1 Malcolm Taylor. His father's obituary names his wife "Josie."

        E2 Bonita Ruth Taylor, b. Mary 17, 1949, Orwell, baptized June 9, 1949, Vernon River. She m. (1) James MacDonald, (2) Richard Collins.

        E3 Linda Taylor.

        E4 Richard Taylor.

        E5 Karen Leigh Taylor, b. December 1, 1962, in Ontario, and worked for the Department of Veterans Affairs, d. January 3, 1989, age 26, in a car accident, buried, Uigg Cemetery. She m. Robert MacLeod, b. Uigg, son of Arnold and Louise MacLeod.

    D2 George Lane MacLean, b. September 6, 1931, Alberry Plains, baptized December 30, 1931, Vernon River, d. June 3, 2001, age 70, Burlington, Ontario, survived by a wife and three daughters living in the Burlington area. He m. Mildred Christine MacDonald, b. June 12, 1934, Grandview, daughter of Ernest Hockin MacDonald and Mabel Bruce, d. February 7, 2002, Burlington, Ontario. George and Mildred were married in 1952.

  D3 Edwin Kenneth MacLean, b. June 30, 1933, Alberry Plains, baptized April 8, 1938, at home.

  D4 Reginald MacLean (Blair), b. August 29, 1935, Orwell, baptized April 9, 1938, at home, d. 1900, Ontario. He served in the Canadian Armed Forces.

  D5 Clarence MacLean (Roger), b. April 24, 1937, Orwell, baptized April 8, 1939, at home, m. Julie [?].

   E1 David Clarence MacLean.

  D6 Glen MacLean, m. Elaine [?].

B6* James Campbell Martin, b. July 30, 1861, in Dundee Road, Uigg, baptized August 17, 1861, Orwell Head, d. October 3, 1930 in Roseneath, PEI, age 68, of cancer, buried Orwell Head. James was a Presbyterian minister and the USA and PEI. He m. Norma A. Livock, b. 1858, d. June 27, 1936, in Charlottetown, age 78, buried Orwell Head. James adopted Norma's two children from a previous marriage to a Mr. Goodwin and also raised his nephew James Albert Beers (1901-198?), who was the son of his sister Emily (one of the triplets, B8 below) and Fred Beers. James Albert Beers later changed his name to James Albert Martin. At the time of James Campbell Martin's death, his two adopted children, Mary and Albert, were living in the USA.

B7 James Martin, b. July 20, 1864, d. in infancy, member of a set of triplets.

B8 Emily Martin, b. July 20, 1864, Kinross, triplet of James and Marjorie, baptized August 2, 1864, Orwell Head, d. in Massachusetts after 1946. She m. Fred Beers, d. in Massachusetts.

  C1 James Albert Beers Martin, b. 1901. He lived with his uncle, the Rev. James Martin, and changed his name from Beers to Martin. He died in the 1980s. He m. Elsa Heden, d. 1980.

   D1 Linda Martin, m. Donald Simmons.

   D2 June Martin, b. 1943, m. Roger Zaklukieweiz.

    E1 Kirsten Zaklukieweiz.

    E2 Wendy Zaklukieweiz.

    E3 Stephanie Zaklukieweiz.

    E4 Amanda Zaklukieweiz.

   D3 Bruce Martin.

  C2 George Beers.

>
> C3 Wilbur Beers.
>
B9* Marjorie Martin, b. July 21, 1864, triplet of James and Emily, baptized August 2, 1864, Orwell Head, d. May 1, 1935, Stanley Bridge, buried, New London Cemetery. She was a teacher. She m. (1) Alexander MacKay, b. September, 1851, Glynde Road, son of William MacKay and Christy Ann MacLeod, d. December 2, 1909, buried New London Cemetery. He was a carriage builder. Marjorie and Alexander were married on February 2, 1886, in the Valleyfield Manse by the Rev. R. MacLean. The bondsman was R.B. Norton and John Martin was a witness.

> C1 Christie Ann MacKay, b. December 23, 1886, Stanley Bridge, d. December 31, 1956, in the USA. She m. Hugh Barclay, b. in Chelsea, Massachusetts.
>
> C2 Sarah E. MacKay (Sadie), b. October 6, 1888, Lot 53, d. December 11, 1972, in Melrose, Massachusetts. She m. Bruce Champion, a contractor who died in Medford, Massachusetts.
>
> C3 William MacKay, b. October 23, 1890, b. October 23, 1890, Lot 53, d. 1968, buried in the People's Cemetery, Charlottetown. He was in England with the army in WWI and married there. He m. Marjorie Stanhope Cortney, who was born in England.
>> D1 Paul Arthur MacKay, b. 1923, Charlottetown, d. 1941, buried, People's Cemetery, Charlottetown.
>>
>> D2 George MacKay, was living in Charlottetown in 2006.
>
> C4* Hugh Samuel MacKay, b. September 7, 1892, Stanley Bridge, d. December 11, 1972, Charlottetown, buried, People's Cemetery. Hugh was a tailor who also served with the armed forces in both WWI and WWII. He m. Pearle MacKay, b. 1898, daughter of Mr. and Mrs. Archie MacKay, Charlottetown, d. 1982. Hugh and Pearle were married September 12, 1921, by the Rev. J.C. Martin. The bondsman was George Rice and witnesses were Mrs. J.C. Martin and Mrs. G.H. Rice.
>> D1 Ralph MacKay (Scottie), b. January 19, 1924, Charlottetown. He m. Marianne [?]. Ralph served in the Canadian Army signal corps during WWII. He was dispatch rider and was wounded in Belgium. He later joined the US Army and served in both Korea and Vietnam. After retiring from the army, he was last known to be living in Las Vegas. The couple had no children.
>>
>> D2 Clive Milton MacKay, b. 1926, Charlottetown, d. 1954, age 28, buried, People's Cemetery, Charlottetown. Clive was in the Royal Canadian Navy during WWII and in

the RCAF at the time of his death. He m. Jean Coffin, b. in Rollo Bay, daughter of Reginald Coffin and Sadie MacKenzie.

    E1   Deborah MacKay, b. July 17, 1953, Brandon, MB. She is a professor of physiotherapy at a university in Vermont. She m. Bernard O'Rourke, who is an architect.

        F1   Matthew MacKay O'Rourke, b. February 18, 1984.

        F2   Sarah Jean O'Rourke, b. January 17, 1986.

    E2   Clive MacKay, b. January 6, 1955, Charlottetown. He is a civil engineer, working for a consulting firm in Calgary in 2006. He m. Elizabeth Soper, a lawyer in Calgary in 2006.

        F1   Aaron Mark MacKay, b. June 11, 1995.

        F2   Brendan Matthew MacKay, b. June 7, 1997.

C5   George MacKay, b. September 28, 1894, d. November 17, 1918, of injuries sustained in WWI. He was unmarried and is buried in England.

C6   Ruth MacKay, b. June 28, 1896, m. Furley Belcher.

C7   Robert MacKay, b. September 3, 1898. He and his brothers James, Earnest and Glen operated a carriage building business in Massachusetts for 48 years. He m. May Lockart in Scotland. They resided in New Durham, New Hampshire.

    D1   Robert MacKay, m. Hilda Auld.

C8*   Emily MacKay, b. September 26, 1900, daughter of Alexander MacKay and Marjorie Martin, d. June 15, 1997 in Prince County Hospital, buried, Cape Traverse United Church Cemetery. She m. (1) Donald Martin [see A2.B4.C4, p. 113, for biographical information about Donald and a list of their children]. After the death of Donald Martin in 1923, Emily returned from Boston to her home in Stanley Bridge. Her obituary lists 11 grandchildren, 19 great grandchildren and a number of great-great grandchildren.

Emily m. (2) Daniel MacDonald

    D1   Eileen MacDonald, b. ca. 1927, m. (1) Russell MacLean, b. ca. 1910, buried, Argyle Shore.

        E1   James MacLean, residing in Oshawa, ON, in 2006, with a daughter, Cathy.

        E2   Laura MacLean, residing in Fredericton, NB, in 2006.

		E3	Wanda MacLean, m. Fred Livingstone, who was a painter. They were residing in Rustico in 2006.
		E4	Garfield MacLean, residing in Summerside in 2006 and working at the tax centre.

              Eileen (D1) m. (2) Arthur MacDonald, buried in Charlottetown.

- D2   Donald MacDonald, d. at age 60, buried, Seven Mile Bay. He m. Marie Landry, b. in Nova Scotia.
  - E1   Ronald MacDonald, m. Rita [?].
    - F1   Rhonda MacDonald, b. ca. 1975. Married with two children.
    - F2   Rae Ann MacDonald, d. from leukemia at age 6 or 7.
    - F3   Roma MacDonald, married to a teacher in Plymouth, England.
  - E2   Faye MacDonald, married with children.
  - E3   Jerry MacDonald, married.
  - E4   Mitchell MacDonald.

        Emily (C8) m. (3) Gavin Burgoyne

- C9   Ernest MacKay, m. Charlotte Forsee. Ernest was a carriage builder. Both he and Charlotte died in Crapaud.
  - D1   Glen MacKay
- C10   Glen MacKay, a carriage builder, m. Evelyn [MacKay]. Glen was a teacher and also at one time mayor of Concord, New Hampshire.
- C11   James A. MacKay, b. 1903, d. 1981. He was a carriage builder. He m. Muriel McNaught

Marjorie (B9) m. (2) Lauchlin MacKay.

- B10   Sarah Martin, b. June 27, 1866, baptized July 16, 1866, Orwell Head, d. February 21, 1941, Granville, Lot 21, buried, South Granville Presbyterian Cemetery. She m. John Gunn MacKenzie, b. July 12, 1856, Granville, Lot 21, son of Charles MacKenzie and Barbara MacLeod, baptized June 9, 1857, Kensington Presbyterian Church, d. April 29, 1925, buried, South Granville Presbyterian Cemetery. Sarah and John were married on February 2, 1887, by the Rev. D.B. MacLeod in Orwell Head. The bondsman and witnesses were Robert R. Gunn, John MacLean and Christy Campbell.
  - C1*   Charlotte MacKenzie, b. August 7, 1888, Granville, Lot 21.
  - C2   Margaret E. MacKenzie, b. March 9, 1890, Granville, Lot 21, d. April 23, 1932. She m. Angus Green. They had no children.
  - C3   Barbara Etta MacKenzie, b. January 9, 1892, Granville, Lot

21, d. July 6, 1907, Granville, Lot 21, buried, South Granville Presbyterian Cemetery.

C4 Sarah A. MacKenzie, b. August 29, 1893, Granville, Lot 21, d. March 11, 1970. She m. Walter Naylor. They had no children.

C5 George Clifton MacKenzie, b. November 10, 1895, Granville, Lot 21, d. September 2, 1918. He was killed during WWI, when he served with the 105th Battalion.

C6 Roberta M. MacKenzie, b. March 17, 1898, Granville, Lot 21.

C7 Samuel Martin MacKenzie, b. September 1, 1900, Granville, Lot 21.

C8 Euphemia Catherine MacKenzie (Phemie), b. May 5, 1902.

C9 Gladys MacKenzie, b. December 10, 1904.

C10 Norma Adelaide MacKenzie, b. May 24, 1907, d. October 12, 2000. She m. George Wesley Paynter, d. October 11, 1988. They were married December 24, 1930, in Long River.

    D1 Muriel Paynter, b. September 21, 1931, m. Norman MacRae, b. December 14, 1925. They were married February 15, 1956.

        E1 Adelaide MacRae, b. May 3, 1954. She m. (1) Allen Clark, b. August 4, 1953, d. July 9, 1976. They were married on August 26, 1972.

            F1 Gail Clark, b. March 20, 1973, m. Randy MacCaull. They were married on May 16, 2002, and later separated.

                G1 George MacCaull, b. January 6, 1992.

                G2 William MacCaull, b. May 28, 1993.

                G3 Donovan MacCaull, b. September 21, 1994.

            F2 Clair Clark, b. August 8, 1974, m. Rachael Reeves.

                G1 Matthew Clark, b. February 4, 2005.

Adelaide (E1) m. (2) Elmer MacAusland, b. October 3, 1934.

            F3 Laura MacAusland, b. October 14, 1977.

                G1 Kale MacAusland, b. April 4, 1997.

                G2 Tyler MacAusland, b. September 10, 1998.

                G3 Logan MacAusland, b. August 26, 1999.

- E2 Ann MacRae, b. December 7, 1956, d. September 20, 2006. She m. Jack Mackie, b. March 10, 1958. They were married on October 21, 1976.
  - F1 Jason Mackie, b. April 9, 1977, m. Colleen Belanger on June 16, 2007.
  - F2 James Mackie, b. January 11, 1985.
- E3 Austin MacRae, b. October 29, 1957. He m. Paula Benett, b. September 18, 1979. They were married December 18, 1982.
  - F1 Michelle MacRae, b. August 18, 1979.
  - F2 Anthony MacRae, b. July 12, 1983.
  - F3 Andrew MacRae, b. January 16, 1990.
- E4 George MacRae, b. June 1, 1962, unmarried.
- E5 Marie MacRae, b. March 28, 1964. She m. Ronald Ramsay, b. September 8, 1963. They were married on September 13, 1986, and later divorced.
  - F1 Natashia Ramsay, b. April 17, 1992.
  - F2 Nathan Ramsay, b. February 24, 1994.
- E6 Cindy MacRae, b. March 16, 1969. She m. Roger Moore, b. July 2, 1962. They were married August 29, 1992.
  - F1 Jenna Moore, b. July 30, 1999.
  - F2 Marcus Moore, b. May 2, 2003.

D2 Gladys Paynter, b. May 21, 1933. She m. Albert Stavert, b. April 21, 1931, d. December 3, 1993. They were married May 4, 1950.
- E1 Wendell Stavert, b. October 6, 1950, m. Linda Sharpe, b. February 3, 1951.
  - F1 Christopher Stavert, b. April 29, 1975. He m. Tanya Gallant in August 2000.
  - F2 Davis Stavart, b. March 2, 1979.
- E2 Reta Stavert, b. October 13, 1951, m. Ivan Bernard, b. September 9, 1947. They were married August 31, 1968.
  - F1 Kimberley Bernard, b. April 3, 1969, m. Karl Jollimore on September 20, 1991.
    - G1 Baylee Jollimore, b. September 7, 1994.
    - G2 Logan Jollimore, b. August 3, 1996.
- E3 Willa Stavert, b. November 20, 1952, m. Floyd Costain, b. January 13, 1950. They were married

August 31, 1968.
- F1 Duane Costain, b. April 16, 1971, m. Karen [?].
  - G1 Kayla Costain, b. January 16, 1992.
  - G2 Adam Costain, b. November 1, 1994.
  - G3 Jessica Costain, b. August 1996.
  - G4 Maranda Costain, b. November 17, 1999.
- E4 Jean Stavert, b. September 9, 1954, m. Garth MacKenzie, b. December 23, 1952.
  - F1 Mitchell MacKenzie, b. May 7, 1982.
  - F2 Tyler MacKenzie, b. January 15, 1984.
- E5 Lowell Stavert, b. July 21, 1960. He m. Wendy Whitehead, b. October 12, 1956. They were married October 7, 1990.
- E6 Gary Stavert, b. October 15, 1965. He m. (1) Shelly Betts on August 18, 1986, and later divorced.
  - F1 Shanae Stavert, b. December 11, 2004.
  Gary m. (2) Sandra MacArthur on September 15, 2007.
- E7 Sharon Stavert, b. March 3, 1969, m. Paul Gallant on June 18, 1988, and later divorced.
  - F1 Richard Gallant, b. January 4, 1989.

D3 Herbert Paynter, b. April 28, 1935. He m. Margaret Somers, b. April 27, 1940. They were married November 22, 1958.
- E1 Brian Paynter, b. September 22, 1959, m. Ellen Blackett, b. September 6, 1963. They were married on July 23, 1984.
  - F1 Ashley Paynter, b. August 11, 1987.
  - F2 Allyson Paynter, b. April 19, 1989.
- E2 Dawson Paynter, b. December 24, 1961, d. January 29, 2002, in a car accident. He m. Christine Carr, b. December 19, 1957, on July 13, 1985.
  - F1 Daniel Paynter, b. March 19, 1986.
  - F2 William Paynter, b. January 12, 1989.
  - F3 Johnathan Paynter, b. January 11, 1992.
- E3 Stephen Paynter, b. April 5, 1963, unmarried.
- E4 Norma Paynter b. October 30, 1964, m. Kenneth MacLeod, b. February 10, 1956. They were

married July 6, 1982.
- F1 Devin MacLeod, b. July 22, 1989.

E5 Martin Paynter, b. December 27, 1966, m. Kathie Brown, b. November 13, 1968.
- F1 Kyle Paynter, b. June 29, 1991.
- F2 Ryan Paynter.

E6 Tracy Paynter, b. December 5, 1968, m. Dennis Phillips, b. April 9 [year unknown]. Dennis had a son from a former marriage, Jeremy, b. April 27, 1978.
- F1 Megan Phillips, b. November 26, 1994.
- F2 John Phillips, b. February 22, 1996.

D4 Douglas Paynter, b. April 28, 1937, d. October 31, 1991. He m. (1) Betty Burgess, b. July 15, 1935. They were married November 13, 1961, and later divorced.

E1 Ronald Paynter, b. March 16, 1963.

Douglas m. (2) Mollie Samways, b. April 30, 1938, in England. They were married March 11, 1966.

E2 Glen Paynter, b. July 6, 1967, m. Sheryl [?].
- F1 Kaylynn Paynter, b. July 27, 1992.
- F2 Bradley Paynter, b. June 17, 1997.

E3 Merle Paynter, b. July 3, 1971, m. Paula [?] on July 10, 2003.

D5 Joan Paynter, b. July 2, 1941. She m. Wesley Cole, b. January 17, 1931. They were married November 26, 1960.

E1 Connie Cole, b. March 25, 1962, m. David Reeves, b. June 10, 1960. They were married May 2, 1981. They have a granddaughter, Lily, b. August 13, 2003.
- F1 Ryan Reeves, b. November 14, 1983.
- F2 Jeremy Reeves, b. July 5, 1986.
- F3 Richard Reeves, b. March 8, 1990.

E2 Linda Cole, b. March 29, 1965, m. Robert Crozier, b. November 15, 1997. They were married August 6, 1983.
- F1 Robbie Crozier, b. April 23, 1994.
- F2 Christopher Crozier, b. December 1, 1986.
- F3 Linden Crozier, b. May 16, 1991.

E3 Barbara Cole, b. July 12, 1969, m. Dennis Dunn, b. July 1, 1963. They were married March 7, 1991.
- F1 Jason Dunn, b. May 31, 1996.

F2 Rachael Dunn, b. July 3, 1998.
E4 Stephen Cole, b. June 5, 1971. He m. (1) Mary Andrews on September 9, 1996, and later divorced. He (2) Sheryl Gill, b. March 31 [year unknown].
D6 Brenda Paynter, b. December 4, 1947. She m. Hugh Baglole, b. April 30, 1946. They were married July 8, 1967, and later divorced.
E1 Rodney Baglole, b. November 9, 1968. He received a B.A. from the University of Prince Edward Island and studied at the University of Dundee, Scotland. He taught English in Japan for over six years. He was residing in Vancouver in 2007.
E2 April Baglole, b. April 10, 1970. She received a B.A. from the University of New Brunswick and a M.A. in library research from McGill University. She has been employed at Houghton Mifflin in Cambridge since 2006.
C11 James Andrew MacKenzie, b. June 23, 1913, d. February 15, 1976. He m. (1) Vera Paynter on March 15, 1933. Vera d. June 1970. He m. (2) Edna MacInnis on February 26, 1972.

B11* John Donald Martin, b. October 25, 1868, baptized, Orwell Head Church of Scotland by the Rev. James McColl, d. April 4, 1922, Eldon, buried in Belfast. He was a farmer and wheelwright. He m. Mary Ella MacKenzie, b. June 30, 1874, daughter of Neil MacKenzie and Catherine Gillis (Katie), d. 1966, buried in Belfast. They were married on September 1, 1896, by the Rev. D.B. MacLeod.
C1 Etta Martin, b. March 24, 1900, Grandview, baptized April 1, 1900, Orwell Head, d. April 4, 1900, buried, Orwell Head.
C2 Harold Neil Martin, b. September 29, 1905, baptized January 12, 1906, Orwell Head, d. February 8, 1998, age 94, in Orwell, buried, St. Andrew's Cemetery, Vernon. He never married.
C3 Catherine Grace Martin, b. June 7, 1907, baptized June 8, 1907, Orwell Head, d. in infancy.
C4 Catherine Martin (Muriel), b. November 17, 1909, Orwell, baptized July 19, 1910, Orwell Head, d. March 27, 1985, buried, Orwell Corner Cemetery. She m. Willard Campbell MacLeod (A1-B3-C2-D2, p. 71), b. June 30, 1908, Kinross, son of Angus Alexander MacLeod and Mary Campbell, baptized August 28, 1909, Orwell Head, d. July 13, 1978, buried, Orwell Corner Cemetery. Catherine and Willard were married January 11,

1932, by the Rev. E.H. Ramsay. The bondsman was Wilfred Gillis.

- D1 Mary MacLeod (Elva), b. April 16, 1932, Kinross, baptized December 2, 1932, Orwell, d. July 5, 1987, age 55, Lyndale, buried, Orwell Corner. She m. Donald Glen Nicholson, b. October 23, 1931, Upper Montague, baptized June 24, 1936.
    - E1 Donald Gordon Nicholson (Gordon), b. November 25, 1953, m. Judith Elizabeth Carver (see A1-B5-C3-D3-E5, p. 87).
    - E2 Douglas Nicholson.
    - E3 Lea Nicholson.
- D2 Donald Malcolm MacLeod, b. July 11, 1933, Kinross, baptized June 21, 1936, Orwell, d. February 11, 1967, Victoria General Hospital, Halifax, buried, February 14, 1967, Orwell Corner Cemetery. He was a sheet metal worker. He m. Lorna May MacDonald, b. July 25, 1937, Orwell, daughter of Ernest MacDonald and Mabel Bruce.
    - E1 Jeffrey MacLeod, b. September 16, 1959, m. Carla Brecken.
    - E2 Donald Andrew MacLeod, b. November 17, 1963, m. Priscilla [?] and later divorced.
        - F1 Jonathan MacLeod, b. May 9, 1997.
        - F2 Kaylee MacLeod, n. May 25, 2000.
    - E3 John MacLeod, b. June 25, 1966.
    - E4 Timothy Ross MacLeod, b. December 3, 1964, baptized October 3, 1965, Vernon River. He m. Nicola Claire Mather, b. in Burlington, ON, daughter of Richard Mather and Catherine Byrnell. They were married June 30, 2001, in Forest Hill United Church, Toronto.
        - F1 Kate MacLeod, b. December 28, 2002.
        - F2 Colin MacLeod, b. March 8, 2006.
- D3 Angus Keith MacLeod, b. October 1, 1935, Kinross, baptized June 21, 1936, Orwell. He was living on the homestead in Kinross in 2008. He m. Catherine Elizabeth Brehaut (Kay), b. 1937, Lyndale, daughter of Robert Brehaut and Annie Richards.
    - E1 Richard Keith MacLeod, b. December 11, 1957, baptized October 5, 1958, Orwell Head. He m.

Pam Kays in Calgary, AB.
- E2 Janice Helen MacLeod, b. Fort McMurray, AB. She m. (1) David Patterson, (2) Charles Gillis, b. Whim Road, son of Wilfred Gillis and Margaret Scott.
  - F1 Amanda Beth Gillis.
- D4 Robert Martin MacLeod (Bobbie), b. July 4, 1937, Eldon, baptized October 8, 1946, Vernon River, d. March 16, 2003, Fairview. He m. (1) Sarah Stewart (Sally).
  - E1 Randy MacLeod.
  - E2 Robin MacLeod.
  - E3 Nancy MacLeod.
  - E4 Mary Louise MacLeod, b. August 11, 1965, baptized May 28, 1967, Vernon River.

Robert m. (2) Edith MacLeod (Clara), b. in Uigg, daughter of Malcolm MacLeod (Mackie) and Marion Hugh. She was a nurse.

- D5 Florence Eleanor MacLeod, b. September 19, 1940, Eldon, baptized October 8, 1946, Vernon River. She m. Munroe Kenneth Wheeler, b. October 16, 1936, son of Christopher William Wheeler and Jean L. Marshall of Hopeville, ON, baptized July 3, 1966, Orwell Head, d. December 30, 2007, age 71, Newmarket, ON, buried, January 4, 2008, Lower Montague.
  - E1 Susan Wheeler, m. Mackie Dixon.
    - F1 Kelcie Jeanette Dixon, b. ca. 1990, Lower Montague, d. June 18, 2006, age 16, in a car accident in Lower Montague, buried, Murray Harbour North Cemetery.
    - F2 Melinda Dixon.
    - F3 John Dixon.
  - E2 Stephen Wheeler, m. Darla [?], living in North Carolina in 2007.
  - E3 Wendy Wheeler, m. James Sharkey, living in Heatherdale in 2007.
  - E4 Paul Wheeler, m. Charlotte [?], lives in Prince George, BC.
  - E5 Leslie Wheeler, m. Terri Anne [?], lives in Cardigan.
- D6 Harold Walton MacLeod, b. May 16, 1946, Eldon, baptized October 8, 1946, Vernon River. He m. Heather

Ann Gillis, b. August 15, 1947, daughter of Lauchlin MacLeod Gillis and Alberta Gertrude Nicholson, baptized in Belfast.
- E1 Gwendolyn MacLeod.
- E2 Kevin MacLeod.

C5 Marion Emily Martin, b. February 2, 1912, Orwell. She m. Harold H. MacKie, b. August 28, 1903, Stanley Bridge, son of Boyce MacKie and Emma Martin, d. June 15, 1971, age 67, buried, People's Cemetery, Charlottetown. He was a farmer and mechanic.
- D1 Jessie Emma MacKie (Bonnie), b. July 9, 1942, m. Fred Burke. Jessie was a teacher and Fred a businessman.
  - E1 Will Burke.
  - E2 Robert Burke (Bob), m. Rosanne [?].
  - E3 Allison Burke.
  - E4 Colin Burke.

C6 Samuel Hugh Martin, b. 1914, d. 1981, buried, Orwell Corner Cemetery. He served in the RCAF during WWII. He m. Mary Annie Bozan in Cape Breton.
- D1 Brenda Martin, m. William Irwin (Bill).
  - E1 Jackie.
  - E2 Billy-Jo.
  - E3 Travis.
  - E4 Bobby-Sue.
  - E5 Jason.
  - E6 Adam.
- D2 Ronald Martin, m. Wanda Smith.
  - E1 Julie.
  - E2 Erwin.
- D3 John Donald Martin, b. and d. 1944, 8 weeks of age, buried, Orwell Corner Cemetery.

C7 Lloyd George Martin, b. 1917, d. January 2006, Montague. The date of his funeral was January 8, 2006, buried in Saint Andrew's Cemetery. He was a farmer. He m. Daisy Johnston Bowles, b. March 27, 1919, Dover, daughter of John Malcolm Bowles and Evelyn Jane MacLure, baptized April 3, 1920, d. September 5, 1986, Queen Elizabeth Hospital, buried, Saint Andrew's Cemetery, Vernon. Lloyd and Daisy were married on June 29, 1957, in Dover by the Rev. J.M. Sheen. Witnesses were Ewen Lamont MacLeod and Lois A. MacLeod.

B12 Malcolm Campbell Martin, b. April 1, 1871, Uigg, baptized August

27, 1871, Orwell Head, d. October 29, 1940, California. He was a minister and chaplain with the AEF in WWII. He m. Ella May Parks.

- C1 June Martin, b. June 15, 1904, California, d. November 29, 1982.
- C2 Margaret Cecelia Martin, b. February 21, 1906, California, d. December 15, 1994.
- C3 Eleanor Katherine Martin, b. June 16, 1916, California, d. April 22, 1996, Oregon.

B13* Samuel Angus Martin, b. September 4, 1873, Kinross, baptized March 8, 1874, Orwell Head Church of Scotland, d. June 20, 1939, Portland, Oregon, age 67. He was a minister and served with the Canadian Army as a chaplain in WWI. He had parishes in Rivers, MB, in 1922, Churchill, MB, in 1930, and Oregon in 1939. He m. Nettie Fielding.

- C1 Wallace James Martin, b. September 21, 1907, d. March 24, 1930, age 22 years, 6 months, buried, Rivers, MB. He died of meningitis the same year he graduated from the University of Manitoba.
- C2 Jean Martin, m. Ernest Yeo. They lived in Veronia, OR, in 1930, and in Portland in 1939.
- C3 Margaret Martin was a teacher, living in Winnipeg in 1930.
- C4 Malcolm Martin, d. before 1930, buried, Rivers, MB.

A5.* The Descendants of Donald Campbell and Christy MacLeod

Donald Campbell, b. ca. 1831 in Uigg, d. September 1, 1913, in Haverhill, MA, age 83, buried September 6, 1913, Orwell Head. His name is not on the headstone, but he is said to be buried with his wife. He worked for the Sutherland Brothers, Montague. He m. Christy MacLeod on November 10, 1852, by the Rev. Donald MacDonald. Christy was b. August 7, 1831, on the Murray Harbour Road, daughter of Archibald MacLeod and Marion MacDonald, baptized March 30, 1832, in Belfast, d. February 22, 1882, Head of Montague, buried, Orwell Head.

B1 James Campbell, b. January 11, 1853, Murray Harbour Road, baptized February 17, 1853, in the Church of Scotland, Orwell Head, d. before 1914 in USA, never married.

B2 Archibald Campbell, b. 1855, Murray Harbour Road, d. before 1914 in USA.

B3 John Campbell, b. October 5, 1856, Murray Harbour Road, baptized November 5, 1856, in the Church of Scotland, Orwell Head, d. after 1914 in Duluth, MN. Married with two daughters:
    C1 Mabel Campbell.
    C2 Euphemia Campbell.

B4* Sarah Campbell (Marion), b. December 23, 1858, Murray Harbour Road, baptized June 13, 1859, Orwell Head, d. October 6, 1916, Head of Montague, buried, Brudenell. She m. Robert James Stewart, b. 1859, New Perth, son of Alexander Stewart and Jessie Dewar, d. October 7, 1913, buried, Brudenell. They were married on March 24, 1890, in Montague by the Rev. O.B. Emery.
    C1 Ira Alexander Stewart, b. August 19, 1893, d. June 17, 1966, buried, Union Cemetery. He m. Margaret May Grant, b. June 26, 1897, daughter of John Amos Grant and Margaret MacQueen, d. June 5, 1993, age 95, buried, Union Cemetery. They were married December 25, 1919, in Montague by the Rev. C.E. Armstrong. Witnesses were Lulu Christine Stewart and H. Penna Moore.
        D1 Robert Alexander Stewart, b. July 9, 1921, New Perth, d. September 8, 1994, age 73, Ottawa General Hospital, buried, Union Road Cemetery.
        D2 Elizabeth May Stewart (Bessie), b. June 30, 1922. She m. William Sinclair MacLean, b. 1919, d. 1964,

Charlottetown, buried, Belfast Cemetery.

    E1   William MacLean (Sinclair), b. April 16, 1964, Charlottetown, m. April MacLean and later divorced.

D3   Edith Joyce Stewart, b. April 6, 1925, d. May 1988 at the Dr. Eric Found Health Centre, buried, Crossroads Cemetery. She m. John Ralph Stewart, b. May 5, 1919, in the USA.

    E1   Gail Charlene Stewart, b. March 18, 1947, Halifax, m. James Joseph Isaac, b. January 31, 1946, Halifax.

        F1   Allison Margaret Isaac, b. June 14, 1976, Halifax, m. Ross Potter.

    E2   Deborah Ann Stewart, b. March 18, 1952, in Halifax. She m. Gerald Ralph Ward, b. September 10, 1950, in Nova Scotia.

D4   Sterling James Stewart, b. June 14, 1928, New Perth. He m. (1) Ruth Constance Namee, b. September 7, 1924, in Ontario, d. April 24, 1987.

    E1   Lesley Margaret Stewart, b. April 23, 1953, m. Michael Hanley, b. July 20, 1951.

        F1   Jason Michael Hanley, b. December 12, 1975, Ottawa, m. Arin Tomson.

        F2   Robyne Lynn Hanley, b. May 18, 1979, Ottawa, m. Bradley Kirk.

            G1   Hunter Stewart Kirk.

    E2   Jeffrey Grant Stewart, b. April 23, 1955, Ottawa, m. Ann Elizabeth McKee, b. February 14, 1955, Ontario.

        F1   Sara Elizabeth Stewart, b. April 30, 1981, m. Liam Breedon.

            G1   Bailey Breedon.

        F2   Katherine Ellen Stewart, b. August 15, 1983, Ottawa.

        F3   Michael Jeffrey Stewart, b. June 1, 1985.

        F4   James Alexander Stewart, b. December 10, 1985.

    E3   Barbara Alexander Stewart, b. July 20, 1956, Ottawa, m. Frank Gratton, b. January 12, 1956.

        F1   Benjamin Raymond Gratton, b. April 26, 1984.

    F2 Patrick James Gratton, b. January 26, 1986.
    F3 Carolyn Rose Gratton, b. March 23, 1988.
  E4 Kimberly Ruth Stewart, b. January 13, 1959, Ottawa, m. John Pollock, b. June 12, 1954.
    F1 Joshua Hart Pollock, b. April 12, 1986.
    F2 Ian Pollock, b. August 8, 1988.

Sterling James (D4) m. (2) Jessie Mary Furey Adam

 D5 Jean Shirley Stewart, b. May 21, 1930. She m. Harold Gordon MacKay, b. March 15, 1928, Charlottetown, d. November 7, 1982, Charlottetown, buried, People's Cemetery.
  E1 Brian Gordon MacKay, b. February 28, 1954, d. June 6, 1954, buried, People's Cemetery.
  E2 Dana Harold MacKay, b. May 1, 1955.
  E3 Kenneth Ira MacKay, b. June 29, 1958, m. Linda Laybolt.
  E4 Lois Leanne MacKay, b. August 2, 1962.
  E5 John Scott MacKay, stillborn on April 16, 1966.
 D6 Hazel Irene Stewart, b. September 3, 1932, New Perth, d. October 9, 1990, Purdys, NY, buried, White Plains, NY. She m. William Philip Merkel, b. 1941.
  E1 Bonnie Eve Merkel, b. June 29, 1967, in Purdys, NY, m. Jeffrey Sexton.
  E2 Laurel Jean Merkel, b. June 19, 1969.
  E3 William Stewart Merkel, b. August 26, 1971, Charlottetown.

C2 Lulu Christina Stewart, b. June 17, 1897, d. March 3, 1986. She m. Harris Penna Moore, b. Union Road, on December 20, 1920 (the date on the marriage licence) in Montague by the Rev. C.E. Armstrong.
 D1 Mabel Moore, b. 1922, m. (1) Robert Chisholm.
  E1 Judy Chisholm, m. Wayne Myers.
    F1 Joanne Myers, m. Roland Proulx.
      G1 Jonathan Proulx.

Mabel m. (2) Clyde York.

 D2 H. June Moore, b. June 14, 1928, m. Myron MacDonald Weeks, b. September 18, 1931.
  E1 David Kevin Weeks, b. October 4, 1955, m. Joan Butcher.
    F1 Will David Weeks, b. August 19, 1991.

	E2	Nancy Jean Weeks, b. February 8, 1957, m. David McGrath.		
		F1	Laura Helen McGrath, b. November 23, 1992.	
		F2	Steven Joseph McGrath (twin of Kelly), June 27, 1995.	
		F3	Kelly Erin McGrath (twin of Steven), June 27, 1995.	
	E3	Paul Wayne Weeks, b. March 6, 1958, m. Frances O'Conner.		
		F1	Chantal Marie Weeks, b. June 8, 1989.	
	E4	Beryl June Weeks, b. September 14, 1959, m. Donald Moses.		
	E5	John Earle Weeks, b. September 20, 1960.		
	E6	Douglas Steven Weeks, b. May 8, 1962.		
	E7	Gordon Weeks (Blair), b. July 13, 1963, m. Shelley Musika.		
	E8	Wendy Faye Weeks, b. February 3, 1965, m. Andrew Oakley.		
		F1	Megan Sarah Weeks, b. February 15, 1991.	
C3	John James Stewart (J.J.), b. April 8, 1900, d. March 11, 1970, buried, Montague Community Cemetery. He m. Hazel Glen Brehaut, b. September 1, 1905, daughter of Russell Brehaut and his wife, buried, Montague Community Cemetery. John James was a merchant in Montague.			
	D1	Hazel Stewart (Ruth), b. December 10, 1930. She m. Carmen Douglas Carle, son of Mr. and Mrs. F.H. Carle of East Florenceville, NB. They were married on September 19 [year unknown] in her parents' home in Montague by the Rev. P.L. Richardson.		
		E1	Heather Carle, m. William Hayward.	
			F1	James Hayward.
			F2	Erin Hayward.
			F3	Lauren Hayward.
		E2	Lynn Carle, m. Robert Poirier.	
			F1	Alyson Poirier.
			F2	Andrew Poirier.
		E3	Beth Carle, m. Roy Piercey	
	D2	Mary Stewart (Fay), m. Robert Marshall.		
		E1	Robert Marshall, m. Frances Fraser.	
			F1	Jocelyn Marshall.

          F2   Matthew Marshall.
     E2   Andrew Marshall.
     E3   John Marshall, m. Sherry MacRae.
          F1   Emilyne Marshall.
          F2   Barett Jay Marshall.

B5   Donald Campbell (Dan), b. July 16, 1861, Murray Harbour Road, baptized August 11, 1861, d. before 1914 in USA.

B6   Malcolm Campbell, b. October 15, 1863, Murray Harbour Road, baptized February 14, 1864, in the Church of Scotland, Orwell Head, d. after 1914 in Warren, ID.

B7   Christy Ann Campbell, b. August 16, 1866, Head of Montague, baptized September 16, 1866, Orwell Head Church of Scotland, emigrated to the USA in 1882, d. after 1914 in Haverhill, MA. She m. Uriah Crossland, b. ca. 1862 in England, emigrated in 1881, d. in Haverhill, MA.
     C1   Ernest Crossland, b. ca. 1897.
     C2   Ada Crossland, b. ca. 1896.

B8   Jessie Campbell, b. December 16, 1868, Head of Montague, baptized May 23, 1869, in the Church of Scotland, Orwell Head, d. 1914 at the home of her sister (Mrs. Uriah Crossland) in Haverhill, MA, buried Hamstead, NH. She went to the USA in 1892 and resided in Haverhill for 23 years. She was a servant with the Nithingham family in 1910.

B9   Angus MacLeod Campbell, b. July 30, 1873, Head of Montague, baptized August 31, 1873, Orwell Head Church of Scotland, d. January 31, 1952, in Duluth, MN. He m. Ina Wilcox, b. October 9, 1873, Waterford, ON, d. October 23, 1925, Duluth, MN.
     C1   Inez MacLeod Campbell, b. August 22, 1900, d. April 15, 1990.
     C2   Angus MacLeod Campbell, b. February 3, 1914, d. October 21, 1999.
     C3   Donald Wilcox Campbell, b. August 10, 1907, d. July 21, 1971.
     C4   Ray Wilkinson Campbell, b. ca. 1904, d. April 15, year unknown.

B10 Margaret Ann Campbell, b. September 18, 1875, Head of Montague, baptized October 17, 1875, in the Church of Scotland, Orwell Head, d. February 23, 1876, Head of Montague, buried, Orwell Head.

A6.* The Descendants of Ann Campbell and Donald Murchison

Ann Campbell, b. 1833, Uigg, d. December 25, 1888, Point Prim, buried, Polly Cemetery. She m. Donald Murchison, b. 1824, son of Neil Murchison and Euphemia MacDonald, d. February 1, 1901, Point Prim, buried, Polly Cemetery. They were married February 12, 1851, by the Rev. Donald MacDonald. Donald was a ship captain. He built vessels and sailed, retiring in 1860, after which he bought a 140 acre farm.

B1   Euphemia Murchison, b. April 14, 1853, m. James Stewart (see A3.B4, p. 123).

B2   Margaret Murchison, b. April 11, 1854, Point Prim, baptized July 18, 1854, Orwell Head Church of Scotland, d. May 12, 1895, age 42, Point Prim, buried, Polly Cemetery. Her headstone reads: "Also four infant children." She m. Alexander MacLeod, b. September 18, 1849, Point Prim, son of Donald MacLeod and Mary Murchison, baptized September 25, 1854, Belfast, d. December 26, 1894, age 48, Point Prim. He was a sea captain. Margaret and Alexander were married on May 10, 1881, at Osborne House by the Rev. J.M. MacLeod.

    C1   Donald M. MacLeod, b. February 21, 1882, Point Prim, baptized June 4, 1882, Zion Church, d. April 8, 1947, age 65, buried, Polly Cemetery. He was a teacher, unmarried, living with his mother's brother and sister, according to the 1901 census.

    C2   Malcolm Murchison MacLeod, b. November 6, 1888, Point Prim, baptized February 12, 1889, Belfast, m. Elizabeth MacPherson. The Murchison book indicates that they had five children, but does not name them.

        D1   Walter A. MacLeod, d. March 12, 1981, Halifax, buried, Murray River Cemetery. He m. Elma Lois Bowles, daughter of John Malcolm Bowles and Evelyn Jane MacLure. Walter's obituary states that he was survived his wife Lois, son Brent, daughter Heather, sisters Ann of Los Angeles, Ruth of Toronto, Alice of Montreal and Bruce of PEI, and that he was preceded by his parents, his daughter Faye and his brother Malcolm.

        D2   Malcolm MacLeod.

        D3   Ann MacLeod.

        D4   Ruth MacLeod.

        D5   Alice MacLeod.

>> D6 Bruce MacLeod.
> C3 Angus Murchison MacLeod, b. May 30, 1893, Point Prim, baptized June 25, 1893, Belfast, d. in San Francisco. He was an optometrist, living with his mother's brother and sister according to the 1901 census.

B3 Mary Murchison, b. January 3, 1856, Point Prim, baptized April 8, 1856, Orwell Head Church of Scotland, d. January 19, 1921, buried, Wood Islands Cemetery. She m. Allan Matheson, b. May 24, 1839, son of Donald Matheson and Catherine MacDonald, d. May 15, 1927, age 88, buried, Wood Islands Cemetery. He was a farmer. Mary and Allan were married on December 4, 1879, at Murray Harbour Road by the Rev. A. Munro. The bondsman was James Stewart.

> C1 Catherine Matheson (Katie), b. December 4, 1879, Belle River, baptized February 13, 1888, Wood Islands Presbyterian Church, d. October 31, 1961, age 81, in the Beach Grove Home, buried, Belfast. She m. Charles Douglas John MacLeod, b. April 13, 1875, Mount Buchanan, son of Charles W. MacLeod and Janet MacLeod (Jessie), d. June 9, 1961, age 86, in the Prince Edward Island Hospital, buried in Belfast. Catherine and Charles were married September 10, 1928, in the Kirk of Saint James by the Rev. T.F. Fullerton. The obituary of Charles states that he was survived by his wife, Katie Matheson, his foster son John, and four grandchildren, and that he was the youngest son of Charles and Jessie MacLeod.
>> D1 John MacLeod (foster son).
> C2 Donald J. Matheson, b. March 27, 1881, baptized February 13, 1888, Wood Islands Presbyterian Church.
> C3 Annie Matheson, b. April 21, 1883, baptized February 13, 1888, Wood Islands Presbyterian Church, d. April 22, 1933, Summerville, MA, buried, Woodlawn Cemetery, Everett, MA. She m. John Alex MacDonald, b. in Cape Breton and living in Boston in 1907. They were married August 24, 1907, in PEI by the Rev. A.S. Stewart. The bondsman was Henry White.
>> D1 Douglas Matheson MacDonald.
>> D2 Hugh Wallace MacDonald.
>> D3 Mary Nichol MacDonald.
>> D4 Janet Murchison MacDonald.
>> D5 Kenneth Gordon MacDonald.
> C4 James Craig Matheson, b. October 30, 1888, baptized August 13, 1889, Wood Islands Presbyterian Church, d. 1951, buried, Wood Islands Cemetery. m. Jessie MacPherson, b. March 31,

The Descendants of James Campbell and Christy MacDonald 167

1889, Heatherdale, daughter of Alexander A. MacPherson and Elizabeth Anne MacDonald, baptized September 12, 1903, Valleyfield, d. 1946, buried, Wood Islands Cemetery. They had no children.

C5 Alexander Matheson, b. May 22, 1891, d. 1921, buried, Wood Islands Cemetery.

C6 Christine Anne Matheson, b. July 13, 1893, Belle River, baptized June 1894, Wood Islands Presbyterian Church, d. November 16, 1978, buried, Belfast. Christine was a nurse and served as a nursing sister during WWI. She m. William Neil Ross, b. September 23, 1891, Garfield, son of Alexander Ross and Isabella MacLeod, baptized February 27, 1892, Belfast, d. March 20, 1980, age 89, Lennox Nursing Home, buried in Belfast. He lived in North Pinette. Christine and William were married October 21, 1920, in the manse, Belfast, by the Rev. J.W. MacKenzie.

   D1 Mary Isabel Ross, b. 1923, d. March 13, 1993, age 66, in the Dr. John Gillis Memorial Lodge, buried, Belfast. She m. Donald A. Morrison, b. 1921, Pinette, d. January 23, 1988, age 66, Queen Elizabeth Hospital, buried, Belfast Cemetery.

      E1 Neil Ross Morrison.

      E2 Donna Morrison, m. James Knox.

   D2 Eleanor Ross, b. September 9, 1926. She m. Donald Alexander MacPherson, b. September 20, 1925, son of Donald MacPherson (Dan) and Catherine Gillis, d. August 26, 1977. They were married on January 6, 1947.

      E1 Sandra Elinor MacPherson, b. September 13, 1947, m. (1) David Benjamin Acorn, b. May 26, 1944. They were married July 1, 1966.

         F1 Julie Lynn Acorn, b. January 21, 1968, m. Randy Mahar on June 10, 1989.

            G1 Logan Alexander Mahar, b. May 13, 1991, Charlottetown.

      Sandra m. (2) Scott John MacPhail, b. June 10, 1935. They were married September 17, 1988.

         F2 Gregory John MacPhail, b. November 29, 1980.

      E2 Bonnie Lynn MacPherson, b. July 13, 1950, d. January 15, 1976.

      E3 Kathy Ann MacPherson, b. August 13, 1954, Clinton, ON.

D3 Alexander Ross, b. ca. 1928, North Pinette, d. August 14, 1975, age 47, Victoria General Hospital, buried, Belfast Cemetery. He m. Marion MacDonald.
    E1   Judy Ross.
    E2   Craig Ross.
    E3   Mary Ross.
    E4   Lorna Ross.
D4 Eliot Ross.
D5 Ann Ross.
D6 Peggy Ross m. Clarence Criss.

C7 Margaret Mary Matheson, b. August 9, 1896, Belle River, baptized January 29, 1909, Wood Islands Presbyterian Church, d. August 11, 1987, buried, Wood Islands. She m. William Alexander MacQueen, b. September 17, 1884, Mount Vernon, son of John MacQueen and Christy Martin, baptized February 15, 1888, Wood Islands, d. 1960, buried, Wood Islands. They were married on November 21, 1917, in PEI by the Rev. J.C. Martin.
    D1   Mary C. MacQueen, b. 1920, d. 1942.
    D2   Barcley MacQueen, b. 1927, d. 1932.
    D3   Katherine MacQueen, m. Carleton MacLeod, b. in Murray River, d. 1986. Katherine saw service during WWII.

B4 Neil Murchison, b. December 12, 1857, Point Prim, baptized February 21, 1858, Orwell Head Church of Scotland, d. 1946 in San Rafael, California. He was a master mariner and farmer. He m. Flora Murchison, b. 1859 in Australia, second daughter of Malcolm Murchison and Catherine MacDonald, d. November 28, 1932. They were married on November 25, 1885, by the Rev. Grant.
    C1   Annie Campbell Murchison, b. 1890, d. 1981, San Rafael, California. She m. Alfred D. Swogger, a minister.
        D1   Flora Elizabeth Swogger, b. in Punjab, India.
        D2   Malcolm M. Swogger, b. in California.
        D3   Alfred Dallas Swogger, b. in California, m. Joyce Wiley.
    C2*   Katie MacDonald Murchison, a teacher.

B5 James Murchison, b. March 5, 1860, died in infancy April 12, 1860.

B6 Christianna Murchison (Christy), b. July 6, 1861, Point Prim, baptized August 17, 1861, Orwell Head Church, d. January 30, 1927, age 65, at her home in Rosebury, buried in Belfast. She m. Robert Stewart, b. 1866, Pinette, son of William Stewart, d. 1937, buried in Belfast. They had no children.

B7 James Campbell Murchison, b. July 7, 1863, Point Prim, d. September

1912, drowned in Portland harbour. He was a seaman and never married.

B8* Ann Murchison, b. February 23, 1865, Point Prim, baptized June 18, 1865, Orwell Head Church of Scotland, d. February 8, 1948, Eldon, buried, Polly Cemetery. She m. Hugh A. Gillis, b. December 12, 1861, North Rustico, d. February 14, 1929, Eldon, buried, Polly Cemetery. He was a farmer. Ann and Hugh were married on June 14, 1899, in Quincy, Massachusetts.

    C1   Edward Gillis.

Hugh's obituary includes the following: "Survived by his widow (nee Ann Murchison), 1 son, Edward, 4 sisters: Rachel of New Hampshire, Anne (Mrs. Cousins), Malden, Massachusetts, Irene (Mrs. Matthews), Alberton, Emily (Mrs. Munroe), New Hampshire. Two brothers and two sisters preceded him."

B9* Peter Simon Murchison, b. October 27, 1866, Point Prim, baptized in Belfast, d. before 1921 in Washington State. Peter was the master of the ship *John Currier*, sailing from San Francisco to Australia. He m. Lucille Trainor, b. Kelly's Cross, d. Aberdeen, WA. They were married in 1894 in San Francisco.

    C1   John Malcolm Murchison.
    C2   Peter Simon Murchison.
    C3   Charles Murchison.
    C4   Louise Murchison, m. Floyd Warner.
    C5   Samuel Murchison was a seaman with his uncle Donald. He died at sea, age 16.
    C6   Muriel Murchison, unmarried.

B10* Donald Murchison, b. November 1, 1870, Point Prim, baptized in Belfast. He m. Mary Ann MacDonald, b. December 8, 1871, Point Prim, daughter of John Ronald MacDonald and Mary Murchison, baptized in Belfast. Donald was a master mariner who sailed for over thirty years to Australia, New Zealand, South America, Mexico and Alaska (*Maple Leaf Magazine*, 1930), and was also master of *Polaris*, a four-master schooner which sailed from San Francisco to the Philippines (*Past and Present Magazine*). He was killed in an accident aboard the steamer Jacobs. The *Maple Leaf Magazine* of June 1929 indicates that the accident took place in Seattle, WA.

    C1   Donald Murchison, b. in Washington State, a graduate of the University of Washington, worked for the Star Line Steamship Company.
    C2   Mary Murchison, b. September 4, 1900, m. L.L. Schaffner. Mary was a teacher.

    C3   John Ronald Murchison, b. in Washington State, drowned at a young age in the Columbia River.

    C4   Margaret Murchison, b. in Washington State, d. March 6, 1930, San Diego, California.

B11   James Donald Murchison, b. November 7, 1870, Point Prim, baptized August 27, 1871, Orwell Head Church of Scotland, a farmer on the homestead, according to the 1926 Atlas, d. 1948, buried Polly Cemetery. He m. Janet Euphemia Stewart, b. April 13, 1877, Murray Harbour Road, daughter of Donald Stewart and Sarah Ann Campbell (Marion), baptized July 1, 1877, Orwell Head Church of Scotland, d. 1962, Mount Buchanan, buried, Polly Cemetery. James and Janet were married on November 26, 1902, by the Rev. Donald MacDonald Campbell, Malcolm's son. The bondsman was James A. Stewart.

    C1   Annie Campbell Murchison, b. 1908, d. August 26, 1979, buried, Belfast. Annie was a teacher. She m. Kenneth John MacRae, b. 1908, d. April 18, 1995. They were married December 8, 1934 (the date on the marriage licence), by the Rev. J.R. Skinner.

        D1   Janet Catherine MacRae, b. November 3, 1936, m. Winston Smith.

            E1   Cynthia Anne Smith, b. May 24, 1957, m. (1) Peter Cyr.

                F1   Shawn Colin Peter Cyr, b. February 22, 1975. His partner is Tracy Collins.

                    G1   Riley Robert Neil Shawn Cyr, b. March 20, 1995.

                F2   Sharilyn Anne Cyr, b. October 11, 1977.

Cynthia Anne m. (2) Andrew Windsor.

                F3   Tobias Franklin Windsor, b. July 17, 1986.

            E2   Catherine Jane Smith, b. April 24, 1959, m. Frank Gendron.

                F1   Jason Matthew Gendron, b. April 7, 1981.

                F2   Michael Stephen Gendron, b. January 18, 1983.

                F3   Sarah Elizabeth Gendron, July 28, 1986.

            E3   Winston Kenneth Smith (Kenneth), b. September 1, 1960, m. (1) Sherri Wade.

                F1   Wade Winston Smith, b. December 21, 1981.

                F2   Jessi-Lynn Elizabeth Smith, b. November 29, 1983.

Winston (E3) m. (2) Patti Mailman.

                F3   Peter Winston Smith (Lucas), b. June 26, 1998.
          E4   Malcolm Smith (Irwin), b. September 23, 1961.
          E5   Mary-Lynn Smith, b. November 3, 1962, m. David Smith.
                F1   Alexander Daniel Pierre Smith (Pierre).
          E6   Susan Gail Smith, b. December 19, 1963, m. Glen Hancock.
                F1   Chelsea Lynn Hancock, b. December 29, 1987.
                F2   Jonathan Glen Hancock, b. May 1, 1990.
    D2   Judith Ann MacRae, b. February 5, 1944. She was a registered nurse. She m. Gordon Richard Hickman, son of Mr. and Mrs. Joseph Gordon Hickman of Annapolis Royal, NS. They were married on July 15, 196[?], in Saint John's Church by the Rev. Donald Nicholson.
          E1   Joanne Catherine Hickman, b. May 2, 1970, m. Peter Boyd.
                F1   Megan Anne Boyd, b. May 24, 2001.
                F2   Benjamin Joseph Boyd, b. September 23, 2003.
          E2   James Gordon MacRae Hickman, b. April 26, 1972.
          E3   Nancy Suzanne Hickman, b. April 7, 1975.
    C2   Leonard [Carr] Murchison, b. 1913 and adopted, d. 1998, buried, Polly Cemetery. He m. Margaret Estelle MacLean (Peggy), b. October 10, 1925, daughter of Angus Leslie MacLean and Daisy Waterman, d. February 20, 1966, buried, Belfast Cemetery. Leonard's headstone reads: "Husband of Peggy MacLean."
B12*   Samuel Alexander Murchison, b. May 20, 1872, Point Prim, baptized July 29, 1872, Orwell Head, d. August 21, 1935, age 63 years and 3 months, in Quincy, MA, of silicosis. He m. Catherine Florence MacLeod (Cassie), b. ca. 1879, Point Prim, daughter of John A. MacLeod and Annie Nicholson, d. February 19, 1979, age 100, in Quincy, MA. Samuel and Catherine were married on November 30, 1905, in Quincy at the residence of Hugh Gillis, by the Rev. W.B. Barr. A newspaper clipping reads: "Married at Thanksgiving. The bridesmaid was Miss Margaret Murchison, sister of the groom, and the best man was Simon Stewart, nephew of the groom."
    C1   Annie Catherine Murchison. b. March 5, 1907, d. April 7, 1907,

age 1 month, 2 days, of influenza.

C2   Dorothy Murchison, b. in MA, d. in 1971 or 1972, Quincy, MA. She m. (1) Mario Buzzi.

     D1   Susan Buzzi, m. Paul Vickers. They later divorced.

Dorothy m. (2) Donald Black.

C3   Edna Florence Murchison, b. ca. 1910 in MA, d. of colon cancer in April 1971, age 61, Quincy, MA. She m. John Einer Andre, b. March 26, 1908, Sweden, son of Carl and Amanda Marie Andre, emigrated in 1911, d. before Edna in Massachusetts. Edna and John were married in 1931 and divorced in 1956.

     D1   John Murchison Andre, b. February 7, 1941, Quincy, MA, d. June 22, 2006, age 65, in Kingham, MA, of cancer. He m. (1) Barbara J. Sorensen on March 21, 1964 and divorced in 1976.

        E1   Jon Christian Andre, b. November 2, 1964, m. Christine Daniels on November 8, 1966 and divorced in 2003.

        E2   Heather Marie Andre, b. July 1, 1967. She m. (1) Ron Ornenstien in 1990 and divorced in 1998. She m. (2) Stephen Breslin in August 2000. Heather has four children: Adam, Courtney, Nicole and Tyler.

John (D1) m. (2) Linda Schmidtke. He m. (3) Lisa Coolidge on June 25, 1988. There were no children from this marriage.

C4   Muriel Murchison, d. in 1971 or 1972 in Quincy, MA. She m. [?] Gilligan.

     D1   Catherine Gilligan, m. [?] Nutter.

     D2   Edward Gilligan (Ned).

C5   John Neil Murchison, d. 1971 or 1972, Point Barrow, Alaska.

B13   John Malcolm Murchison, b. July 24, 1874, baptized August 23, 1875, Church of Scotland, Orwell Head, d. February 12, 1895. He was a seaman and drowned at sea.

B14   John Neil Murchison, b. April 28, 1876, d. November 17, 1901. He was a master mariner and drowned at sea (Barbados).

B15*   Margaret Ann Murchison, b. January 1, 1878, d. in Quincy, MA. The Murchison book lists the following children: Florence, Alice, and John M. Her husband's name seems to have been J. MacPherson.

B16   Harriet Elizabeth Murchison, b. July 1, 1880, Point Prim, d. in South Andover, Maine. She m. Charles Smith, b. in Maine and d. South Andover, Maine.

C1 David Smith, b. in Maine.
C2 Donald M. Smith, b. in Maine.
C3 John Neil Smith, b. in Maine.

A7. The Descendants of Christy Campbell and Joseph Beers

Christy Campbell, b. October 27, 1839, Uigg, d. May 3, 1909, at the home of her nephew Samuel Campbell, buried, Belle River cemetery. She m. Joseph Beers, b. 1840, Belle River, son of Benjamin Beers and Hannah Nickerson, d. February 6, 1866, age 46, Belle River, buried, Belle River Pioneer Cemetery. Christy and Joseph were married on August 27, 1872, by the Rev. Thomas Duncan.

Editor's note: *Beers* and *Bears* are used interchangeably in sources.

B1   Moses Beers, b. July 21, 1873, Belle River, baptized August 10, 1873, Church of Scotland, d. February 3, 1890, Belle River, buried Belle River cemetery.

B2*   Christena Ann Beers (Christy), b. October 21, 1847, Belle River, baptized October 24, 1874, Church of Scotland, d. February 25, 1954, Wallaceburg, ON, buried, Murray River Cemetery. Her headstone reads: "born 1873." She m. (1) John Vere Wheeler, b. April 14, 1868, Murray River, son of John Wheeler and Eleanor Elizabeth Saunders, baptized June 7, 1868, Murray River, d. August 15, 1907, Murray River, buried, Gladstone Cemetery. His wife and two children are buried in the same plot. His headstone reads: 1869-1907. Christena and John were married on November 15, 1899, and separated after 1913.
    C1   George Herbert Wheeler, b. August 13, 1900, baptized in Belle River, d. December 30, 1975, buried, Gladstone Cemetery. He was unmarried.
    C2   Beatrice Wheeler, b. March 21, 1902, baptized Murray River Church of Scotland, d. July 1, 1987, Tawas City, MI. She m. William Millar, b. September 10, 1890, Scotland, d. July 6, 1968, Detroit. William emigrated from Scotland to Detroit just before the outbreak of WWI. He soon crossed the border to Windsor, ON, and joined a Scottish regiment. He saw service at the front for the duration, enduring numerous gas attacks.
        D1   William M. Millar, m. Virginia [?].
    C3   Lucy May Wheeler, b. October 24, 1904, baptized Murray River Church of Scotland, d. November 27, 1970, Mount Clements, MI, buried, Gladstone Cemetery, PEI. She m. Thomas DeNike.
        D1   James DeNike, b. ca. 1940, MI, d. December 15, 2000, Detroit.

The Descendants of James Campbell and Christy MacDonald

C4   John Vere Wheeler, b. December 2, 1907, Murray River, baptized December 20, 1907, Toronto (PEI), d. January 23, 1986, age 78, Windsor, ON, buried, Geddie Memorial Cemetery. He m. Bessie May Marks, b. May 16, 1905, Long River, daughter of Adonijah Marks and Elizabeth Campbell, d. August 8, 1988, Windsor, ON, buried, Geddie Memorial Cemetery. John and Bessie were married on May 30, 1935, in Long River. Information following John's death indicates that he left the following children: William, Gerard and daughter Evelyn (Roy) Cornish of Saint Eleanor's.

       D1   John William Vere Wheeler, b. June 5, 1936, French River, d. September 29, 1900, Windsor, ON. He m. Elizabeth Johnson, b. February 9, 1944, Windsor, ON.

       D2   Gerard Heath Wheeler, b. May 27, 1940, Charlottetown. He m. Verlie Pauline White, m. December 9, 1941, New Westminster, BC.

       D3   Mary Evelyn Wheeler, b. March 29, 1944, Montague. She m. Roy Cornish, b. in PEI, on April 5, 1961, in Summerside.

       D4   Beatrice Ann Wheeler, b. September 25, 1947, French River, d. July 18, 1948, French River, buried, Geddie Memorial Cemetery.

Christena (B2) m. (2) Neil MacLeod, b. in French River.

B3   Benjamin Beers, b. April 30, 1876, Belle River, baptized May 30, 1876, Church of Scotland, d. 1956, Cambridge, Mass. He was ordained a minister by the United Pentecostal Assemblies of God in 1930.

B4*   James Campbell Beers, b. December 7, 1877, Belle River, baptized January 6, 1878, Church of Scotland, d. October 14, 1932, Packard Heights, MA, buried, Rural Cemetery, New Bedford, MA. James designed metal working tools and machines. He m. Annie Jardine, b. February 2, 1877, Freetown, daughter of Christopher Jardine and Annie Clow, d. January 6, 1964, Athol, MA, buried, Rural Cemetery, New Bedford. James and Annie were married on October 5, 1899, in Mansfield, MA.

    C1   Christina Beers, b. March 26, 1901, in MA, d. August 24, 1902.

    C2   Hannah Myrtle Beers, b. May 2, 1903, in MA, d. March 6, 1978, buried, Silver Lake Cemetery, Morristown, NJ. She m. Farrell B. Richards, d. November 1977.

       D1   Donald Richards.

    C3   Clara Martha Beers, b. July 4, 1904, MA, d. June 18, 1998, Winnebago, IL. She m. Harold Trolander.

C4   James Milton Beers, b. October 6, 1905, New Bedford, MA, d. November 22, 1990, Rockford, IL, buried in Scandinavian Cemetery, Rockford. He m. Marcella R. Fritz on July 1, 1933, in West Hartford, CT. Marcella d. May 22, 1989.
- D1   James Beers.
- D2   Caralou Beers, m. Norman Erickson.

C5   Dorothy Christina Beers, m. Herman King.

C6   Jennie Belle Beers, b. January 12, 1913, Athol, MA, d. April 16, 1997, Worcester, MA. She m. (1) [?] Hinckley.
- D1   James Hinckley.
- D2   Joan Hinckley.
- D3   Lianne Hinckley.
- D4   Barbara Hinckley.

Jennie Belle m. (2) [?] Carter, (3) [?] Klingenberg.

C7   Joseph Christopher Beers, b. 1915, Athol, MA, d. July 12, 2001, in Warner Robins, GA, buried Magnolia Park Cemetery. His wife's name is unknown.
- D1   Margaret Ann Beers.

C8   Harold Benjamin Beers, b. October 1, 1916, Athol, MA, d. January 20, 1987, Rockford, IL, buried, Scandinavian Cemetery, Rockford. He m. (1) Helen M., who died before 1977. He m. (2) Helen Thomas on October 8, 1977.

Appendix: Obituaries, Weddings, Other Documents

The following documents have been transcribed from clippings or handwritten papers provided by Roy and Maida Campbell. Many lack information about their source and date, but all will be of interest to those interested in the Campbell family and Prince Edward Island history and genealogy.

Malcolm Campbell (A1), p. 65

In the name of God, Amen.

I, Malcolm Campbell of Kinross, Lot Number 50, Queens County, in the province of Prince Edward Island, farmer, being frail in body but of sound deposing mind, memory and understanding do make and publish this as my last will and testament.

1) I give, devise and bequeath to my beloved wife Janetta Campbell and to my dutiful son Malcolm Hector Campbell all my real and personal estate, goods, chattels and effects subject to the following conditions, that is: my said wife to have, hold and enjoy one half-part of my said estate for and during her natural life, and after her demise to revert and become the property of my said son Malcolm Hector Campbell, said real estate consisting of one hundred and five acres of land, a little more or less, to have and hold the same with appurtenances thereto belong[ing] unto the said Malcolm Hector Campbell, his heirs and assigns forever subject to the condition aforesaid. I also [make] the following bequests, the same to be paid when ordered, by my executor hereinafter named.

2) I give and bequeath to my dutiful daughter Flora Campbell a home while she is single or wishes to stay on the homestead, and at her marriage or when she may leave her present home to get six sheep and two cows or an equivalent in cash.

3) I give and bequeath to each and every one of my other children, males and females, the sum of one dollar (to each as aforesaid).

4) And lastly, I appoint John S. Martin as executor of this my last will and testament.

In testimony whereof I have hereunto set my hand and seal this nineteenth day of January, A.D. 1893, and publish and declare this as my last will and testament.

Signed, sealed and published and declared by the said testator in our presence and in the presence of each other who by his request have signed our names as witnesses thereto.

John S. Martin
Donald MacLeod
Signed, *Malcolm Campbell*

This will was proved on the 22nd December 1906 on the oath of John S. Martin, one of the subscribed witnesses thereto, and was filed and registered the same day. Probate was also granted same day to the executor thereto named.

As certified by *R. Redden*, Judge Probate

David A. MacLeod (A1-B3-C2-D3-E1) p. 71

The death occurred at the Queen Elizabeth Hospital on Tuesday, September 1, 2009, of David (Sleepy) MacLeod of Charlottetown, age 65 years. Beloved husband of Joanne (nee Lord). Brother of Bill (Cher) and Ian (Paulette). Son of the late Constance and Alistair MacLeod. Uncle of Nicole, Christina and Alex. Resting at MacLean Funeral Home Swan Chapel. Funeral Friday from St. Paul's Anglican Church at 10 a.m. Interment in the People's Cemetery. If so desired, memorials to the Queen Elizabeth Hospital would be appreciated. Visiting hours on Thursday from 2 to 5 p.m.

Christina Laura Campbell (A1-B3-C8) p. 73

The death in the Prince Edward Hospital on Sunday, October 8th, of Mrs. Alexander Martin of Grandview, has brought much sorrow to that community.

Mrs. Martin, who was twenty-nine years of age, was the wife of Mr. Alexander Martin, merchant, who is a son of Dr. Martin Martin. Mrs. Martin's maiden name was Laura Campbell, and she was a daughter of Mr. and Mrs. Donald Campbell of Uigg.

She leaves to mourn, besides her deeply bereaved husband, an aged mother and father, five sisters, Mrs. Owen Coluse of Lynn, Mass., Mrs. William Dempsey of Dorchester, Mass., Mrs. William Cummings of Lynn, Mass., Mrs. Angus Alexander MacLeod of Kinross, Mrs. Sam Hume of Uigg, also two brothers, William and Hector, both of Charlottetown.

The deceased had been ill for only two weeks.

Mr. and Mrs. Martin had entered into the enjoyment of their lovely new home only a short while when death brought its heavy shadow of affliction.

Mrs. Martin was a woman of beautiful qualities of mind and heart, greatly beloved by all who knew her. The large funeral, one of the largest seen in that locality for many years, which took place on Wednesday last, testified to the high regard for Mrs. Martin and to the sincere sympathy for the grief stricken relatives.

Two of her sisters, Mrs. Coluse and Mrs. Cummings, arrived from the United States the day before the funeral.

DONALD WILLIAM HUME (A1-B3-C9-D1) P. 73

Pilot Office Donald William Hume, only son of Mr. and Mrs. Samuel Hume of Uigg, P.E. Island, was killed in a reconnaissance bomber crash on June 6th, when the plane of which he was observer plummeted to earth soon after taking off from Goose Bay, Labrador. At the time of the tragedy, Pilot Office Hume was attached to the RCAF base at Dartmouth, NS. He is survived by his wife, formerly Miss Catherine Shaw, and a six weeks old son, John. A graduate of Prince of Wales College, Charlottetown, Donald was interested in engineering, and prior to his enlistment in the Air Force, was employed in that capacity with the Department of Public Works and Highways, and after passing the civil service examinations accepted a position as draftsman in the construction of an air base at Charlottetown and at Greenwood, NS. He enlisted in 1942 and went on active service in January 1944, taking his basic training at Belleville, Ontario. Pilot Officer Hume was twenty-three at his untimely death, an excellent type of officer, being tall, well built, and of a friendly and cheerful disposition, a prime favourite among old and young. A memorial service was held in the Church of Scotland at Kinross on July 31st and was largely attended by friends from many parts of the province.

JOHN WILLIAM HUME (A1-B3-C9-D1-E1) P. 73

The funeral for John W. Hume was held Friday, June 26, 2009, from Belvedere Funeral Home to St. Andrew's United Church, Vernon Bridge, where the service was conducted by Reverend Ian MacLean. The organist was Linda Sharpe. The congregational hymns were "When the Roll is Called up Yonder" and "I'll Fly Away." Honorary pallbearers were Malcolm MacLeod, Boyd and Margie Campbell, Elwood and Marion Robbins, Ken and Sandra Lea, Ron and Brenda MacKinnon, Harold and Mary Hager, Keith and Kay MacLeod, Arnold and Louise MacLeod, Reggie and Caryl MacPherson, Ken and Elsie MacLeod, and David and Linda Clow. Flowerbearers were Trina Lavers, Stacey Hynes, Angela McCallum and Donna MacLeod. Granddaughter Kieren Hume read "Guess How Much I Love You" on behalf of his grandchildren. Words of remembrance were shared by brother-in-law Kevin Quinn. The recessional was "Wind Beneath my Wings." Interment took place in St. Andrew's United Church Cemetery, Vernon Bridge. Those attending the funeral service included representatives from Island Construction, Limited. A Masonic memorial service was held at Belvedere Funeral Home on Thursday, June 25, 2009, at 9 p.m. It was conducted by Gordon MacKenzie assisted by the Master and Chaplain of Mizpah Lodge #17, Eldon. In attendance was the Grand Master of Masons of PEI, Rowan Caseley, along with brethren of Mizpah Lodge #17 and other visiting brethren from PEI.

James Alex Stewart (A1-B4-C1), p. 74

Residents of Grandview, Mount Buchanan and vicinity learned with regret of the sudden death of Jas. A. Stewart. He was the son of the late Donald and Sarah (Campbell) Stewart, formerly of Grandview and later of Mount Buchanan. He passed peacefully away Monday, October 14th, at the home of Mr. and Mrs. Behm, aged 68 years.

His two sisters, Mrs. Murchison and Mrs. Cantelo, were with him in his last hours. He was tenderly nursed by Mrs. Behm. Mr. Stewart spent his life in various places. He carried on ranching in Montana, USA, later was farming in Mount Buchanan and later in Grandview. Mr. Stewart was an upright Christian man and good neighbour. Besides his sorrowing friends and neighbours, he leaves to mourn his widow Mazie Lamont, one daughter Sadie (Mrs. McKinnon), two grandchildren, all of Quincy, Mass. Several children predeceased him some years ago. Four brothers and four sisters are also left to mourn, namely, Malcolm in Los Angeles, Cal., Hector and Donald M. in Quincy, Mass., Allan C. in Brittania, BC. One brother, Roderick M., predeceased him some years ago. The sisters are Janet (Mrs. J.D. Murchison), Margaret (Mrs. Nelson Cantelo), Euphemia (Mrs. McInnis, BC), Christine (Mrs. Will Ross of Quincy, Mass.).

The funeral took place from the home of his sister, Mrs. Nelson Cantelo, Mount Buchanan, on October 15th. Rev. W.B. McPhail officiated at the house and the grave. The pallbearers were Messrs. John McKinnon, Benson Carver and Harold Behm, all of Grandview, Daniel Murchison, Cameron McPhee and Everett MacAulay, all of Mount Buchanan.

Burial took place in Polly Cemetery, Mount Buchanan, beside his children.

Margaret Priscilla Stewart (A1-B4-C4) p. 74

On the 28th of July, 1909, Mr. Nelson Cantelo of Mount Buchanan and Miss Margaret Priscilla Stewart, daughter of Donald A. Stewart of the same place, were united together in marriage at Watermere by the Rev. Daniel MacLean. The groom was supported by Donald MacKinnon and the bride was attended by Miss [Mabel?] Isabell MacLeod. Immediately after the ceremony the happy couple started for their future home followed by the best wishes of a large circle of friends and acquaintances as the young couple are very popular in the community in which they have lived all their lives. The Guardian extends its congratulations to Mr. and Mrs. Cantelo, wishing them a prosperous journey through life.

Edison Campbell Stewart (A1-B4-C9-D2), p. 79

Stewart Edison Campbell (Cam), March 1, 1915-November 14, 2008. Born in Vancouver, Cam grew up in Britannia Beach. Following his service in the RCNVR during WWII, Cam and Betty moved to Comox in 1946 where Cam took up a teaching position at Courtenay High School. There he spent twenty years as teacher, vice-principal and principal. Cam and Betty and four of their six children travelled for a year in Europe and, on their return to Canada in 1967, Cam became a superintendent of schools, first in Terrace and Smithers, and then in Lake Cowichan and the Gulf Islands. Retiring in 1975, Cam and Betty returned to their Comox Valley home, and Cam lived there until his death.

Predeceased by Betty and grandson Ben, Cam leaves his six children: Maryl, Sandy (Edie), Donald (Elizabeth), David (Diane), Anne (Alex) and Cliff (Ann); grandchildren: Angus (Danita), Eric (Katrina), Morgan (Andrea Mears), Cathy (Eric) Nordgren, Shawna (Dale) Melvin, David and Georgia; and great grandchildren; Charlie and Laney Stewart, Ainsley Mears, Fynn and Annika Nordgren, Isabelle and Olivia Melvin. Cam was very active in the Comox United Church. The family thanks the medical staff at St. Joseph's, Doctors Thomas Gornall, Steve Millar and Jack Bryant, and his many friends and neighbours who have supported him in his decision to live independently in his home on the beach. A memorial service will be held in the Comox United Church at 1:00 pm on Saturday, November 29.

Maryl Elaine Stewart (A1-B4-C9-D2-E1) p. 79

Stewart, Maryl Elaine, 1944-2010. Maryl passed away on February 21, one day after her birthday. Predeceased by her parents, Cam and Betty Stewart of Comox and nephew, Ben Stewart, of Victoria, Maryl is lovingly remembered by sister Anne (Alex) of Bamfield, and brothers Sandy (Edie) and Donald (Elizabeth) of Victoria, David (Diane) of Kamloops and Cliff (Ann) of Vancouver; nieces and nephews David, Angus (Danita) and Eric (Katrina), Morgan (Andrea), Cathy (Eric) Nordgren and Shawna (Dale) Melvin and Georgia; great-nieces and nephews, Cathy and Laney, Ella, Ainsley, Fynn and Annika and Isabelle and Olivia. Born in Quesnel, Maryl grew up in Comox, graduated from UBC and then studied in France. Returning to Canada, she taught for fifteen years in the Halifax area before coming home to the West Coast in 1982 and teaching for 24 years at Hillside Secondary, where she specialized in French and English as a Second Language. As a teacher, Maryl was legendary for her particularly unusual, creative and practical assignments. While at West Vancouver Secondary, her work with students outside the regular classroom was influential in creating a student interest in Amnesty International and other service opportunities for youth. Her sponsorship of many student trips from Halifax and West Vancouver, both within Canada and overseas, and her leadership in the Multicultural Week at West Vancouver Secondary both had their roots in her lifelong belief in promoting international peace through knowledge and friendship. As a consequence of this work, Maryl was the recipient of a Unity in Diversity award from the Baha'i Community of West Vancouver for promoting understanding and respect among students of diverse races, cultures, genders and social class. Maryl was much loved and very active in the West Vancouver First Church of Christ, Scientist, where she held many leadership roles in the spiritual life of her church family. In lieu of flowers, Maryl's brothers and sisters ask that donations go to the Harvest Project (201 Bewicke Avenue, North Vancouver, BC V7M 3M7) where Meryl was an active volunteer and supporter. A celebration of Maryl's life will be held at 1:00 p.m. on Saturday, March 27, in the hall at Shaughnessy Heights United Church, 1550 West 33rd Avenue. Maryl saw the best in all people and enhanced many lives. The ripples from her example and quiet, loving wisdom will continue.

MALCOLM JAMES MACPHERSON (A1-B5-C1) P. 84

Port Elgin, NB, February 25—After four days of pneumonia, death Sunday morning claimed Rev. Malcolm James MacPherson, minister of the Presbyterian Church here. Deceased was 60 years of age and was a native of Prince Edward Island. He came to Port Elgin one year ago, having previously held pastorates in Ontario for many years, as well as in Prince Edward Island and New Brunswick, being formerly located in Woodstock and Sussex in the latter province. He preached at the Presbyterian Church on the Sunday of the week previous to his demise.

The late Rev. Mr. MacPherson had not been in the best of health for several years, although always able to fulfill his pastoral duties. Since coming here he had won the respect and esteem of the residents of this village, and deep regret at his passing is heard generally expressed. He is survived by his wife and one son, Paul.

Funeral service will be held in the Presbyterian Church here Thursday afternoon, conducted by Rev. J.A. Kennedy of this place, and Rev. A. Craise of Sackville, after which the body will be taken to deceased's old home in Uigg, PEI, for interment.

Rev. Malcolm James MacPherson was born at Murray Harbour Road, PEI, and had charges in different parts of the Maritimes during his long career as a minister.

His wife, who survives him, was formerly Miss Ella Stavert, Kelvin. She is a sister of Mrs. MacLean, wife of Mr. A.E. MacLean, MP.

Rev. Mr. MacPherson was brought up by his grandfather, the late Mr. Malcolm Campbell, at Uigg, PEI. He was a graduate of Prince of Wales College at which institution he won honours as a brilliant student. His last charge on Prince Edward Island was a circuit in the western section of the province when he ministered to the congregations of Hampton, Bonshaw and Tryon.

Of recent years his health failed him and for a time he had to give up his ministerial duties. He preached for a time in Ontario and had charges at Woodstock and Sussex before going to Port Elgin.

Donalena MacPherson (A1-B5-B7) p. 88

A pretty wedding took place at the home of Mrs. H. Willard, 59 South Main Street, Ipswich, Mass., on Monday evening, December 26th, when her son Claude LeRoy and Miss Dolena MacPherson, daughter of Neil and Mrs. MacPherson, Uigg, PEI, were united in marriage by Rev. F. Ward of the Baptist Church, Rowley, Mass., assisted by Rev. H.B. Smith, Ipswich. The bride looked charming in a princess gown of white with bridal veil and orange blossoms and was attended by her sister Mary, while Harvey MacKay acted as best man. A beautiful floral arch occupied the corner of the room under which the young couple heard the words that pronounced them man and wife. After receiving the congratulations of those present, a dainty wedding lunch was served to about sixty guests. The numerous gifts displayed in the gift room testified to the popularity of the young couple. Mr. and Mrs. Willard will reside in Ipswich.

John Murdoch Campbell (A1-B7) p. 89

The death of John Murdock Campbell occurred at his home in Eureka, Montana, on December 6th, 1937.

He was a son of the late Malcolm Campbell and Janet Murchison and was born at Uigg, PEI, in the year 1860.

When a young man, he went to Montana where he settled as a rancher.

His wife, Annie McRae of Point Prim, predeceased him six years ago, also two sons, Donald and Malcolm, and one daughter, Euphemia.

There are left to mourn two daughters, Annie Laura at home and Janet, Mrs. Andrew of Eureka, and eight grandchildren; also two brothers, Donald of Uigg, Simon A., Salmon Arm, BC, and one sister, Mrs. Daniel MacKinnon, Forest Hill, PEI.

The Rev. Donald MacDonald Campbell (A1-B10), p. 94

Rev. Donald Campbell of Uigg, Prince Edward Island, also studied for the ministry at Pine Hill College, Halifax, Nova Scotia, and was ordained on October 11, 1894, as a minister of the Church of Scotland in Prince Edward Island (MacDonaldite Section) in the Kirk at Birch Hill by a committee of the Synod of Nova Scotia (the same committee which ordained Rev. John Goodwill and Rev. Daniel MacLean, the two ordinations were on the same day) with Rev. John Goodwill and Rev. Daniel MacLean assisting, and the Rev. Donald Campbell was declared a member of the Egerton Presbytery. Mr. Campbell became the pastor and minister of the Eastern Parish where he laboured for ten years, resigning from the Charge of the Eastern Parish in 1904. After his resignation from the Eastern Parish of the Church of Scotland in Prince Edward Island (MacDonaldite Section), Rev. Donald Campbell, for a short time, ministered to the Cambridge congregation, Cambridge, MA, U.S.A. Mr. Cambridge accepted an appointment from the Presbyterian Church in Canada to labour in Saskatchewan. He passed to his rest on June 11, 1935.
The Church of Scotland on Prince Edward Island (MacDonaldite Section)
by the Rev. J.H. Bishop

Euphemia MacLean (A1-B11) p. 94

Mrs. Simon Campbell died at her home in Silver Creek, British Columbia, on February 21st, 1937. Mrs. Campbell was Euphemia McLean, daughter of John McLean and Mary Murchison, of Point Prim, PEI.

She leaves to mourn her husband, three sons and three grandsons, all living at Sterling Creek.

Mrs. Campbell has been in failing health for the last year, suffering from high blood pressure and general breakdown.

She was an earnest Christian and will be greatly missed in her home, church and community. In health, she was always ready to minister to others, and leaves a beautiful life record and was loved by all.

Services were held in the Seventh Day Advents [sic] Church, conducted by Minister E.M. Chapman of Armstrong, BC. She was laid to rest in the Silver Creek Cemetery, awaiting the call of the Master.

JOHN CAMPBELL (A2), P. 96

The Indenture made this sixteenth day of November, A.D. 1897, between John Campbell of Uigg, Lot or Township number 50, Queens County in the province of Prince Edward Island, farmer, of the first part, and Simon D. Campbell of same place, son of the said John Campbell, farmer, of the second part. Witnesseth that for and in consideration of the covenants, provisions and conditions hereinafter mentioned, to be observed, kept, done, performed by the said Simon D. Campbell, that is to say that he, the said Simon D. Campbell or his legal representative will pay or cause to be paid from and (D.M.L.)* out of the personal property of John Campbell aforesaid to his son James M. Campbell, the sum of fifty dollars and also to pay in like manner to his daughter Emily Campbell the sum of forty dollars, the same to be paid within six months after the decease of the said John Campbell or at any time previous that might be suitable or convenient, which payments must be received in due form and the same Simon D. Campbell doth hereby consent, promise and agree to maintain and support his father, the said John Campbell, with all the necessities of a comfortable living and in every way that may be possible conform to his wants and wishes and to occupy and make use of a share in the dwelling house, barns and outhouses as long as he want the same for his own use and he, the said Simon D. Campbell, doth hereby further bind himself to do, abide by and perform all and every [of] the covenants and provisions above enumerated, or intended so to be.

And he the said John Campbell for the faithful performance and observance of all and every [of] the above covenants and provisions doth hereby give, devise and bequeath to his son Simon D. Campbell his heirs and assigns forever all and every his real and personal property. It being understood by the parties hereto that they are to assist each other about the farm.

In witness thereof the said parties to these presents have hereunto their hands and seals subscribed and set the day and year above written.

Signed, sealed and delivered in presence of

Signed, *John W. MacLeod*
Donald McLeod
Signed, *John Campbell*
Simon D. Campbell

* De minimus non curat lex ("The law does not care about trivial matters"), a legal principle meaning that trivial details of the payment are not the concern of the law and not addressed in this legal document.

NEIL CAMPBELL (A2-B2), P. 100

Neil M. Campbell was born on Prince Edward Island, in Canada, Nov. 29, 1854, and died at his home near Woodburn, Oregon, Sunday morning, May 21, 1911, of paralysis, at the age of 56 years, 5 months and 22 days.

His parents came from the Highlands of Scotland to Prince Edward Island about 80 years ago. His father was a ruling elder in the Presbyterian Church of Canada for many years and noted for his fidelity and zeal in Christian life. Brother Campbell lived on the Island until 21 years of age, when he went to North Dakota, where he married Miss Effie McKenzie. Six children were born to this union, five boys and one daughter.

Brother Campbell came to Oregon about 6 years ago, and to Woodburn 2 years ago. Wherever he lived he was recognized as a man of unsullied honor, intergrity and uprightness of character, ever winning the respect and confidence of his friends.

He leaves a bereaved wife, six children, three brothers and three sisters to mourn his departure just in the prime of life, also many relatives and friends, some in the State of Washington and California, but only two in Oregon, the Rev. M.C. Martin and Mr. J.D. McDonald of Portland.

Brother Campbell was trained in a Christian home, Christian influences followed him all his life. Last year, at the Taylor evangelistic meetings in our city, he renewed his covenant with his maker and united with the First Presbyterian Church of Woodburn, remaining faithful, loyal and devoted to the service of the King until called home last Sunday morning.

The funeral was Tuesday, services being held at the Presbyterian Church, Rev. T.T. Vincent officiating. The church was filled with sorrowing friends, the Modern Woodmen, of which he was a member, attending as a body. At the grave at Belle Passi cemetery the Modern Woodmen had charge of the services. There was a profusion of flowers.

This account of the family of Neil Campbell was written by Alice Ainsworth

These are stories my mother, Myrtle Campbell Little, told me about her home. I will not attest to their complete accuracy, but this is the way I remember the stories she told me about her family.

Her father, Neil Campbell, homesteaded in Jamestown, North Dakota, then went back to Prince Edward Island and married Effie MacKenzie. She lived on the farm next to him and was nine or ten years younger than he was. Neil wanted to leave Prince Edward Island, because he didn't want his boys going off to sea, like many men in PEI.

According to the book, Pioneers of PEI [*Skye Pioneers and "The Island"* by Malcolm Macqueen?], Neil Campbell was a sea captain, however, I hadn't heard that before, Mother never mentioned it, and Walter McKenzie didn't know anything about it. I would guess that information is inaccurate.

Double cousins, Murchisons, contemporaries of my mother, had four sons who were sea captains. One of them lived in San Anselma. Tim Murchison, a developer in Sacramento, is related to them and us.

Effie Campbell was a teacher, Mother said she taught high school. More research needs to be done on this. Her name was on the elementary schools of PEI as a teacher [Uigg school, 1887]. This school has been turned into a community centre. She graduated from McGill University [?]. She had seven sisters and four brothers—all tall. Mother said Grandma was thankful to be one of the shortest. She had brothers and sisters six feet and over. The girls were known for their beauty.

Effie loved to help the boys with their homework, Latin, math. Her sister Margaret married Alex Faulkner (not certain of the spelling). They lived in Quincy, Massachusetts. He came from Scotland. According to Uncle Don, he built monuments from stone, a stone mason. He was very wealthy. His house may still be standing. The address is 46 Independence Avenue, Quincy, Massachusetts. The Falconers came to visit the Campbells in North Dakota, bringing nice presents. I have a small gold watch they gave Mother. Sister Margaret had a chance to go to Europe with her husband, but went to visit Effie in North Dakota instead. Her husband, Alex, had been married before. His wife and three children died in an epidemic (diptheria, scarlet fever?). His was loss was so painful he didn't want to have any more children. Margaret died before her husband. He remarried, left his money to the city of Quincy, according to Don.

Norman the oldest brother settled in North Dakota and is the father of Walter McKenzie. Walter is a real authority on the McKenzie family and has a terrific personality.

The relatives we saw in PEI are Alex's children.

Every morning the family gathered around the table and their father read from the Bible and pray[ed]. Neil was very community-spirited. He was a member of the school board, helped start the Presbyterian church, and participated in various organizations. A strict disciplinarian, he made the boys work hard—a no nonsense person. He didn't want my mother to work outside. With so many brothers, he was afraid she would become a tomboy. In the evening the family listened to someone read books aloud. Uncle Falconer got the nickname Shook, from a character in the Hoosier Schoolmaster, a book the family read aloud. In the story, Shook was a very mischievous boy. They thought Falconer, who was three or four at the time, resembled him.

Their parents would go to church and leave Jim, Jack and Myrtle at home.

Jim and Jack would go out in the barn and try riding the unbroken horses and cows. Mother said Uncle Jack especially liked to pick the wildest horse. She would stand by the barn and cry. She was so afraid they would be hurt or killed.

During the harvest season, they had a cook wagon. The cook was a black man, who made wonderful pies, and was very nice to my mother. He came every year and cooked for the harvesters in the field.

They had a hired girl from the Polish settlement nearby. She had never seen anyone with red hair. She wanted to take mother home with her to stay overnight. Mother did and they all stood around and marvelled at her red hair.

My grandmother went by herself to visit her family in PEI several times. In later years, she took my mother with her, so Mother got to meet the PEI relatives. They remembered her when she saw them last summer.

Mother said Uncle Jack learned to read at a very early age. When they lived in Woodburn, the boys had to hoe the fields to grow potatoes. Uncle Jack said the ferns would grow overnight. They'd work all day and get most of the ferns out. The next day the field would be full of ferns again.

They had just moved to Portland when their father died at 56. He suffered from hypertension. Mother felt he didn't take care of himself. In Portland all the boys worked at anything they could to earn money. Most had paper routes at some time during their youth. Neighbours said they could set their clock by the paper Don delivered. It was always on time. In Portland, they never sat down to a meal without having at least two or three extra people at the table, friends of the boys. My dad said there were always lots of dishes to do. He helped Mother by drying the dishes.

Uncle Jack boxed to earn money. Uncle Glenn gave blood. The older boys went together and bought a suit for their graduation for the younger boys. The older boys pooled their money to buy football shoes so Uncle Glenn could play football in high school.

American Naturalization Certificate for Neil M. Campbell

UNITED STATES OF AMERICA
DISTRICT COURT, STUTSMAN COUNTY
FIFTH JUDICIAL DISTRICT OF NORTH DAKOTA

BE IT REMEMBERED that on the 31st day of October, in the year of our Lord one thousand eight hundred and ninety-one, personally appeared before the honorable Roderick Rose, Presiding Judge of the District Court of Stutsman County, in the District aforesaid, Neil M. Campbell, an alien born, above the age of twenty-one years, and applied in open Court to be admitted to become a naturalized citizen of the United States of America, pursuant to the several acts of Congress heretofore passed on that subject. And the said Neil M. Campbell, having thereupon produced to the Court record testimony showing that he had heretofore reported himself and filed his declaration of his intention to become a citizen of the United States, according to the provisions of said several acts of Congress, and the Court being satisfied as well from the oath of the said Neil M. Campbell, as from the testimony of A. McKechmi [?] and S.L. Glaspell [?] who are known to be citizens of the United States, that the said Neil M. Campbell, has resided within the limits and under the jurisdiction of the United States, for at least five years last past, and at least one year last past within the State of North Dakota, and that during the whole of that time he has behaved himself as a man of good moral character, attached to the principles contained in the Constitution of the United States, and well disposed to the good order, well being, and happiness of the same, and two years and upwards having elapsed since the said Neil M. Campbell reported himself and filed his declaration of intention as aforesaid:

IT WAS ORDERED, That the said Neil M. Campbell be permitted to take the oath to support the Constitution of the United States, and the usual oath whereby he renounced all allegiance and fidelity to every foreign Prince, Potentate, State or Sovereignty whatever, and more particularly to the Queen of Great Britain and Ireland, whereof he was heretofore a subject, which said oath having been administered to the said Neil M. Campbell by the Clerk of said Court, it is ordered by the Court that the said Neil M. Campbell be admitted to all and singular the rights, privileges and immunities of a naturalized citizen of the United States, and that the same be certified by the Clerk of this Court, under the seal of said Court, which is done accordingly.

Roderick Rose, Judge
Attest: *F.F. Brauch [?]*, Clerk

In testimony that the foregoing is a true copy of the proceedings, taken from the record of the proceedings of the Court aforesaid, I subscribe my name hereunto and affix the Seal of the District Court this 16 day of October, in the year of our Lord one thousand nine hundred and eight.

George T. Richmond, Clerk
by [blank line] Deputy

Euphemia MacKenzie (Mrs. Neil Campbell, A2-B2), p. 100

This is an account of Euphemia MacKenzie's grandparents, taken from a 1930 newspaper article concerning the centennial celebration of the MacKenzies coming to PEI.

Norman MacKenzie and his wife, Catherine MacKay MacKenzie, came from families who lived chiefly in the Western Isles of Scotland, his native home being Raasay, a detached portion of the Isle of Skye. Both families were typical Highlanders and were closely associated with the life of their respective clans. Norman was by profession a gardener, and served in this capacity for some years in the employ of one of the Seaforth MacKenzies.

His wife belonged to a family of noted musicians among whom were the famous MacKay pipers. One of these was piper to Queen Victoria; another, piper to His Royal Highness, the Duke of Sussex; and a cousin of theirs, Donald MacKay, was piper until his death in 1894 to His Royal Highness, Edward Prince of Wales.

Other members of their family served for upwards of two centuries in various positions in the royal household.

Norman MacKenzie with his wife and family sailed from Portree, the capital, at that time, of the Isle of Skye, in September of the year 1830.

His family consisted of six of their children: James, Malcolm, Margaret, Mary, Christie and Jessie.

The family landed on what is now known at Dickieson's Point and remained here with friends while they built their log cabin home on the farm now owned by Norman's grandson, Alexander MacKenzie, in Long Creek.

They became tenants of the Wright estate, and paid ground rent to the proprietors of this estate until the act passed under the administration of the Hon. Louis Davies (afterwards Sir Louis Davies) forced the proprietors to sell to the tenants their holdings, thus becoming freehold settlers.

Here they remained, and on the death of Norman MacKenzie in 1863, his son, Alexander, came into possession of the farm and held it until he sold it to his nephew, Alexander MacKenzie, who is now the owner.

The pioneer life in the home of Norman MacKenzie and his wife resembled closely that beautiful example described in Burns' "Cottar's Saturday Night," for though husband and wife both enjoyed social merriment, especially when connected with Scotch music and other Scottish associations, they were in the main of a deeply religious and devout turn of mind, and always began the day's work with morning devotions and ended it in like manner.

Real want they never knew, but plain living and high thinking was then the order of the day in most homes in Prince Edward Island, and their home was no exception to that rule.

Dainties were not unknown, for the women of Scotland carried from their native land an art of fine cooking peculiar to their own, and there is no doubt a dinner served up by them for a wedding or New Year's celebration would surprise and delight even the guests who are partaking of the last word in good cooking at this centenary.

Nevertheless, it is pretty certain that their regular fare in the early days consisted largely of "the wholesome parritch, chief o' Scotia's food," oat cake, good potatoes and an abundant supply of the best fish in the world. And when they ate their hearty meals they no doubt often sang in the spirit and words of Burns:

> That though on hamely fare we dine,
> Wear hodden grey and a' that,
> Gie fools their silks, and knaves their wine,
> A man's a man for a' that.

The account of one example of heroic endeavour and courage on the part of Mrs. MacKenzie is handed down to their descendants and may be of interest especially to the women and girls who are now accustomed to move easily in nice cars.

The father of the family would start out and walk three miles to a point in Canoe Cove shore, where he would join with friends and row to their fishing nets, where they generally secured a good catch of fish which they landed and cleaned on the beach.

In the meantime, at the home the mother cared for her children, clothing and preparing them for their morning meal.

Then she extinguished the chimney fire to ensure the safety of the little ones. After this, she too walked the three miles and joined her husband on the shore, and returned with him, carrying her share, a switch basket, known as a creel and containing a bushel of green fish, which were salted for the winter.

Despite these and other hardships, this vigorous and rugged couple from the Highlands lived to a ripe old age, the husband to reach the age of seventy-five and the wife the great age of ninety years, the father having around his deathbed all his sons and daughters whose history is as follows, the names being in order of age:

James MacKenzie, married Ann Martin of Uigg. They had thirteen children, eleven of whom grew to manhood and womanhood, seven girls and four boys.

Malcolm MacKenzie, married Catherine MacNevin of Argyle Shore. They had ten children, nine of whom grew up, five boys and four girls.

Alexander MacKenzie, remained unmarried.

Margaret MacKenzie, married John Currie. They had five girls and two boys, five of whom grew up, four girls and one boy.

Mary MacKenzie, never married. She made her home always on the homestead with Alexander.

Christie MacKenzie, married Alexander MacNeill and was left a widow with three girls in 1860. Shortly after this, she returned to her home and here her little ones were all taken away during an epidemic of diphtheria. After this she, too, always made her home with Alexander and Mary.

Jessie MacKenzie, married John Darrach and left no family.

Catherine MacKenzie, married John MacKenzie of Rose Valley. They had seven children, five boys and two girls. This family moved to western Canada many years ago and their recent history is unknown to the committee. One of their sons was one of the first white men killed in the Northwest Rebellion, being enlisted in the first forces organized to suppress the rebels.

Flora MacKenzie, married Hector MacLean. They had twelve children, ten of whom grew up, four boys and six girls.

Through these children have come a very large number of descendants (including to date seven great-great-great-grandchildren), two hundred and fifty descendants in all, over seventy of whom are present at this centenary, the total number of friends and relatives presently being 158.

Norman MacKenzie not only bequeathed a large number of descendants to his adopted land, but he also bequeathed a heritage in the memory and record of his integrity and uprightness of character. This character, we pray, may ever be perpetuated in his descendants. The outstanding slogan of the father to his children was: "Always regard your honour above the world."

This account of Euphemia MacKenzie in her old age appeared in a magazine in 1931.

A woman of fine personality in San Bernadine is Mrs. Effie Campbell, native of Uigg, near Belfast, PEI. She has four sons, one in the medical profession, and three of them doctors of dentistry. One of them occupies with his good mother. I found Mrs. Campbell a splendid entertainer and a well preserved woman for her years. She spoke of the religious training in early days on the Island and the effect it has had to give the country its present reputation, namely, a land without divorce. Mrs. Campbell first left her home 43 years ago. She has made her residence in Portland, Oregon, for the past 20 years. Her husband was the late Neil Campbell, who passed away in 1911. They were ranchers in South Dakota. They have a married daughter who lives in Modesto. Neil Campbell was a brother of our friend James Campbell, the bank cashier in Ceres, California. Mrs. Campbell's maiden name was Effie MacKenzie.

"Canadians in California" by Dr. R.E. Delaney,
The Maple Leaf Magazine, 1931

Peter Murchison (A2-B3), p. 104

The death of Mr. Peter Murchison of Kinross, PEI, which occurred very suddenly on the evening of Tuesday, November 4, 1913, at the age of 63 years, removes one who, by his peaceable and true Christian character, won the respect and friendship of all who knew him. He had been in his usual good health and worked hard all day Tuesday. In the evening while sitting by the fireside, his eyes closed in death. He leaves a sorrowing widow, seven sons and three daughters, who feel keenly the loss of a kind and faithful husband and father. Of the family, John and John N. reside in Sydney, NS, Mrs. A.A. MacDonald (Sarah) in Cambridge, Massachusetts, Simon in Saskatchewan, Murdoch and Donald in Vancouver, James in Calgary, and Joseph, Euphemia and Isabel are now at home with their mother. Mr. Murchison had for some years been an elder in the Church of Scotland. He was active in duty and lived a life consistent with his Christian profession. The blow to the family and friends is severe in its suddenness, but there is the comfort of knowing that this departed friend had the blessed assurance of God's favour and the Hope of Glory. The funeral was held on Friday the 7th, and was largely attended. The service at the home was conducted by Rev. E. MacDougall. The brethren of the Loyal Orange Association, of which the deceased was a member, paid their tribute of respect at the burial service at the grave. Sincere sympathy is felt for the family and friends.

Euphemia Campbell (A2-B3), p. 104

There passed peacefully away after an illness of four days at the home of her daughter, Mrs. Angus MacDonald, Somerville, Massachusetts, on February 6th, Euphemia Campbell, beloved wife of the late Peter Murchison of Dundee, Lot 50, age 70 years. Deceased was a woman of sterling character, a good Christian, kind and hospitable to all. Her husband predeceased her fourteen years ago, and she resided in her old home until a few years who when she removed to Somerville, Massachusetts. She leaves to mourn, besides a large number of friends and relatives, six sons and three daughters. John A. and John N. in Sydney, NS; Simon and James in Maizond, Saskatchewan; Joseph and Murdoch in Vancouver, BC; Donald (deceased); Sadie (Mrs. MacDonald), Somerville; Euphemia (Mrs. Hopkins), Miami, Florida; Isobel (Mrs. MacAllister), Concord, NH; also, the following brothers: John M., California; Samuel and Simon D., Uigg; and one sister, Mrs. Hugh Martin, Uigg. Her daughter accompanied the remains to the home of her brother Simon D., where the funeral took place, to the cemetery of Orwell Head Church. The religious services at the house and graveside were conducted by her pastor, Rev. Ewen MacDougall, who spoke very touchingly of the exemplary life of the departed.

John Neil Murchison (A2-B3-C4), p. 105

Sydney steel workers and fellow workers, along with many other friends and acquaintances, turned out in large numbers on Sunday afternoon to pay their last respects to the memory of Neil Murchison of MacLeod Lane, whose untimely passing at his work came as a shock and with profound regret to the community and to his wide circle of friends and sorrowing family. Many cars were in the lengthy procession.

Service at the home was conducted by Rev. Dr. Alexander Murray and Rev. John MacKinnon and hymns sung were "Rock of Ages" and "Safe in the Arms of Jesus." Pall bearers were: Alexander Mombourquette, Andrew Morrison, Seymour Hines, William Darby, M. Brown and T. Gray.

Interment took place in Hardwood Hill Cemetery.

In addition to his widow and children, Mr. Murchison is survived by three sisters, Mrs. Robert A. McAllister of Concord, New Hampshire, who is here having arrived for the obsequies and is leaving this evening for her home; Mrs. A.A. MacDonald of Summerville, Mass.; and Mrs. G.D. Hopkins of Palm Beach, Florida; five brothers, John A., Murdock, Joseph and James in British Columbia; Simon in Saskatchewan.

Mr. Murchison was a son of the late Peter Murchison and Euphemia Kinrose of Prince Edward Island. He had resided in Sydney about thirty years, during which time he won the esteem of many people through his quiet and unassuming nature.

Sydney Post Record, February 23, 1937

Christy Ann Campbell (A2-B4), p. 107

Dominion of Canada
Province of Prince Edward Island
Marriage License
By His Honor Jedediah Slason Carvell, Esquire,

Lieutenant Governor of the Province of Prince Edward Island, &c., &c., &c.

To *Hugh Martin of Kinross, Lot 57, Bachelor,* and *Christy Ann Campbell of Uigg, Belfast, Spinster.*

Whereas, it hath been signified unto us that you have resolved to proceed in the solemnization of true and lawful Matrimony, and are desirous to have the same solemnized without proclamation of Banns, and we being willing that these your good intentions shall take effect, and under and by virtue of an Act of the General Assembly of the said Island, made and passed in the second year of the reign of His late Majesty King William the Fourth, intituled "An Act to conform and render valid certain Marriages heretofore solemnized within this Island, and also to declare to whom and in what manner Marriages shall be celebrated in future, and to provide for the public registry of the same," do hereby grant this our License and Faculty, as well to you the parties contracting as to *Rev. D. B. McLeod* in the said Island, to solemnize the said Marriage openly, without publishing Banns; provided there shall hereafter appear no lawful impediment, by reason of cosanguinity, affinity, or any other cause whatever, and if in case hereafter appear any such impediment, then these presents shall be void and of no effect in law, inhibiting you the said *D.B. McLeod* in any of the premises come to your knowledge, from proceeding to the celebration of the Marriage.

Given under my hand and Seal, at Charlottetown, this twenty-sixth day of December, in the year of our Lord One Thousand Eight Hundred and eighty-nine.

By command,
Arthur Newberry
Assistant Provincial Secretary
J.S. Carvell
Lt. Governor

Recorded *April 26th, 1899*
Liber *13*, Folio *96*
Names of Parties Married
Hugh Martin of Lot 57, PEI (B)
to
Christy Ann Campbell of Uigg, Belfast, PEI (S)

Date of License *December 26th, 1889*
Date of Ceremony *January 1st, 1890*
By whom performed
Rev. Donald B. McLeod, Kinross, PEI
Filed *April 26th, 1899*

Certificate of Solemnization of Marriage
(Form as required by 2nd William IV., Cap. 14.)

Names of Parties: *Hugh Martin, bachelor*
Christy Ann Campbell, spinster
Date of Celebration: *January 1st, 1890*
By License or Bann: *License*
Names of Witnesses: *Samuel Campbell, Catherine McPherson*

I hereby certify that the above named Parties were Married by me this day under License from the Lieutenant Governor, in the presence of the above named Witnesses.

Dated at *Orwell*, this *1st* day of *Jan'y*, A.D. *1890*
(Signature) *Donald B. McLeod*
(P.O. Address) *Kinross*

Hugh Martin (A2-B4) p. 107

On August 3rd, 1940, Hugh Martin passed away at his late residence, Uigg. He was a son of the late Donald Martin and Flora (MacDonald) Martin. And was born the first day of March 1861. He had enjoyed fair health until about three days before his death, when he came suddenly ill.

He will be greatly missed in the community in which he lived and in which he had many friends and kinfolk. Much might be written of his honesty, his sincere attention to duty, his hospitality and his humble devotion. He walked humbly with God and found peace in Jesus Christ.

His wife, Christy Ann Campbell, daughter of the late John Campbell, Uigg, predeceased him on June 27th, 1939. Two sons and one daughter also passed away. They were John C., Donald and Euphemia. There are left to mourn the loss of a true father, Ernest of St. Eleanors, Mrs. Arthur Ladner of Cambridge, Mass., Mrs. Lloyd Robbins of Uigg and Miss Sadie of Cambridge. There are also thirteen grandchildren, one brother, Duncan of Kinross, all surviving.

The funeral took place on Monday, August 5th, at 2 p.m. The service was conducted by Rev. A.J. Ebbutt. The hymns sung included "The Lord's my Shepherd" and "Abide with Me." A solo, "No Night There," was beautifully sung by Mrs. James Gillis. Many attended to pay a tribute of respect to the departed and to extend sympathy to the family and friends.

The pall bearers were Simon D. Campbell, John S. Campbell, Samuel Martin, Alex H. MacDonald, D. John MacLeod and Malcom A. MacDonald.

Euphemia Martin (A2-B4-C1) p. 107

The community of Orwell was shocked to learn of the sudden death of Miss Euphemia Martin, eldest daughter of Mr. and Mrs. Hugh Martin of Kinross, PEI, which sad event took place in Cambridge Hospital, Massachusetts, Tuesday, October 13, 1913. Miss Martin left home in good health about a month ago to resume her profession in Cambridge, word came a few days ago that she had symptoms of typhoid fever, and yesterday came the tidings of her death. The deceased was a faithful daughter and loving sister, and greatly beloved by all. She was a beautiful Christian girl, 22 years old, a member of Orwell Head church and choir, and will be sorely missed. Her remains will arrive in Charlottetown, Thursday evening. Funeral to Orwell Head Cemetery on Friday at 2 o'clock.

Euphemia MacLeod Jordan (A2-B4-C2-D1) p. 108

Euphemia Jordan (nee MacLeod) of Elmhurst, formerly of Oak Park, Illinois. Born June 29, 1916, passed away April 27, 2001. Beloved wife of John P.; loving mother of Ann (Alfred) Anastasiou of Riverside, Illinois; Grace (Robert) Slawinski and Margaret (Craig) Bixler, both of Elmhurst, Illinois. Devoted grandmother of Christiana and Juliana Anastasiou; Sara and John Slawinski; and Emily, Jordan and Lauren Bixler. Dear sister of Hugh Robbins, Florence MacLean, Elwood and Preston Robbins and the late James, John and Sterling Robbins, all of Prince Edward Island; fond aunt of many. Funeral mass 10 a.m. Saturday, May 5, at Ascension Church, 815 S. East Avenue, Oak Park, Illinois. Interment Queen of Heaven Cemetery in Hillside, Illinois. In lieu of flowers, donations to the Alzheimers Assocation of Greater Chicago, 4709 Golf Road, Suite 1015, Skokie, Illinois 60076, would be appreciated. Funeral information: (708) 383-3191.

The Guardian, May 3, 2001

Hugh Martin Robbins (A2-B4-C2-D3) p. 108

Peacefully at the Kings County Memorial Hospital, on Saturday, February 15, 2014, with saddened hearts the family announces the passing of their father Hugh Robbins, age 86, of Montague, beloved husband of the late Helen (nee Behm) Robbins. Hugh is survived by his loving children, Anne (Harvey) MacEwen, Terry (Doris), Donnie (Yolanda), Leslie (Kathy), Joyce (Mike) Cavanaugh and Phillip (Faye), sister Flo MacLean, brother Preston (Winnie), 18 grandchildren, 7 great-grandchildren, many cousins, nieces and nephews. He was predeceased by a sister, Phemie Jordan, and brothers James, John, Stirling and Elwood.

Resting at Ferguson Logan Montague Funeral Home, with visiting on Wednesday, February 19, 2014, from 2 to 4 and 7 to 9 p.m. Funeral service will be held at the St. Andrew's United Church, Vernon Bridge, on Thursday, February 20, 2014, at 11 a.m. Interment to take place at a later date in the St. Andrew's United Church Cemetery. In lieu of flowers, donations to the St. Andrew's United Church Cemetery Fund or the Kings County Hospital Equipment Fund would be appreciated by the family. Mizpah Lodge #17 in Eldon will hold a Masonic Memorial Service on Wednesday, February 19, 2014, at 9:00 p.m.

Helen Behms Robbins (A2-B4-C2-D3) p. 108

With grace and dignity as she had lived, Helen Robbins (nee Behm), Order of PEI, passed away at the Kings Memorial Hospital in Montague on Wednesday, April 29, 2009. She leaves to mourn her devoted husband and best friend, Hugh Robbins, Montague. Children Anne (Harvey) MacEwen, Summerside; Terry (Doris), Bedford, NS; Donnie (Yolanda), Belfast; Leslie (Kathy), Kilmuir; Joyce (Mike) Cavanaugh, Kemptville, Ont.; and Phillip (Faye), Charlottetown. Loving grandmother to 18 and "Grammie Great" to three. She will be greatly missed by her siblings, Thelma MacLeod, Orwell; Wynn (Maggie) Behm, Rosedale, BC; and Sheila (Brian) Kerr, Bayside, NB. Predeceased by her much loved parents, Harold and Sally Behm and her brother, Teryl, at 14 months. Resting at Ferguson Funeral Home until Saturday then to St. Andrew's United Church, Vernon, for funeral service at 10:30 a.m. Interment in the church cemetery. Visitation Friday 2-4 and 7-9 p.m. If so desired, memorials to Kings Memorial Hospital, St. Andrew's United Church Memorial Fund or the Junior Curling Program, Montague.

FLORENCE ELLEN ROBBINS (A2-B4-C2-D4), P. 110

The death occurred peacefully at the Dr. John M. Gillis Memorial Lodge, Belfast, on Wednesday, April 23, 2014, of Flora "Flo" MacLean, of Victoria Cross, aged 85 years. Born in Uigg, she was the daughter of the late Lloyd and Flora Ann "Honey" (Martin) Robbins. Survived by her sons Sterling (Mary Ellen), Stanley Bridge; Lester (Jian Zhi "Snow"), Victoria Cross; grandchildren Mark, Marven (Shauna), Shawn (Donna), Jeff (Patricia), Jennifer (Sam) Sanderson, Xue Li; brother Preston (Winnie) Robbins; sister-in-law Marion Robbins; and by numerous nieces and nephews. Predeceased by her husband Haywood MacLean; children Carl Lydell, Darrell Lloyd, Darlene Kathryn Ann and Sharon Lynn, all in infancy; sister Phemie Jordan; and by brothers James, Hugh, John "Jackie," Sterling and Elwood Robbins. Resting at the Moase Funeral Home, Summerside, until Saturday, then transferred to the Belvedere Funeral Home, Charlottetown, for visiting hours on Saturday from 6-9 p.m. Funeral service will be held at the Belvedere Funeral Home Chapel, Charlottetown, on Sunday at 1:30 p.m. Interment in the St. John's Presbyterian Church Cemetery, Belfast. Memorial donations to the St. John's Presbyterian Church Cemetery Fund would be appreciated.

JOHN CAMPBELL ROBBINS (A2-B4-C2-D5), P. 110

Passed away at Scarborough General Hospital on Wednesday, December 20, 2000, in his 71st year. Loving husband of Carole. Dear father of Lloyd, David and Jacqueline and Bob Lane, all of Mississauga. Stepfather of Cherly and Blair Borland of Scarborough; Marty Lamoureux and Kathy Salter of Markham and Greg of Ajax. Loving Granddad of Darlene and Steve Fournier, Laurie and Emily Lane, Corrie, Chris and Kirsten Robbins, Alexander and Carolee Borland, Dean Lamoureux, Kate and Alexandra Salter. Great-grandfather of Chanel and Tori Robbins. Brother of Phimi and Jack Jordon of Chicago, Ill.; Hugh and Helen, Flo MacLean, Elwood and Marion, Preston and Winnie, all of PEI. Uncle Jackie to many nieces and nephews. Friends may visit the Pine Hills Visitation Chapel and Reception Centre, 625 Birchmount Road (just north of St. Clair, east side) on Saturday, December 23, from 1-3 p.m. Service in the chapel to follow at 3 p.m. Interment Pine Hills Cemetery. If desired, donations to the Heart and Stroke Foundation or to the Diabetes Association would be appreciated.

Sheila Mary MacKinnon [Mrs. Sterling Robbins] (A2-B4-C2-D6), p. 111

The private funeral for Mrs. Sheila Robbins, wife of Dr. Sterling Robbins, was held on Tuesday afternoon, August 30, 1977, from the Jenkins Funeral Home with service conducted by Rev. Elmer MacLean. Acting as pallbearers were five brothers-in-law and a cousin, James Robbins, Elwood Robbins, Hugh Robbins, John Robbins, Preston Robbins and William Stearns. Flowerbearers were Donnie Robbins, Sterling MacLean, Peter Robbins, Jeffery Robbins, Sandy MacKinnon, Gary Robbins and David Robbins, all nephews of the deceased. Interment was in Uigg Community Cemetery with Rev. Elmer MacLean officiating.

John Campbell Martin (A2-B4-C3), p. 112

Pte. John Campbell Martin, the eldest son of Mr. and Mrs. Hugh Martin, was born in Kinross January 16th, 1885. He was killed in action in France on August 7th, 1917; aged 22 years and 7 months.

In the death of John C. Martin another brave Island son has made the supreme sacrifice to his country's cause.

The regret of officers and men of his Battalion the 13th RHC for the loss of their comrade on "Hill 70" on August 15th has been tendered the sorrowing family through the chaplain, Capt. C.E. Graham.

The sorrow of his parents, sisters, brothers and friends is assuaged as far as these things bring comfort, by the knowledge of the service this noble young man rendered to the cause of righteousness. In the final contrasting of life's values he indeed won the highest reward.

John C. was a worthy son, kind and dutiful in the home, genial and wholesouled among his companions.

When the call came for men, he was among the first in his community to respond. He enlisted November 17th, 1915, a week later he began to train in Charlottetown. He left with the 105th on June 13th, 1915, for Valcartier, and on the 13th of July sailed for England where he arrived two weeks later. He was early drafted for France and left for there on the 29th of November last, and in January 1917 went to the trenches. He was off and on in action till the day he was killed in August.

His parents and friends have in common with all parents and friends of heroic sons, the gratitude of the nation for their protection from a merciless enemy. They have the sympathy of all who knew them. They have the assurance of the sympathy of Him who in all his people's affliction "He himself is afflicted." Also the high tribute paid to all who die on behalf of others by

Him who in the consummation of His life work died upon the Cross, who said, "Greater love hath no man than this, that a man lay down his life for his friends."

Charlottetown *Guardian*, October 26, 1917

RETA HICKEN MARTIN (A2-B4-C7), P. 114

The death occurred at Kings County Memorial Hospital, Friday, December 2, 1994, of Reta F. Martin, Uigg, wife of the late Ernest Martin, Uigg, in her 87th year. Beloved mother of Margaret LeBlanc, West Royalty; George Martin, Baltimore, Maryland; Muriel Davies, Richmond Hill, Ontario; John Martin, Uigg. Also survived by ten grandchildren and eight great-grandchildren. Resting at Jenkins Funeral Home, Millview, with funeral Monday, December 5, from St. Andrews United Church, Vernon, with service 2 p.m. Interment in the Orwell Head Cemetery. Visiting hours Sunday 2-4 p.m. and 7-9 p.m. If so desired, memorials to St. Andrews United Church memorial fund or Southern Kings Hospice Association would be appreciated.

SAMUEL CAMPBELL (A2-B6), P. 115

On May 14th, 1933, Samuel Campbell of Uigg passed away at the Prince Edward Island Hospital. He was a son of the late John Campbell and Euphemia (Murchison) Campbell, and was born on the 15th day of April, 1864. He had always enjoyed fair health until about five days before his death when he became suddenly ill with an intestinal trouble which required immediate attention. He was taken to the hospital and an operation performed. Owing to complications which were discovered, his case was considered critical. His daughter-in-law came from the home to wait on him. He remained comparatively bright until the last two days. Many prayers were offered for his comfort which indeed came to him in a greater measure than man could dispose, for God took him.

He will be greatly missed in the community in which he lived and in which he had many friends and kinsfolk. He was a consistent member of the Church of Scotland and was a member of the Kirk Session. Much might be written of his honesty, his sincere attention to duty, his hospitality and his humble devotion. He walked humbly with his God and found peace in Jesus Christ. He is survived by two brothers and one sister, James Murdock Campbell of California, and Simon Donald Campbell and Christy Ann, wife of Hugh Martin, of Uigg.

He was twice married. His first wife was Catherine MacLeod, daughter of the late John S. MacLeod, [and his second wife, Isabel MacLeod], daughter of Malcolm MacLeod of Victoria Cross. Both were estimable women. His first wife died when the family were quite young, and they were most kindly treated by their step-mother. The family have grown up and scattered. They are: John S. at home; J.D. Wilfred of Long Island, NY; Euphemia, wife of Alan Stewart of Brittania Beach, BC; Mary Isabell, RN, New York; Ada Ruth, wife of William Benson of Norwood, Mass., and Eva Emily, wife of Samuel Cantello of Quincey, Mass.

The funeral took place on Thursday, May 18th, at 2 pm. The services were conducted by Rev. Ewen MacDougall assisted by Rev. Mr. Pierce of Orwell and Rev. Mr. Sinclair of Valleyfield. Many attended to pay a tribute of respect to the departed and extend sympathy to the family and friends.

The pallbearers were Finley MacDougall, Francis Cook, James Cantello, R.C. MacLeod, Samuel MacLeod and Samuel Hume.

CATHERINE MACLEOD (A2-B6), P. 115

The death of Mrs. Samuel Campbell of Uigg occurred at the PEI Hospital on the 6th of April. Mrs. Campbell was an estimable woman, who by her good qualities endeared herself to all those who had the pleasure of her acquaintance, and her death at the early age of forty-one years is greatly regretted. Besides a sorrowing husband and six children, there are left to mourn a mother, the sister Mrs. Angus Gillis, Head of Montague, a brother Malcolm R. McLeod, Orwell, and four brothers in the West.

The death took place at the PEI Hospital on Saturday, April 6th, of Catherine MacLeod, beloved wife of Samuel Campbell, Uigg. Mrs. Campbell only went to the hospital on the previous day and her early death was a great shock to her many friends. She leaves to mourn a mother, five sons and one daughter. The funeral which took place on Tuesday, April 8th, was largely attended, the funeral service being conducted Rev. Mr. Meikle.

SAMUEL EWEN CAMPBELL (A2-B6-C1-D1), P. 116

(Proprietor of Campbell's Tree Farm and retired CPR engineer after 47 years of service)
Passed away peacefully at the family farm, Montague Township, on Monday, March 29, 2010, Samuel Ewen Campbell at the age of 80. Beloved husband for over 56 years of Norma (Trodden) Campbell. Loved father of John (Margaret) of RR #5, Smiths Falls, Donald (Ruth) of Otter Lake, Douglas (Wendy) of Calgary, Marilyn (Pierre) Sincennes, of St. Lazare, Quebec and the late

David in 1960. Sadly missed by his thirteen grandchildren, Samuel, William, Simon, and Maria Campbell, Andrea, Ashley and Abraham Campbell, Michael, David and Amy Campbell, Nicholas, Benjamin and Emily Sincennes. Dear brother of Roy (Maida) and Clarence (Dot), all of Charlottetown, PEI, and Eva (Marcel) Pronovost of Windsor and the late Rebecca Williams and Sheldon Campbell. Predeceased also by his parents, John and Edith (MacNeill) Campbell. Sam will also be fondly remembered by many nieces, nephews, extended family and friends. Friends may pay their respects at the Blair and Son Funeral Home, Smiths Falls, on Wednesday, March 31, 2010, from 2 to 4 and 6 to 8 p.m. Funeral service will be held at Calvary Bible Church, 15 Beech Street, Smiths Falls, on Thursday, April 1, 2010 at 1:00 p.m. Interment, Hillcrest Cemetery. In remembrance, contributions to Gideon International or the Kingston Regional Cancer Centre (Kingston General Hospital) would be appreciated.

VIRGINIA JEAN (GINNY) BROWN CAMPBELL (A2-B6-C1-D2-E1), p. 117

We are heartbroken to announce the passing of our wife, mother, daughter and sister. Ginny passed away peacefully and surrounded by family, at home in Windsor Junction, NS, on August 28, 2013, after a long and valiant struggle with malignant melanoma. She is survived by her husband of 25 years, Jim; daughter, Corey; son, Derek; parents, Stewart and Jean Brown; and sisters, Shirley Borgal (Skip) and Faye Brown (Bob). Born on December 5, 1958, in Wolfville, NS, she graduated from Cornwallis District High School in Canning, NS, and received a B.Sc. from Acadia University. Ginny worked for several years at Maritime Life before starting a career as an optician. Family was always her highest priority and she stayed home for most of Corey and Derek's school years. Jim, Corey and Derek will forever cherish her strong, constant love and support. Ginny's warmth and selflessness won her many friends—her family will always be grateful for the love, support and prayers she and they received, especially in the last few months of her illness. Special thanks to Dr. Mimi Davis for her compassionate care during Ginny's two-year battle and the Nova Scotia Capital Health Continuing Care/Palliative teams for all their comforting care during her last weeks. Cremation has been completed. Visitation will be held on Monday, September 2, 2013, at 1:30 p.m. in the Saint John's United Church Hall at 3360 Highway 2 in Fall River, NS. A funeral service in the church will be held at 2:30 p.m., followed by a reception in the church hall. Ginny's wish was that people wear a bright colour as they help celebrate her life. Interment will follow at a later date. In lieu of flowers, memorial donations to Melanoma Network of Canada or a charity of your choice would be appreciated.

Rebecca Catherine Campbell (A2-B6-C1-D3), p. 117

The death occurred at Chilliwack, BC, March 20, of Rebecca Katherine Williams (Campbell), aged 46 years.

Born in Uigg, PEI, she later moved to Toronto and finally to BC. Surviving are her husband Ronald and children Andrew and Elizabeth at home, Winston of Prince George, BC, and Katherine (Mrs. Campbell) of Charlottetown, her brothers Roy and Sheldon of Charlottetown, Clarence of Dartmouth, NS, Sam of Smiths Falls, ON, and one sister, Eva, of Toronto.

The funeral will be held in Chilliwack today. In lieu of flowers, donations to the Gideons or the Canadian Cancer Society would be appreciated.

Marcel Pronovost (A2-B6-C1-D6), p. 119

Marcel passed peacefully after a brief illness on Sunday, April 26th, 2015, at 84 years of age. Born on June 15, 1930, in Lac La Tortue, Quebec. Loving son of the late Leopold and Juliette (Beaudoin). Marcel is survived by his wife, Eva, of 21 years, predeceased by his first wife, Cindy (1993). Cherished father of Michel (Marie), Brigitte and Leo (Tina). Adored grandfather of Tannis, Melissa and Ryan. Dearest brother to Roger (deceased) (Denise), Gaston (Jeanine), Rene (Jeannine), Claude, Jacques (Louise), Benoit (Denise), Monique (Mike, deceased), Nicole (Michel), Andre (Gisele), Jean (Diane) and Liliane. Dear brother-in-law to Dr. Clarence Campbell (Dot), Dr. Roy Campbell (Maida) and many other family members. Marcel's family kept him grounded throughout his life.

Hockey was Marcel's passion, from a boy who played the game on frozen ponds to the man who played on the biggest stage in hockey. Marcel was always involved in the sport, as a player, a scout, a coach. A decorated player with 8 Stanley Cups to his name (5 as a player with the Detroit Red Wings and Toronto Maple Leafs and 3 in management with the New Jersey Devils). Early in his career he played for the Windsor Spitfires and Windsor remained his home. He is an honouree with the Hockey Fall of Fame (1978) and a member of the Windsor, Omaha, Michigan, Shawinigan and Saint Maurice Sports Hall of Fame.

Special thanks to Dr. Frank DeMarco for his long time care and friendship and thanks to the medical staff at Windsor Regional Hospital Ouelette Campus and Complex Care on Prince Street. Special thanks to Father Parent and to the many friends and family that have supported Marcel throughout his life.

If you so desire, memorial donations to the Heart and Stroke Foundation or the Canadian Cancer Society would be appreciated by the family. Visiting Thursday, 2-5 and 7-9 p.m. Prayers Thursday, 4:30 p.m. at Families First, 3260

Dougall Avenue, South Windsor, 519-969-5841. On Friday, family and friends are invited to meet at Our Lady of Mount Carmel Church (440 Mount Royal Drive, Windsor, Ontario) after 9:30 a.m. until time of funeral mass at 10:30 a.m. Interment Heavenly Rest Cemetery.

JOAN BEVERLY CANTELO (A2-B6-C6-D1) p. 120

Kellogg—Joan Cantelo. Daughter of Samuel and Eva Cantelo of Quincy, Massachusetts. She died suddenly in her home on October 30. She is survived by her husband Dwight and her children and spouses, Kim K. Devoe (Alan), David D. (Shannon) and Jenny E. (Ryan Miller) and by her grandchildren, Malcolm, Bryce and Cameron Devoe and Nathaniel D. Kellogg. She was a graduate of Boston University and taught fifth grade in Quincy and Brooklyn, NY, before starting a family. She devoted her life to her family and community. She was an active member of the Rye Presbyterian Church Women's Association, Rye Women's Interfaith Committee and the Goshen (CT) Garden Club. She was a founding member of the Women's Center of Huntington, LI, which remains a vibrant organization after more than thirty years. She loved life and all those in her life. She uplifted us all. A memorial service will be held at Rye Presbyterian Church on November 23.

MARGARET BRUCE (A2-B8), p. 122

The death occurred at Uigg on Monday last, the 14th inst. of Margaret Bruce, aged 41, daughter of the late Alexander Bruce and wife of Simon Campbell. The deceased had been ill for some time and had suffered greatly. She leaves to mourn a sorrowing husband and six children, the eldest aged twelve, and the following brothers and sisters: James in Regina, Lauchlin and Daniel in Montana, John in Kingsboro, PEI, Alexander in Boston and D.A. in Charlottetown, Mrs. David Bruce in East Baltic, Mrs. John T. Harper in Boston and Mrs. James Ching in Boston. The funeral which was very well attended took place at Orwell on Wednesday last. Rev. D.H. MacLeod officiating at the ... [remainder of clipping lost].

JOHN CHESTER CAMPBELL (A2-B8-C2), p. 122

Early Sunday morning, May 28, 1944, the many friends in Trenton, NS, and other parts of Pictou County, as well as in his native province of Prince Edward Island, were given a distinctive shock when it was learned John Chester Campbell, 46, had met tragic death by suffocation, when his snug little one-roomed home on Bruce Street had been completely destroyed by fire of an unknown origin.

Born at Dundee, PEI, he spent many years employed at his trade, a painter, in the Canadian West, being employed in that capacity with one of the Transcontinental Railways.

Mr. Campbell came to Trenton a few years ago. He had been an employee of the Trenton Steel Works; also of the Power House at the Eastern Car Plant. At both these industrial plants he enjoyed the respect and high esteem of all his fellow associates.

Possessing a jovial and friendly personality, he was a general favourite with a wide circle of friends in the Steel Town. Exceptionally fond of children he was always thoughtful of them, and many here will always cherish tender memories of his generosity. The very quintessence of kindness, he loved doing for others; but in such a quiet manner that only those thus befriended knew of his charitable qualities. While resident here he followed his trade and was real skilled at the art of interior and exterior decorations.

Following the fatality, his remains were taken to Howard Ross Funeral Home in New Glasgow where they rested until Wednesday morning when they were conveyed by motor hearse to Bay View, the ferry terminus of the M.V. *Prince Nova*, Cariboo to Wood Island ferry. Arriving at Wood Island, the remains were conveyed by hearse to a Montague funeral home thence to Orwell Head United Church, where at 2:30 o'clock in the afternoon tribute to the late Mr. Campbell was eloquently paid when relatives, neighbours and friends gathered in large numbers to pay their final tribute to him, whom in life all deeply revered.

Rev. A.S. Weir of the Orwell and Vernon Charge conducted the solemn service, the choir under the direction of Mrs. Samuel Martin led in the singing of "Nearer My God to Thee," "Oh God, our Help in Ages Past" and "What a Friend We Have in Jesus." The pastor left solacing messages with the sorely bereft family, who were called upon to mourn the loss of a beloved son and brother, in such a sudden and tragic manner.

Those officiating as pallbearers were: Messrs. Samuel Hume, Ernest Martin, John Campbell, James Martin, Lloyd Robbins, John MacDonald. Interment took place in the family plot.

Surviving are his parents, Mr. and Mrs. Simon D. Campbell, Dundee, PEI, three sisters, Euphemia, Mrs. Gordon Morris, Arlington, Mass., Margaret, Mrs. Archibald MacKinnon, Cambridge, Mass., Jessie, Mrs. Parker MacDougall, Waltham, Mass., two brothers, Arthur, Belmont, Mass., Alexander, Milwaukee, Wis. His wife predeceased him a number of years ago.

John Samuel Martin (A4-B3) p. 129

A widely known and much esteemed citizen of Kinross passed away at the home of his daughter, Mrs. W.A. Jenkins of P.E. Island, on June 29th, 1946, at the advanced age of almost ninety-one years. He was a son of the late Samuel Martin and wife Sarah Campbell and was born at Kinross, August 3rd, 1855. He attended the Uigg School and for a time as a young man taught school. Later he carried on farming at the old Martin homestead. He was also a skilled carpenter and built a great many homes in the neighbourhood. He was an elder in the Church of Scotland and also acted as precentor. He was a good Gaelic scholar. He was a Conservative member of the P.E. Island legislature from 1912 to 1919 and for four of those years was Speaker of the House.

His wife, the former Hattie MacKenzie of Charlottetown, passed away in 1942. All of his six brothers predeceased him. They were James, who died in childhood, Hugh, Rev. J.G. Martin, John D., Rev. Malcolm C. and Rev. Sam A. Martin. Five sisters also predeceased him, Margaret (Mrs. Martin), Christy (Mrs. Wood), Catherine (Mrs. Kenneth MacLean), Sarah (Mrs. John MacKenzie) and Marjorie (Mrs. A. MacKay). One sister, Mrs. Emily Beer of Medford, Mass., survives him. He is survived also by three sons—Samuel of Vernon, and James and Hugh of Kinross; also by two daughters, Mrs. W.A. Jenkins of Vernon and Mrs. Alex MacLeod of Charlottetown. One daughter, Sadie, predeceased him, also one son, Pte. John W. of the 105th Battalion. His has eighteen grandchildren and thirteen great-grandchildren.

The funeral took place from the home of his daughter, Mrs. W.A. Jenkins, to Orwell Head Church. The service was conducted by the Rev. Carlyle Webster, assisted by the Rev. A.S. Weir. There was a large attendance of friends from many places. Interment took place in the Orwell Head Cemetery beside the church. The pallbearers were Wm. A. [and] Lloyd Martin, grandsons, and Malcolm MacLean, Sam. H., Lloyd and Harold Martin, nephews.

Mr. Martin lived a long and useful life and his name will be long remembered and held in high esteem by the entire community [in which] he used to dwell.

Mary Emily Martin (A4-B3-C2), p. 130

There passed peacefully at the Prince Edward Hospital on January 16, 1957, Mrs. Alexander MacLeod. The late Mrs. MacLeod, nee Mary Emily Martin, was born in Kinross, PEI, June 23, 1887, a daughter of the late John S. and Harriet MacKenzie Martin.

She received her early education in Uigg School and later graduated from Gordon Perry Hospital, Boston, Mass., with an RN degree. Her kindly disposition and patience left fond memories with the many patients entrusted to her care.

In June 1912, she married Alexander MacLeod and lived in Montague, PEI, moving to Charlottetown in 1923.

Mrs. MacLeod was a faithful member and attendant of Trinity United Church, and her place was seldom vacant. For some years she was a member of the choir under Prof. Fletcher. During the time her late husband was treasurer of Trinity Church, Mrs. MacLeod gave untiring assistance at all times.

Her illness of the past year was borne with remarkable Christian fortitude and she was never heard to complain.

She leaves to mourn her passing a daughter Jessie, Mrs. M. Arthur MacLeod, and three grandsons, David, Donald and Roger MacLeod, in whose welfare and advancement she was keenly interested. Her husband predeceased her three and a half years ago, and a son, John, predeceased her in 1932.

A brother, Samuel Martin of Vernon, and a sister Annie, Mrs. W.A. Jenkins of Charlottetown, survive. One sister, Sadie, and three brothers, John, Hugh and James, predeceased her.

The funeral, which was largely attended, was held from Trinity United Church on Saturday, January 19, 1957. The service was conducted by Rev. A. Frank MacLean and Rev. Howard Christie. The Trinity Quartet sang "God is Waiting." Interment was in Valleyfield Cemetery, with service at the grave conducted by Rev. Mr. MacLean and Rev. Mr. Sheen. Pallbearers were Harold MacKie, Harold White, Harold Martin, Munroe MacLeod, Ernest S. Coffin and E. Edgar Jardine.

The many floral tributes, letters and cards of sympathy testified to the esteem in which the deceased was held. [A list of those giving flowers followed.]

LLOYD IRWIN MARTIN (A4-B3-C4-D8), P. 133

At the Queen Elizabeth Hospital on Tuesday, February 13, 2007, of Lloyd Martin, veteran of Second World War, of Stratford, age 84 years. Beloved husband of Lucinda (Dickie) Martin (nee McKinnis) and loving father of Barry (Sharleen), Clayton (Sherry Kacsmarik), Debbie Thomas (Charlie) and Donald (Lauren Redmond). Lloyd is also survived by his grandchildren, Mike Thomas (Nancy), Laurie Thomas (Ryan Brehaut) and Billy, Mary Beth, Jennifer and Vanessa Martin; great-grandchildren, Noah and Reeve Brehaut; sisters, May MacDougall (Everett), Leida Lea (Clifford) and Donna Green; sister-in-law, Alfreda Martin; and numerous nieces and nephews. He was predeceased by his parents, Sam and Mary Martin; foster parents, Truman and Annie Jenkins; brothers, MacLeod, William and Donald; and sisters, Sadie, Evelyn and Doris. Resting at Hillsboro Funeral Home, 2 Hollis Ave.,

Stratford, for visitation on Thursday, 2-4 and 7-9 p.m. Funeral service will be held on Friday, February 16, at St. Andrew's United Church, Vernon Bridge, at 11 a.m. Interment will follow later at the church cemetery. As an expression of sympathy, memorial donations to St. Andrew's United Church or to QEH Foundation would be appreciated. Royal Canadian Legion Charlottetown Branch No. 1 will hold a tribute service at the funeral home Thursday evening at 6:45 p.m. Completion of funeral arrangements have been entrusted to Hillsboro Funeral Home, Stratford.

ANNIE (JOYCE) MARTIN (A4-B3-C6-D1), P. 134

At MacMillan Lodge, May 9, 2014, of Joyce Drake (nee Martin). Formerly of Vernon Bridge. Aged 83 years. Wife of the late Perley Drake. Dear mother of Allison (Ardyth), Florence (Dr. Rob) Hennessy, Gwen (Dr. John) Chow, Cindy (Michel) Gaudet and daughter-in-law, Jean Drake. Survived by sisters, Mildred Robbins (Ron Fenney), Molly (Don Drake); brother, Bob Martin (Joan); sister-in-law, Ann Martin. Also survived by 10 grandchildren and eight great-grandchildren. Predeceased by husband, Perley; sons, Gary, Melvin, Derrill; granddaughter, Shelley; and brother, Doug. Transferred from the Jenkins Funeral Home, Millview, to the Hillsboro Funeral Home, Stratford, for visitation on Monday from 2 to 4 and 7 to 9. Funeral Tuesday from St. Andrew's United Church, Vernon, with service at 11 a.m. Flowers gratefully declined. If so desired, memorial contributions can be made to the Heart and Stroke Foundation or the Canadian Cancer Society. Arrangements entrusted to the Jenkins Funeral Home, Millview.

JOHN DOUGLAS MARTIN (A4-B3-C6-D3), P. 136

Peacefully at Norfolk General Hospital, Simcoe, Ontario, on July 7, 2012, in his 79th year after a courageous battle with vascular dementia and heart disease. He leaves behind his loving wife of 55 years, Ann. Dear father of Deborah, William, Troy and his wife Susie. Proud grandfather of Michael and Amanda, Jesse and Molly Hunter and Kendra. Also survived by sisters Joyce (late Perley), Mildred (Ron), Molly (Don) of Prince Edward Island, and his brother Bob (Joan) of Bolton. Brother-in-law of Maud (Bill) of Burlington and George (late Terry) of Elliot Lake. He will be fondly remembered by many nieces and nephews, cousins and good friends in Prince Edward Island, Ontario and the USA. Predeceased by parents Hugh and Bessie. Doug was a retired employee of Canada Post with over 35 years service. A special thank you to the doctors and nurses at NGH for their compassion and care and also to Carla Sywak and staff at Thompson Waters Funeral Home for their kindness and direction. Cremation has taken place. A memorial service will be held at St. Andrew's United Church, Prince Edward Island, date to follow. For those wishing, donations to Queen Elizabeth Hospital, Norfolk General Hospital or charity of choice would be greatly appreciated. Arrangements have been entrusted to Thompson Waters Funeral Home, Port Dover, Ont., 519-583-1530.

James Boyce Martin (A4-B3-C7), p. 137

The body of Mr. James Boyce Martin, missing Grandview man, was discovered at 3:00 o'clock yesterday afternoon on the east bank of Fullerton's Marsh, about 300 yards north of the bridge over the marsh. The discovery of the body was made by Mr. Everett MacDougall, Vernon, who with Mr. Martin's brother was searching in the area.

The deceased was missing from his home since October 2nd. Royal Canadian Mounted Police, with the help of relatives and friends, had been conducting an unsuccessful search during last week. Previous to this time it had been thought that he had gone to Ontario, because of plans that had been made to go to the Upper Canadian Province.

A coroner's jury was empanelled by Dr. C.A. Cody and after viewing the remains were instructed to meet at 7:30 on Friday evening for the inquest at City Hall. The following comprise the jury. William P. Crane (foreman), Vernon; James Alex Beaton, Bonshaw; George A. Burhoe, Mt. Herbert; George A. Smith, Charlottetown; Arthur L. MacPherson, Grandview; and Samuel A. MacLeod, Kinross. The late Mr. Martin conducted a general business at Grandview and at times worked in carpenty. He is survived by his widow, the former Katherine Bruce, Lyndale, and three children. The children are Loren, in the RCAF at Halifax, Emily (Mrs. Harold White), City, and Marilyn at home. Two brothers are two sisters are also left to mourn his passing: they are Samuel, Vernon Bridge; Hugh, Kinross; Emily (widow of the late Alex MacLeod), Malpeque Road; and Annie (Mrs. William Jenkins), City.

The Guardian, October 19, 1953

James Campbell Martin (A4-B6), p. 147

Friends throughout the province will learn with deep regret of the death yesterday afternoon at his home, Roseneath, of Rev. James C. Martin. The deceased, who was sixty-eight years of age, had been in failing health for some months and had recently undergone treatment at Camp Hill Hospital, Halifax, whence he returned home a week ago. All that loving care and attention could do proved to be unavailing, Mr. Martin passing peacefully away at 2 p.m.

Born at Uigg, son of the late Mr. Samuel Martin and his wife Sarah Campbell of that district, Mr. Martin received his early education at Uigg public school and Prince of Wales College, completing his studies in the United States where he entered the Presbyterian ministry. From Abbotsford, Wisconsin, he returned to his native province in 1910 as pastor of the Cardigan church.

Enlisting during the war as Chaplain of the 87th Battalion, Mr. Martin served his country with patriotic zeal and distinction, retiring from his military duties with the honorary title of Major.

After the war, Rev. Mr. Martin preached at Wood Islands. He then went to California, whence he returned to take charge of the Presbyterian church at Mount Stewart, later removing to the pastoral charge at Lot 14 and 16. Some three and a half years ago he retired from active ministry and settled at Roseneath.

Mr. Martin was an ardent supporter of church union and entered the United Church during the latter years of his ministry.

He was a member of the Temperance Alliance and a strong advocate of Probibition.

Of genial disposition, Rev. Mr. Martin made friends wherever he went. He was widely known and esteemed for his Christian character and sincerity, and his loss to the community and the province will be deeply felt.

He was for many years an active member of the Masonic and Orange orders, taking a great interest in everything pertaining to the welfare of the community.

Survivors are his widow, Roseneath, and two adult children, Albert in [illegible] and Mary, New York, to whom the Guardian extends much sympathy.

Marjorie Martin (A4-B9), p. 148

Dominion of Canada
Province of Prince Edward Island
Queens County

Know all men by these presents, that we, *Alexander MacKay*, *Bachelor* of *Cardigan*, and *Rupert Bovyer Norton* of *Charlottetown*, *Merchant*, are held and firmly bound by His Honor the Honorable Andrew Archibald Macdonald, Lieutenant Governor of the Province of Prince Edward Island and its Dependencies, &c., &c., &c., and to his successors in office, in the sum of One Hundred Pounds, lawful money of Great Britain, to be paid to the said His Honor Andrew Archibald Macdonald or his certain Attorneys, Executors, Administrators or Assigns, for the true payment whereof we bind ourselves and each of us by himself, for the whole and every part thereof, and the Heirs, Executors and Administrators of us, and each of us, firmly by these presents, sealed with our seals, dated the 30th day of *January*, in the year of our Lord One Thousand Eight Hundred and Eighty *Six*.

The condition of this obligation is such, that, if hereafter there shall appear any lawful let or impediment, by reason of consanguinity, affinity, or any other lawful means whatever, why the said *Alexander McKay* and *Marjorie S. Martin* of *Orwell, Spinster*, may not lawfully solemnize Marriage together, and in the same afterwards to remain and continue for man and wife, according to the law in the behalf provided; and if the above bounden *Alexander MacKay* and *Rupert Bovyers Norton* do save harmless the said His Honor Andrew Archibald Macdonald, and other his officers whatsoever, by reason of the premises, then this obligation to be void, or else to remain in full force and virtue.

Signed, Sealed and Delivered in the presence of
Arthur Newberry
Alex. McKay
R.B. Norton
(Rev. Rod'k McLean)

Hugh Samuel MacKay (A4-B9-C4), p. 148

The death occurred at the Garden of the Gulf Nursing Home Monday, December 11th, 1972, of Hugh S. MacKay, well known Charlottetown tailor.

He was a son of the late Alexander and Marjorie (Martin) MacKay of Stanley Bridge, PEI, and was a veteran of World Wars One and Two. He went to England with the 105th P.E. Island Regiment and later to France, Belgium and Germany with the 26th Machine Gun Battalion until the end of hostilities. During World War Two, at the request of the late Col. Fred Andrews, he became the popular tailor at the No. 62 Canadian Army Basic Training Centre at West Royalty, where he was highly regarded by officers and men.

On his return to civilian life, he was with the Department of Transport for a short time when he accepted the position of tailor with the New Method Cleaners, Charlottetown, until his retirement.

Although in failing health the past year, the end came suddenly. By a sad coincidence, an older sister, Sadie (Mrs. Bruce Champion), passed away the same day in a nursing home in Melrose, Mass.

Left to mourn his passing are his wife (the former Pearle MacKay), Charlottetown, one son, Ralph (Scottie), Salt Lake City, Utah, and two grandchildren,

Debbie and Clive MacKay, students at Dalhousie University, Halifax. A younger son Clive passed away in 1954 at the early age of twenty-eight. Also left to mourn are the following sisters and brothers: Mrs. Ruth Belcher, Cambridge, Mass.; Mrs. Emily Burgoyne, Borden, PEI; Robert, New Durham, New Hampshire; James, Coleman, PEI; Ernest, Crapaud, PEI; and Glen, Melrose, Mass. Two brothers predeceased him, George, a casualty of World War One and William, Charlottetown.

Many relatives and friends came from far and near to pay a last tribute to a beloved relative and friend. The funeral service at the MacLean Funeral Home was conducted by his beloved pastor, Rev. Donald A. Campbell of Zion Presbyterian Church and Mrs. Hugh Lowry. Dr. Campbell spoke of his keen sense of humour, his kindness and consideration for others; his love for his family and church and his patient endurance in his illness. By request of the deceased, his cousin Lloyd Martin sang "How Great Thou Art." The congregational hymns were "The Lord's My Shepherd" and "Nearer my God to Thee."

The pallbearers were Sinclair MacKay, Gordon MacKay, Reginald Coffin, Murdock Nicholson, Lewis H. Simmons and Wendell Phillips.

The Legion service was conducted by Joe Weaver. On Tuesday evening, the Oddfellows service was conducted by Lewis H. Simmons (Noble Grand) and William M. Stewart (Chaplain).

The remains were placed in the MacLean Memorial Vault, later to be interred in the People's Cemetery.

Emily MacKay Burgoyne (A4-B9-C8), p. 149

At the Prince County Hospital, Summerside, Sunday, June 15, 1997, of Emily Burgoyne of Borden-Carleton and formerly of Kensington, aged 96 years. Wife of the late Gavin T. Burgoyne and the late Daniel MacDonald and the late Donald Martin. Daughter of the late Alexander and Marjorie (Martin) MacKay. Mother of Marjorie Paynter, Borden-Carleton, and Eileen MacDonald, Charlottetown. Grandmother of 11 grandchildren, 19 great-grandchildren and a number of great-great-grandchildren. Sister-in-law of Charlotte MacKay, New Hampshire, and Julia MacKay, O'Leary. Predeceased by her son Donald MacDonald and the following brothers and sisters: William, Robert, Hugh, George, Ernest, Glenn and James MacKay, Annie Brackley, Ruth Belcher, Sadie Champion, granddaughter Rachel Paynter, sons-in-law James Paynter and Russell MacLean and sister-in-law Marie MacDonald. Resting at the Davison Funeral Home, Kensington, for visitation Monday from 2-4 and 7-9 p.m. Funeral Tuesday in the Davison Funeral Home Chapel at 1:30 p.m. Interment in Cape Traverse United Church Cemetery.

Charlotte MacKenzie (A4-B10-C1), p. 150

On December 20, 1917, at the home of Mr. and Mrs. John G. McKenzioe, South Granville, their daughter Charlotte married Andrew McNeill, a prosperous farmer of Malpeque. Performed by the bride's uncle, Rev. J.C. Martin, Wood Islands.

Charlottetown Guardian, December 28, 1917

John Donald Martin (A4-B11), p. 155

The death occurred at his home in Eldon at 5 o'clock yesterday morning of Mr. John D. Martin, in the 53rd year of his age.

Mr. Martin had been unwell for a year, but his illness was not considered serious, so that his passing comes as a great shock to relatives and friends.

Mr. Martin was a son of the late Samuel Martin of Kinross. For a time he was engaged in carriage building, but his main occupation was farming, and for a number of years he has been the owner of the splendid property formerly owned by the late Hon. James M. Nicholson.

He was a man of irreproachable character, upright, honourable and independent in his views.

He was treasurer of the Presbyterian Church at Belfast for years and a member of the choir, and as prominently identified with the O.L. of which was a Past Master.

Mr. Martin came of a family of fifteen, there being three children at one birth, two of whom grew to womanhood and are still living. It is also worthy of note that three of his brothers are clergymen and were Chaplains overseas, namely Rev. James C. Martin, Mt. Stewart, Rev. M.C. Martin, Santa Paula, California, and Rev. S.A. Martin, Rivers, Manitoba. Two other brothers, Hugh Martin, in Sheboygan, Wisconsin, and John S. Martin at Kinross, ex-Speaker of the Legislature, and four sisters, Mrs. Kenneth MacLean, Alberry Plains, Mrs. Fred Beer, Sommerville, Massachusetts, Mrs. Marjorie McKay of Stanley Bridge and Mrs. John G. MacKenzie, South Granville, survive him.

He leaves to mourn a widow, nee Miss Ella MacKenzie, three sons, Harold, Samuel Hugh, Lloyd George, and two daughters, [Illegible] and Katherine, all at home. John has over one hundred nephews and nieces living.

The funeral will be held on Thursday, at 2 p.m., to the Belfast Cemetery.

Rev. J.C. Martin and Mrs. Martin of Mt. Stewart came to the city Monday and were not aware of the very critical illness of the former's brother, so that they received quite a shock when they heard the sad news of his death yesterday morning.

Samuel Angus Martin (A4-B13), p. 159

One of the best known and beloved missionaries of the North country, Rev. Samuel Angus Martin, formerly of Churchill, Manitoba, died in his 67th year at his home in Portland, Oregon, Tuesday morning. He was known to have been in poor health for several years.

Mr. Martin, who earned for himself the name of "the man who put the church in Churchill," was born at Orwell, Prince Edward Island, in 1873. He was the youngest of a family of 15 children, born to Samuel Martin and Sarah Campbell Martin, who emigrated from Scotland to Orwell in 1829.

Mr. Martin came to Manitoba 31 years ago as field secretary of the Christian Endeavor Union and was transferred from the Presbyterian Church in the United States to the Presbyterian Church in Canada. In 1927, when he was minister of the United Church at Hamiota, he received the appointment of missionary-at-large on the Hudson Bay railway, and from then until his health failed in 1934, he ministered to the bands of construction men along the line.

He will be remembered by a host of men from all parts of Canada, who followed the construction of the railway to the sea. On that stormy day in March 1929, when "steel" reached the tidewater at Churchill, Rev. Sam Martin was at hand to wrap some tinfoil around "the last spike" of the Hudson Bay railway and drive it home.

During his period of service in the north, Mr. Martin built two churches along the railway, the first at Gilliam in 1927, and other at Churchill in 1929. It was while he was building the latter that a young banker at Churchill, passing him one day busy working on the church, pointed him out to a friend, saying: "There is the man who is putting the church in Churchill." That catchy phrase stuck to Mr. Martin for years and helped make him a popular and familiar figure on the lecture platform.

As a boy, Mr. Martin attended Moody Institute in Chicago, Illinois. Here he met Nettie Fielding, who late became his wife. Of Mr. Martin's brothers and sisters, 13 reached maturity, four were school teachers, and two were successful clergymen. These two brothers and Mr. Martin himself served as chaplains with the Canadian army overseas. Eight nephews also served overseas, three of whom were killed in action.

Following his resignation from the Rock Lake presbytery of the United Church last June, Mr. Martin, with his family, moved to Portland, Oregon, where he resided until his death.

Immediate members of his family who survive him are his wife; and two daughters, Margaret, a teacher at Melita High School; and Mrs. Ernest Yeo, of Portland. One son, Wallace James, died in 1930.

He is also survived by two brothers, John S. of Kinross, PEI, and Malcolm

C., Portland, Oregon, three sisters, Mrs. Catherine MacLean, Charlottetown, Mrs. Fred Beer, Boston, and Mrs. Sarah MacKenzie, Hunter River.

Mr. Martin visited this province about eight years ago at which time he delivered an address in Trinity Church on the mission work in Churchill.

Charlottetown *Guardian*, June 27, 1939

Christy MacLeod Campbell (A5), p. 160

At Head of Montague on February 22nd in the 50th year of her age, Christy, the beloved wife of Donald Campbell, leaving a husband, six sons [and] three daughters to mourn the loss of an affectionate wife and mother.

The Presbyterian, March 2, 1882, p. 5

Sarah Campbell (A5-B4), p. 160

At Montague on October 6th, 1916, Sarah Campbell, the daughter of the late Donald Campbell and wife of the late Rob't Stewart, passed to her eternal reward after a lingering illness of paralysis. Mrs. Stewart was 58 years of age, leaves to mourn her loss and revere her memory one living and very faithful daughter Lulu and two sons, Ira and Jay, all at home, also one sister in the United States and three brothers who too are absent from their native province. The deceased was a devoted Christian, a loving mother, and a kind and affectionate wife. In disposition, she was quiet and retiring, and the esteem in which she was held was attested to by the many floral tributes which were placed by loving hands upon her casket. The funeral service was conducted by Rev. G.C. Henry of the Christian Church of which she was a loyal member. The interment took place in Brudenell Cemetery, and not withstanding the cold day, a large crowd gathered to pay their last respects to one so dearly loved and so highly honoured. The only daughter and sons have the sincere sympathy as they mourn for the kind and loving mother.

Ann Campell (A6, p. 165).
Neil Murchison is Ann Campbell's father-in-law

In the Name of God, Amen.

This is the last will and testament of one Neil Murchison of Point Prim, Queens County, Prince Edward Island, farmer. In the first place, I commit my body to the earth and resign my soul unto my Blessed Redeemer, fully relying on his son, who has blessed me with such worldly affairs as I am now possessed of and now distribute the same as follows.

I give, grant and bequeath to my dear and beloved son John the eastern half of my farm, and to my dear and beloved son Malcolm, I give, grant and bequeath the other, western half of my farm. The fire wood and longers are to be equally enjoyed no matter what side of the division line their growth is on. It is understood there will be no obstruction on either side from carting manure or seaweed until the lines are run, and then John is to furnish one half materials and labour in building a bridge along the marsh on Malcolm's share of the land, both parties are to have free access along the bank to haul sea weed or anything else to their respective roads. I give, grant, and bequeath to my dear and beloved son Simon the sum of ten pounds (£10.0.0) currency to be equally paid by John and Malcolm in produce or cattle as they conveniently spare. I give, grant and bequeath to my dear and beloved son Donald the sum of five pounds (£5.0.0) currency to be paid the same way as Simon is to be paid, give, grant and bequeath to each of my four daughters the sum of two pounds (£2.0.0) currency to be paid out of my goods and chattles, and the residue of my goods and chattles, I give, grant and bequeath to my said son John. I do hereby nominate, constitute and appoint my dear and beloved sons John and Malcolm to be my executors to carry this my last will and testament into effect as witness my hand this ninth day of December A.D. 1854.

Neil Murchison, X His Mark

Witness
Signed by the testator in our presence and each of us in the presence of each other.

Samuel Murchison
Simon Murchison
Donald Murchison

The written will having been presented for probate, Samuel Murchison, one of the subscribing witnesses thereto, made oath that he was present and did see the testator Neil Murchison subscribe his name by affixing his mark thereto and heard him publish and declare the same as [illegible] for his last will and testament, that when Testator so did he was of sound disposing mind and memory to this Deponent's best discerning, that he subscribed his name as witness thereto in the presence of Testator and that Simon Murchison and Donald Murchison subscribed their names as witnesses thereto at the same time.

Sworn to at Chambers this 27 February A.D. 1855,
Sam Murchison,
before me, *Charles Young*, Judge of Probates

Donald Murchison (A6), p. 165

In the name of God, Amen.

I, Donald Murchison, Senior, of Point Prim, Parish of St. John and Province of Prince Edward Island, being in a weak state of bodily health but of unimpaired memory, judgment and understanding, and considering the uncertainty of this transitory life, do make, publish and declare this my last will and testament.

In the first place, I commend my soul to Almighty God and order my body to be interred in a decent, Christianlike manner, the expenses of my funeral to be paid out of my personal estates.

I order and bequeath to my son Alexander Murchison all my landed property consisting of one hundred acres more or less, viz. that one hundred acres upon which I myself now live, with all the buildings and improvements upon them, to be held by himself and his heirs or assigns forever.

I also bequeath to my beloved wife Anne Murchison all the stock upon the farm consisting of horses, cows, sheep, etc., to be disposed of as she shall see fit.

I order and appoint the sum of six pounds currency in cash or value to be given to my grandson Donald Murchison, Neil's son, as a small token of my regard and also the sum of two pounds to my son Peter Murchison. These small bequests to be paid out of my personal property.

In consideration of my leaving the bulk of my property to my son Alexander, I expect that he will prove to his mother a dutiful and affectionate son and maintain her in a comfortable, decentlike manner, seeing that it is both his duty and interest to do so.

I hereby revoke and annul all former wills. In witness whereof I have hereunto set my seal this twenty-eighth day of August in the year of our Lord, one thousand eight hundred and [?]-seven.

Donald Murchison, X his mark

Signed, sealed, published and declared in the presence of us who have hereunto subscribed our names in the presence of said testator and in the presence of one another.

John McLellan, witness
Simon Murchison, witness, his mark
Neil Murchison, witness

The many friends and relatives of Capt. Donald Murchison will hear with regret of his death, which took place at his residence in Point Prim on Friday morning, February 1st, at the age of 77 years. The deceased was a generous and kind hearted father and was loved and respected by all who had the pleasure of his acquaintance. His intelligence was above the average. He leaves to mourn seven sons and six daughters. The interment took place at Mount Buchanan Cemetery on the 4th inst., the body being followed to its last resting place by a large number of people from different sections of the country.

Guardian, February 19, 1901

KATIE M. MURCHISON (A6-B4-C2), P. 168

A memorial service for Katie M. Murchison, retired San Anselmo teacher, will be 1:30 p.m. Tuesday at the First Presbyterian Church of San Anselmo.

Miss Murchison, who was 94, died Wednesday, August 5, 1987, in her home in San Rafael.

She was born and reared in San Rafael and was a lifetime resident.

She began her teaching career at the Lagunitas School in 1918. The following year, she joined the faculty of the old Robert Dollar School in San Anselmo. When that school was abandoned in 1930, she transferred to the Red Hill School, later renamed the Isabel Cook School, where she spent the rest of her career. She retired in 1957.

Miss Murchison was a member of the First Presbyterian Church.

Her only survivors are two nephews, Malcolm and Dallas Swogger.

Private burial will be in Mount Tamalpais Cemetery in San Rafael.

HUGH A. GILLIS (A6-B8), P. 169

The people of Eldon and vicinity were saddened to learn of the sudden death of Thursday, February 14th, 1929, of Mr. Hugh A. Gillis of that place.

The late Mr. Gillis was born at North Rustico in the year 1861 but for the last twenty years made his home in Eldon. He was a prosperous and enterprising farmer, taking an active interest in all that pertained to the good of the community, both spiritually and materially.

His devotion to his home and family was a beautiful trait of his kind and friendly nature. Stranger and friend received a cordial welcome in his home where current topics were intelligently discussed. Mr. Gillis was a life long member of the Christian Baptist Church but believed that "wherever God's people meet, there they behold the Mercy Seat," and always seeing the good in all Christian denominations. He was a regular attendant and staunch supporter of the Belfast United Church.

The funeral services at the house and grave were conducted by the Rev. Donald Sinclair of Valleyfield. Interment in Mount Buchanan Cemetery.

There are left to mourn their loss, besides his widow (nee Annie Murchison,

Point Prim), one son, Edward, four sisters, namely Rachel of New Hampshire; Annie (Mrs. Cousins) of Malden, Mass.; Irene (Mrs. Matthews) of Alberton, PEI; Emily (Mrs. Munroe), New Hampshire. Two brothers and two sisters predeceased him. The sympathy of the community goes out to the bereaved family.

Peter Simon Murchison (A6-B9), p. 169

The bond between newspaper and shipping was strong in the early 1900s. Shipping records were well documented in order to cover commerce and tourism. Shipping bonded the elite to the common man and still attracted the adventurous spirit of those excited by the constant dangers of sailing.

Captain Peter Simon Murchison, 1866-1919, followed the Murchison tradition as a ship captain, but left Prince Edward Island, Canada, for the growing city of San Francisco, California. Here, his journeys and travails were well documented. He met his wife and raised his family. Their lives were honored with attention in the social pages as well as the shipping columns.

Raised in Point Prim, Prince Edward Island, Canada, Peter took up the family tradition of sailing. Like his father, he quickly became Captain and Master Mariner, which gave him the privilege of leading transcontinental commerce. As a young captain, he lost a vessel, the *John Currier* in Washington with details related in the Prince Edward Island papers.

It seems at this point he took his skills to San Francisco, married and raised his family. The most significant article in San Francisco occurred following the tragedy of the death of his younger brother in 1909. Captain Peter dutifully relates the horrific details of his efforts to save his young brother, who was clinging to a line in rough seas before being lost.

Tragically, Captain Peter also lost a son to the sea about 15 years later. Of his 15 siblings, 8 of whom were brothers, he lost 5 brothers and a brother-in-law to the sea. His siblings and nephews are tragically lost year after year. The 1881-1901 census records of Prince Edward Island document the sad decline of the full household becoming a home of orphans raised by spinster aunts and widows living in the house of Peter's parents, who have both passed away by 1901.

The successful voyages are also listed in the San Francisco pages. Mere notes in the column of "Shipping Intelligence." They relay a very prolific career. There is a chance that many or perhaps up to half of these entries should be credited to his brother, Captain Neil Donald Murchison. His brother was also a Master Mariner and lived in San Rafael, California, just north of San Francisco. But his brother's name, nor his initials, are ever listed in the pages, so the details will never be known. Captain Peter is often listed by name, and even his wife's social events are mentioned a couple of times. It's amazing to see the history year to year as Captain Murchison travels the coast for lumber and resources for the growing demands of early San Francisco.

The following is an example of a news article about Captain Peter Simon Murchison.

THE STORY OF THE SHIPWRECK

Seattle, Washington, September 24

The revenue cutter *Thetis* arrived here today with the survivors of the American ship *John Currier*. Wrecked in Nelson's Lagoon, Bristol Bay, on August 9th. There were 110 white men, 120 Japanese and Chinese, and the wife and five children of Captain Murchison in the party.

According to Captain Murchison, the *Currier* was driven ashore on August 9th by a fierce gale that came up during a fog. Before the Commander could make out his bearings, his ship had been piled up on the rocks. The crew and the passengers were gotten off safely and the following morning, when the fog lifted, the crew took off all the ship's stores and the baggage of the passengers and crew.

It was estimated thirty days' supplies were on hand, but Captain Murchison, given command of the party by tacit understanding, ordered everybody on two meals a day. No warning was given, but it was thoroughly understood anyone stealing supplies would be shot. As a result there was no pilfering. Ten days after the party landed on a coast so bleak and barren that there was neither shelter nor food supplies, the *Currier* dashed herself to pieces on the rocks. From that time until the revenue cutter *MacCullock* appeared, September 11th, not a ship hove in sight.

Immediately after landing, two members of the crew were sent away with an Indian guide to seek help, and this company intended to set out again just as the revenue cutter *MacCullock* appeared on September 11th. The *MacCullock* transferred her passengers to the *Thetis*, which brought them here. A bread line on the *Thetis* was formed at meal hours. Captain Murchison and crew will be sent to San Francisco, the fishermen and the Orientals to Astoria, Oregon.

MARY MACDONALD MURCHISON (A6-B10), P. 169

I met in Seattle the widow of the late Captain Murchison who passed away over a year ago in Seattle. She is a daughter of John Ronald MacDonald of Point Prim, PEI, her maiden name being Mary A. MacDonald. The late Captain

Murchison was a son of Captain Murchison of Charlottetown. The son sailed the seven seas for a period of thirty years, his good wife accompanying him on many a voyage to Australia, New Zealand, South America, Mexico and Alaska. Their family consists of two daughters and one son. One daughter is Mrs. Mary Schaffner of the faculty of Snohomish High School. Their son Donald is a graduate of the University of Washington and is now in the office of the Star Line Steamhip Co. Mrs. Mary Murchison owns a fine home in Tacoma.

Maple Leaf Magazine, 1930

Samuel Alexander Murchison (A6-B12), p. 171

Thanksgiving night (March 30, 1905), after the good old custom, Samuel A. Murchison and Miss Catherine MacLeod were united in marriage at the home of Hugh Gillis, 46 Albertina Street, by Rev. W.B. Barr. The bridesmaid was Miss Margaret Murchison and the best man was Simon Stewart, a nephew of the groom. The bride was beautifully gowned in a white Persian lawn trimmed with lace; she wore a bridal veil, and carried a bouquet of white carnations. The bridesmaid was dressed in white lawn trimmed with all overlace and carried a bouquet of pinks. After the ceremony a supper was served. There were about forty guests present from Boston, Cambridge, Milford, North Abington, Wollaston and the west. Mr. and Mrs. Murchison received many beautiful ornamental and useful presents. The supper was served on the second floor in their own apartments which are already furnished for housekeeping. These are two of our popular young people and their numerous friends extend congratulations.

Quincy Herald

(Mr. Murchison is the son of the late Captain Donald N. Murchison of Point Prim and his bride is also from the same place, being the second daughter of the late John A. MacLeod. Their many friends on P.E. Island join in wishing them many years of happiness.)

Margaret Ann MacPherson (A6-B15), page 172

Mrs. Margaret A. MacPherson, 66, wife of John E. MacPherson of 197 Center Street, Quincy, Mass., died last night at the Quincy Hospital after a three weeks' illness. Born in Canada, she had been living in Quincy for 44 years. She was a member of the Golden Circle of the United Presbyterian Church.

Mrs. MacPherson leaves her husband; three daughters, Miss Ruth MacPherson, Mrs. Alice Tillson and Mrs. Florence Almquist; one son, John MacPherson;

two sisters, Mrs. Charles Smith of Maine and Mrs. Annie Gillis of Canada; two brothers, James D. Murchison of Canada and Capt. Neil Murchison of California; and two grandchildren.

Rev. William Nicholl, minister of the United Presbyterian Church, will officiate at the funeral services to be held at the Wickens and Troupe funeral home, 26 Adam Street, Wednesday, at 2:30 o'clock. Burial will be in Mt. Wollaston Cemetery. Mrs. MacPherson was formerly of Point Prim, PEI.

Christena Ann Beers [Bears] (A7-B2), p. 174

Her given name is also spelled Christina in some documents. Christena's birth date and the spelling of her name from her own family Bible have been used here. Baptismal records show her birth date as October 21, 1874. The ages given in the 1881, 1891 and 1901 censuses seem to agree with the date in the baptismal record, so 1874 is probably correct.

After the death of her husband [John Vere Wheeler] in August 1907 and the birth of her last child, John Vere, in December of the same year, Christena left the old homestead near Murray River and moved to numerous locations, trying to make a living to raise her young family, working mainly as a housekeeper. She is known to have worked in Boston, MA, New Glasgow, NS, French River, PEI, and Detroit, MI. She sometimes was able to keep some or all of her children with her, and at other times they would stay with various relatives.

Christena was postmistress of French River post office from August 1918 until May 1919. While at French River, she married Capt. Neil MacLeod, 1856-1928, sometime after 1913. They separated after a few years. In 1919, she moved to Detroit with all her children, where she bought and operated a boarding house until the children were grown. The two daughters married and lived in the Detroit area. The sons returned to PEI.

Notes from Maida Campbell, edited by John Westlie

James Campbell Beers (A7-B4), p. 175

James Campbell Beers got a job at Morse Twist Drill in New Beford, MA. From there he went to work at the L.S. Starrett Company in Athol, MA. From there he went with his son, James Milton Beers, to Rochester, MI, where he worked as a shop superintendent for the National Twist Drill Company, where they made drill bits. While at Rochester, he was also a design engineer, and that is where he built and designed the automatic screw machine. Greenlee Company of Rockford, IL, purchased the rights to manufacture the machine. James Campbell Beers was hired by Greenlee to help develop the machine.

During the depression, Greenlee sent James Campbell Beers to New England as an Eastern District Manager. Around 1941-1942, James Campbell's wife, Annie Jardine, received some royalties from the machine for one or two years. James Campbell Beers was highly respected by his employers because of his knowledge.

     Information supplied by granddaughter Joan Bonner

Index of Names

A

Ackley
 Ted 29, 101
Acorn
 David Benjamin 60, 167
 Florence Melva 16, 70
 Julie Lynn 61, 167
Adam
 Jessie Mary Furey 58, 162
Affleck
 Alexander Eugene 25
 Carly 25, 90
 Jack Harrison 25, 90
 Percy Thorne 25, 90
Ainsworth
 Bill 30, 102
 Isabella 30, 102
 Jean 29, 102
 Julie 30, 102
 Laurence 29, 102
 Lorraine 29, 102
 Sarah 30, 102
 Timothy 29, 102
Alex
 Breeanna 24, 87
 Randy 24, 87
 Ricky 24, 87
 Shaun 24, 87
Anastasiou
 Alfred 32, 108
 Christina 32, 108
 Juliana 32, 108
Andre
 Heather Marie 63, 172
 John Einer 63, 172
 John Murchison 63, 172
 Jon Christian 63, 172
Andres
 Adam John 18, 76
 Alex. See Charles Alexander
 Catherine Jean 18, 76
 Charles Alexander 18, 75
 Clara Jane 18, 75
 David Allan 18, 75
 Emma Anne 18, 76
 Grau Alice 18, 76
 Jamie Stewart 18, 75
 John Milton 18, 75
 Margaret Gray 18, 76
 Paul MacLeod 18, 75
 Phillip Campbell 18, 76
Andres-Larsen
 Declan Phillip 18, 75
Andrew
 Clarence A. 24, 89
Andrews
 Mary 55, 155
Anstie
 Leona 22, 85
Aspin
 Danita 20, 79
Auld
 Hilda 52, 149
Authier
 Nadia 33, 109
Ayars
 Dorothy Carolyn 15, 68
 Ernest James 16, 69
 Ernest Uriah 15, 68
 Karen 16, 69
 Mildred 16, 69
Azmier
 Elizabeth Gough 20, 79

B

Baden
 Bob 20, 80
Baglole
 April 55, 155
 Hugh 55, 155
 Rodney 55, 155
Balzer
 Emma 41, 126
Barber
 May 42, 127
Barclay
 Hugh 52, 148
Bauer
 Molly Heather Martin 47, 136
Bears. See Beers
Beaton
 Debbie. See Deborah
 Deborah 36, 114
Beavon
 Anapuma 14, 67
 Brianne 14, 67
 Chester 14, 66
 Cindy 14, 67
 Donald Neil 14, 67
 Eric 14, 66
 Everyl Armson 14, 67
 Fred 14, 66
 Frederick John Malcolm 14, 67
 Harold 14, 66
 Samantha 14, 67
 Terra 14, 67
 Trudy Lee Ann 14, 67
Beers
 Benjamin 63, 64, 174, 175
 Caralou 64, 176
 Christena Ann 63, 174, 223
 Christina 64, 175, 176
 Christy. See Christena Ann
 Clara Martha 64, 175
 Dorothy Christina 64, 176
 George 52, 147
 Hannah Myrtle 64, 175
 Harold Benjamin 64, 176
 James 64, 176
 James Campbell 64, 175, 223
 James Milton 64, 176
 Jennie Belle 64, 176
 Joseph v, 63, 174

Joseph Christopher 64, 176
Margaret Ann 64, 176
Moses 63, 174
Wilbur 52, 148

BEHM
Helen Margaret 33, 108, 198

BELANGER
Colleen 53, 152

BELCHER
Furley 52, 149

BELDEN
Donna Jean 21, 82

BELYA
Constance 17, 71

BENETT
Paula 53, 152

BENSON
Barbara 39, 120
Bill. See William
Braun 43, 129
Brett 43, 129
William 39, 120, 181

BERAULT
Brittney Lynn 16, 69
Joshua Alan 16, 69
Mark Edward 16, 69

BERNARD
Ivan 54, 152
Kimberley 54, 152

BERRY
Gavin 27, 95
Jeff 27, 95
Raymond 27, 95

BERUSCHI
Sharrin Catherine 21, 82

BESHTOEV
Maurat 47, 137
Olivia 47, 137

BETTS
Shelly 54, 153

BIEREN
Linda 17, 73

BIGNEY
Angela 26, 92

BIRDIE
Dave 29, 100

BISHOP
Adam 32, 107
Angela 19, 77
Becky Lyn 42, 127
David 42, 127
Esther 42, 127
Greta Dority 32, 107
Janice 42, 127
William 42, 127

BIXLER
Craig 33, 108
Emily 33, 108
Jordan 33, 108
Lauren 33, 108

BLACK
Donald 63, 172
Richard 23, 85

BLACKETT
Ellen 54, 153

BOGLE
Teresa Martine 38, 118

BOGSTIE
Wendy 37, 116

BONNETT
Pamela Dianne 50, 144

BOOTH
Margaret 43, 128

BORG
Connie 30, 103

BOWERS
Florence 25, 91

BOWLES
Daisy Johnston 57, 158
Elma Lois 60, 165

BOWMAN
Barbara May 24, 88

BOYD
Benjamin Joseph 62, 171
Megan Anne 62, 171
Peter 62, 171

BOYER
Diana 35, 112

BOYLE
Debbie 24, 87
Diane 24, 87
Peter S. 24, 87

BOZAN
Mary Annie 57, 158

BRADLEY
Alesia 42, 128
Allison 42, 128
Amanda 42, 128
Barbara Jean 42, 128
Carolyn Joyce 42, 128
Dennis Patrick 43, 128
George 42, 128
Hal 43, 128
Hugh 43, 128
James, Jr. 42, 128
James Michael 42, 128
Joshua 42, 128
Richard Allen 43, 128
Rusty. See James, Jr.
Sharon Ann 43, 128
Todd 42, 128

BRASSARD
Nicole 21, 82

BRECKEN
Carla 56, 156

BREEDON
Bailey 58, 161
Liam 58, 161

BREHAUT
Catherine Elizabeth 56, 156
Hazel Glen 59, 163
Kay. See Catherine Elizabeth
Noah Thomas 45, 133
Ryan 45, 133

BRESLIN
Stephen 63, 172

BRETON
Tracey 26, 93

BREZENSKI
Christine 44, 129

BRIANT
Heather Rose 49, 143
MacLean Alexander 49, 143
Sandy 49, 143

BRIGNELL
Jonathan Charles Thomas 49
Jonathan Weston Fraser 143

Robert 49, 143
Robert Charles Thomas 49, 143
BROWN
    Anthony Ronald 48, 139
    Jennifer Catherine 48, 139
    Kathie 54, 154
    Norma 27, 95
    Virginia 37, 117, 203
BRUCE
    Katherine 47, 138
    Katie. See Katherine
    Margaret 40, 122, 182, 205
BRYAN
    Helen Ann 50, 144
BRYANT
    Cindy Louise 39, 119
BUDGE
    Lesley 34, 111
BURGESS
    Betty 55, 154
BURGOYNE
    Gavin 52, 150
BURKE
    Allison 56, 158
    Bob. See Robert
    Colin 57, 158
    Fred 56, 158
    Robert 56, 158
    Will 56, 158
BURNER
    Hugh 43, 129
    James A. 42, 127
    James 43, 128
    May Margaret 42, 128
    Richard 43, 129
BUSSEY
    Dot 39, 119
BUTCHER
    Joan 59, 162
BUTTS
    Doris Emma 31, 105
BUZZI
    Mario 63, 172
    Susan 63, 172

C

CAIN
    Michael 29, 101
CALDWELL
    Eric 39, 120
    Laurel 39, 120
CAMERON
    Rhena Louise 48, 140
CAMPBELL
    Abraham Samuel 37, 116
    Adam Frank 30, 103
    Ada Ruth 39, 120
    Albert 15, 68
    Alexander Bruce 40, 122
    Alexander Everette 30, 103
    Alexander James 25, 90
    Ally Virginia 30, 103
    Amy Pearl 37, 116
    Andrea Rebecca 37, 116
    Angus MacLeod 60, 164
    Ann 30, 32, 37, 60, 99, 115, 165, 216
    Ann Evaline 17, 73
    Annie Laura 24, 89
    Archibald 57, 160
    Ashley Elizabeth 37, 116
    Bradley David 30, 103
    Brennan 29, 101
    Buddy. See Samuel Wilfred
    Caroline 27, 95, 107
    Catherine Grace 38, 117
    Cathy. See Catherine Grace
    Cheryl 27, 95
    Chester Gilmore 14, 67
    Christina Catherine 25, 89
    Christina Grace 26, 30, 94, 103
    Christina Laura 17, 73, 178
    Christine 27, 95
    Christine Catherine 26, 93
    Christopher Scott 29, 101
    Christy Ann 32, 59, 107, 164, 194
    Christy 63, 150, 174
    Cindy 29, 101
    Clarence Murdoch 39, 119
    Clinton James 28, 96
    Coleen 27, 94
    Corey Jean 37, 117
    Dan. See Donald
    Daryl 27, 95
    David Alan 40, 121
    David James 37, 116
    David Stuart 30, 103
    Deborah Jean 25, 90
    Derek Roy 37, 117
    Donald Bruce 29, 101
    Donald 14, 16, 24, 26, 29, 37, 57, 59, 67, 71, 78, 79, 89, 91, 94, 101, 106, 116, 117, 160, 164, 177, 178
    Donald MacDonald 26, 94, 177, 184
    Donald Murdock 25, 91
    Donald Neil 30, 102
    Donald Wilcox 60, 164
    Donald William 40, 121
    Doreen 28, 96
    Douglas 30, 37, 104, 116
    Edith Rachel 17, 73
    Edward Watson 40, 121
    Effie. See Euphemia
    Ellen Letitia 29, 100
    Emily 36, 40, 113, 115, 122
    Erin J. 29, 101
    Etta. See Euphemia
    Euphemia 16, 17, 18, 24, 30, 37, 39, 40, 69, 72, 75, 89, 99, 104, 115, 120, 122, 160, 179, 180, 193
    Euphemia Janetta Mac Kay 26, 94
    Eva Elizabeth 39, 119
    Eva Emily 39, 120

Evelyn Anne 39, 119
Everett Glen 40, 121
Falconer Everett, Sr. 30, 102
Falconer Everette, Jr. 30, 102
Flora 26, 37, 93, 115
Florence 38, 117
Franklin Everette 30, 103
Genevieve Marie-France 38, 117
George 15, 68
Gertrude 37, 115
Glen Stuart 30, 102
Gordon Robert 28, 95
Heather Ann 38, 117
Heather 27, 95
Hector 16, 71
Herbert 15, 68
Holly Anne 30, 103
Ian Hugh 38, 117
Inez MacLeod 60, 164
Irene Harriet 15, 68
Jack. See John Gordon
James. See also John Campbell
James Arthur 29, 40, 100, 122
James Arthur, Jr. 29, 100
James Arthur, Sr. 29, 100
James 14, 27, 28, 57, 66, 71, 94, 98, 100, 122, 147, 160, 168, 175, 179
James Garnet 25, 91
James Harris 37, 117
James Murchison 27, 94
James Murdoch 26, 37, 93, 115
James Reginald 40, 122
Jamie 28, 96, 100
Janet 15, 24, 68, 89, 93
Janet Irene 15, 68
Janetta 24, 89
Janette 17, 72
Jason 28, 96
Jean 29, 101
Jean Florence 26, 91
Jeffery Britt Benoit Josiah 28, 96
Jeffrey Stuart 30, 103
Jeremiah Andrew 40, 121
Jessie. See Janette
Jessie 60, 164
Jessie Florence 40, 122
Jill Elizabeth 25, 90
Jim 29, 101
John 28, 37, 39, 46, 57, 95, 98, 99, 110, 112, 115, 116, 119, 135, 160, 185
John Chester 40, 122, 205
John Clarence 29, 101
John Collins 29, 101
John Donald 40, 121
John Gordon 29, 101
John MacLeod 37, 115
John Malcolm 40, 121
John Murdoch 24, 89, 183
John Ronald 40, 121
Jonathan Donald 40, 121
Jon Brian 29, 100
Julie Anne 38, 117
Katherine Louise 15, 68
Katherine Taylor 30, 103
Kenneth 30, 103
Kevin James 29, 100
Kirk 30, 103
Kyle 30, 103
Latba 15, 68
Laura 14, 15, 67, 68, 73
Laura Elizabeth 14, 67
Lindsay 30, 104
Mabel 160
Mabel Isabel 120
MacKenzie 30, 103
Malcolm Archibald 25, 89
Malcolm 14, 24, 28, 59, 65, 66, 89, 97, 99, 158, 164, 177
Malcolm Hector 28, 97
Malcolm James 25, 89
Malcolm Neil 14, 66
Margaret Ann 60, 164
Margaret Bruce 40, 122
Margaret 15, 22, 40, 68, 84, 123, 124
Maria Elise 37, 116
Marian Elinor 14, 67
Marilyn Jane 37, 116
Marion. See Sarah
Marjorie 15, 26, 68, 94
Marjorie Elvera 28, 96
Marnie Gail 28, 96
Mary 37, 71, 115
Mary C. 16, 71
Mary Isabel 39
Matthew Alexander 25, 90
Matthew Martin 40, 121
Maynard 28, 95
Maynard V. 14, 66
Meg. See Megan Marcellina Ungar
Megan Marcellina Ungar 38, 117
Melvin 15, 68
Merle 27, 94
Michael Dale 37, 116
Michael Phillip 30, 103
Michael Wyndham Darrough 29, 100
Michelle 27, 95
Mikael John 28, 96
Murdoch 24, 25, 89
Murray 27, 95
Myrna 14, 66
Myrtle Euphemia 29, 102
Natasha 27, 95
Neil 16, 24, 27, 70, 89, 94, 99, 186
Neil Murchison 29, 100, 184, 186
Nicole May 28, 96
Norman 15, 68
Olive 26, 94
Oscar. See Falconer Everette, Jr.
Paul Aaron 29, 100
Ray Wilkinson 60, 164
Rebecca Catherine 38, 117, 204
Richard 27, 95
Robert Alexander 28, 95
Robert Douglas 30, 103

Robert Gordon 29, 101
Ronald David 40, 121
Ronald Donald 28, 96
Roy. See Donald
Ruth 15, 68
Ruth M. 26, 94
Sadie Jeanette 39, 120
Sally 29, 101
Samantha Ann 30, 103
Samuel 37, 99, 107, 115, 122, 174, 180, 181, 182, 201
Samuel Ewen 37, 116, 202
Samuel John 37, 116
Samuel Wilfred 40, 121
Sandy. See Alexander James
Sarah Ann 18, 25, 40, 73, 74, 89, 123
Sarah 26, 41, 57, 94, 126, 160, 216
Scott Daniel 30, 103
Scott John 28, 96
Scott Ungar 38, 117
Shane MacLean 28, 97
Sharon 29, 101
Sheldon James 39, 119
Simon Alexander 22, 25, 27, 84, 89, 94
Simon Donald 40, 122, 181
Simon Thomas 37, 116
Stella Dyan 17, 72
Taylor 30, 104
Walter 30, 104
Wayne Alan 40, 121
Wilfred. See John Donald
William 26, 73, 94
William Isaac 37, 116
William Malcolm 17, 72

CAMPBELL-BIRDIE
Jamie 29, 100
Kaitlyn 29, 100

CANTELO
Joan Beverly 39, 120, 205
Nelson 18, 74
Sam. See Samuel Watson
Samuel Watson 39, 120

CARLE
Beth 59, 163
Carmen Douglas 59, 163
Heather 59, 163
Lynn 59, 163

CARR
Christine 54, 153
Leonard 62, 171. See also Leonard Murchison

CARROLL
Esther 33, 109
Fred 37, 115

CARVER
Charles Frederick 23, 85
Evelyn Joyce 23, 85
Fred. See Charles Frederick
Judith Elizabeth 23, 55, 87, 156
Margaret Jean 23, 85
Mary Jeanette 23, 86
Matilda 124
Muriel May 23, 86
Robert 23, 86
Samantha Marie 23, 86
Tillie. See Matilda

CASEY
Margaret 47, 138

CATHERWOOD
Heather Lynn 30, 103

CAVANAGH
Brendan Shanley 34, 110
Connor Hugh 34, 110
Keelan Michael 34, 110
Michael 34, 110
Mike. See Michael

CHAMPION
Bruce 52, 148

CHISHOLM
Judy 58, 162
Robert 58, 162

CHOW
John 46, 135
Laura Christina 46, 135
Sarah Elizabeth 46, 135

CHURCHILL
Darry. See Thomas Darwin
Jenna 28, 96
Karl James 28, 96
Kathrine Dawn 28, 96
Kim Doyle 28, 96
Larry James 28, 96
Nadine Edna 28, 96
Scott 28, 96
Thomas Darwin 28, 96
Travis 28, 96
Victor Darwin 28, 96

CLARK
Allen 53, 151
Clair 53, 151
Gail 53, 151
Laura 16, 71
Matthew 53, 151

CLAYTON
Sandra Charlene 16, 69

COFFIN
Jean 52, 149

COLE
Barbara 55, 154
Connie 55, 154
Linda 55, 154
Peter 32, 107
Stephen 55, 155
Wesley 55, 154

COLEMAN
Ruth 37, 116

COLLINS
Richard 51, 146
Tracy 62, 170

CONE
Ann Elizabeth 15, 68
Bruce Eldridge 14, 67
Bryan 14, 67
Cindy 15, 67
Daniel 15, 68
Donald Campbell 14, 67
Edwin A. 15, 68
Edwin 14, 67
Gratia 15, 67
Jennifer 15, 68
Kevin 14, 67
Ronda 15, 67
Sean 15, 67

COOLIDGE
Lisa 63, 172

CORNISH
  Roy 63, 175
CORREY
  Joan Catherine 47, 137
CORTNEY
  Marjorie Stanhope 52, 148
COSTAIN
  Adam 54, 153
  Duane 54, 153
  Floyd 54, 152
  Jessica 54, 153
  Kayla 54, 153
  Maranda 54, 153
COTTON
  Beth. See Margaret Elizabeth
  Margaret Elizabeth 36, 113
COVENTRY
  Al 44, 131
  John 44, 131
CRISS
  Clarence 61, 168
CROSSLAND
  Ada 60, 164
  Ernest 59, 164
  Uriah 59, 164
CROSSMAN
  Cindy 44, 131
  Harold 44, 131
  Michael 44, 131
  Samuel 44, 131
CROUSE
  Florence 17, 72
  John Everett 17, 72
  Owen 17, 72
  Walter 17, 72
  Walton 17, 72
CROZIER
  Christopher 55, 154
  Linden 55, 154
  Robbie 55, 154
  Robert 55, 154
CUDMORE
  Andrew Keith 48, 141
  Carrie Jeanne 48, 141
  Heather Ruth 48, 141

John Barry 48, 141
  Peter Clayton 48, 141
CULPEPPER
  Henry 43, 128
CUMMINGS
  Beatrice 17, 72
  Douglas Lee 17, 72
  Jean. See Katherine Jean
  Katherine Jean 46, 135
  William 17, 72
CYR
  Peter 62, 170
  Riley Robert Neil Shawn 62, 170
  Sharilyn Anne 62, 170
  Shawn Colin Peter 62, 170

D

DALTON
  Maybelle 30, 102
DANIELS
  Christine 63, 172
DARROUGH
  Susan 29, 100
DAVIS
  Anne 37, 115
  Bill. See William
  Bill, Jr. 37, 115
  Carol 37, 115
  Wendy 37, 115
  William 36, 115
DAY
  Catherine 31, 105
DEMPSEY
  Florence 17, 72
  Frances 17, 72
  Malcolm 17, 72
  William 17, 72
  William P. 17, 72
DENIKE
  James 63, 174
  Thomas 63, 174
DENNIS
  Ariel 29, 102
  Rachiel 29, 102
DERUITER

Elizabeth 26, 91
DESROCHES
  Marie 36, 113
DEVEAU
  Melvin 24, 88
DEVITT
  Alexandra Heather 25, 91
  Brent. See Donald Campbell Devitt
  Donald Campbell 25, 91
  Douglas Gregory Campbell 26, 91
  Heather Lynn Campbell 25, 91
  Jessica Julie 25, 91
  Ryan 25, 91
DEVOE
  Alan Daniel 40, 120
  Bryce 40, 120
  Cameron 40, 120
  Malcolm 40, 120
DEVORE
  Nancy 20, 78
DIXON
  John 56, 157
  Kelcie Jeanette 56, 157
  Mackie 56, 157
  Melinda 56, 157
DORITY
  Deidre 32, 107
  Heather 32, 107
  Millard 32, 107
DOWNEY
  Margaret Ann 14, 67
DRAKE
  Adam Randall 47, 137
  Adenara Gail 46, 135
  Aiden John 46, 135
  Allison. See William
  Austin Donald 47, 137
  Barbara Dianne 47, 136
  Cindy Dianne 46, 135
  Courtney Jean 46, 135
  Derrell Hugh 46, 135
  Donald William 47, 136
  Ethan 46, 134
  Florence Darlene 46, 135
  Gary Francis 46, 134

Gregory Tyler 46, 135
Gwen. See Sheila
Ian Frederick 47, 137
Jill Caroline 47, 137
John 46, 135
Larry Wade 47, 137
Leslie Randall 47, 137
Lynn. See Vivian Lynn
Melvin. See John
Nicholas Larry 47, 137
Patrick Donald 47, 137
Paul Douglas 47, 136
Perley Sterling 46, 134
Rodney Trevor 46, 134
Ryan Sterling 46, 135
Sarah Christina 47, 137
Sheila 46, 135
Shelly Marie 46, 135
Vivian Lynn 47, 137
William 46, 134, 136

DRAZNIN
Charlie 42, 127
Debra 42, 127
James 42, 127
Katherine 42, 127
Leif James 42, 127
Martin 42, 127
Sol 42, 127

DREW
Frank 36, 114

DRISCOLL
Jason 38, 117
Joe. See Joseph
Joseph 38, 117
Vanessa 38, 117

DUNCAN
Ada 51, 145

DUNLOP
Ernest John 131
John 44

DUNN
Dennis 55, 154
Jason 55, 154
Rachael 55, 155

E

EISENBOOTH
Jeffry 41, 127
ELLIS
GORDON 50, 144
Jack. See O.R. John
June 50, 145
O.R. John 50, 144
EMERSON
Alison Hilary Kaitlyn 16, 69
Anita Inez 15, 68
Ariel Elizabeth Rebecca 16, 69
Kenneth Harvey 15, 68
Richard Kenneth 16, 69
Robert James 16, 69
Robert Kenneth 16, 69
Traci Lynn 16, 69
ERICKSON
Norman 64, 176
ESPLIN
Jean. See Margaret
Margaret 21, 81
EVANS
Mark 19, 78

F

FAGHERTY
Amanda Jean 28, 96
Arielle Jade 28, 97
Pat 28, 96
FARLEY
Connor Weston MacLeod 50, 143
Neala Siobhan 50, 143
Rick 50, 143
FAVELL
Rosalie 23, 87
FEINBURG
Shelley 42, 128
FENNELL
Thelma 28, 96
FERGUSON
Bruce 45, 132
May 16, 71
Megan 45, 132
FERRARO
Gildo 43, 128
FIELDING
Nettie 57, 159
FINDLAY
Kristine 22, 83
FISHER
Gary 45, 133
FITZGERALD
Alice Ellen 29, 100
FITZPATRICK
Robert 22, 85
FLEMING
Elizabeth Anne McKenzie 38, 118
Jack. See John Cuthbertson
Jason William 38, 118
John Cuthbertson 38, 118
FOLKENBERG
Katelyn Ann 16, 69
Kathi Lynne 16, 69
Randall Thomas 16, 69
Robert Stanley 15, 68, 69
FOLLOWS
Benjamin Peter 50, 143
Dalton Thomas 50, 143
Peter 50, 143
FORD
Dianna 28, 96
Douglas Kelly 28, 96
FORSEE
Charlotte 52, 150
FOURNIER
Ashley 34
Eric 34, 111
Natalie 34, 111
Steve 34, 111
FRASER
Frances 59, 163
FREER
Andrea Kathleen 21, 81
FRENCH
David 49, 142
Laura Ruth 49, 143

Lorely 42, 127
Mark David 49, 142
Tamara Ann 49, 142
Tammy. See Tamara Ann
FRITZ
  Marcella R. 64, 176
FROHMANDER
  Ida 14, 66
  Kathryn 15, 68
  Malcolm 15, 68
  Ruth 15, 68
  William 15, 68
FURST
  George Bradley 43, 128
  James 42, 128
  James Kadden 43, 128
  Natalie 42, 128
  Robert 42, 128
  Sarah Jane 42, 128

G

GADSBY
  Florence 32, 106
GALLANT
  Paul 54, 153
  Richard 54, 153
  Tanya 54, 152
GARRETT
  Ada 16, 70
  Arthur Daniel 16, 70
  David Wallace 16, 70
  John Caleb 16, 70
  Katherine Margaret 16, 70
  Marjorie Faye 16, 70
  Neil Campbell 16, 70
  Valerie. See Ada
GARRIE
  Jean 21, 82
GAUDET
  Michael 46, 135
GAUVIN
  Adrienne Weston 49, 143
  Charles Eric 49, 143
  Danielle Heather 49, 143
  Eric. See Charles Eric

Mark 49, 143
Scott. See Adrienne Weston
GENDRON
  Frank 62, 170
  Jason Matthew 62, 170
  Michael Stephen 62, 170
  Sarah Elizabeth 62, 170
GERVAIS
  Brian Edgar 25, 90
  Danielle Courtney 25, 91
  Mary Elizabeth 25, 91
GIBSON
  Audrey Ann 15, 68
GIFFORD
  Helen 36, 114
GILL
  Sheryl 55, 155
GILLESPIE
  Euphemia 26, 94
GILLIGAN
  Catherine 63, 172
  Edward 63, 172
  Ned. See Edward
GILLIS
  Amanda Beth 56, 157
  Charles 56, 157
  Edward 61, 169
  Elmer 23, 85
  Ewen 44, 130
  Heather Ann 56, 157
  Hugh A. 61, 169, 219
  Kevin Frederick 23, 86
  Terry Lynn 23, 85
GILMOUR
  Harriet Elizabeth 14, 66
GOLLEHER
  Alicia 19, 76
GORMLEY
  Frances 33, 109
GOSSE
  Charlotte Winifred 35, 112
  Winnie. See Charlotte Winifred
GRANT
  Fred 45, 133
  Margaret May 57, 160

GRATTON
  Benjamin Raymond 58, 161
  Carolyn Rose 58, 162
  Frank 58, 161
  Patrick James 58, 162
GREEN
  Angus 53, 150
  Erroll Lloyd 46, 134
  Heather 46, 134
  Lorna 46, 134
  Wendy 46, 134
GREENSHIELDS
  Donna 44, 132
  John 44, 131, 132
  Wanda 44, 131
  Wayne 44, 131
GREGOR
  Karen Louise 47, 137
GRIER
  Michael 47, 137
  Sydney 47, 137
  Wesley 47, 137
GRIESE
  Kirsten Rose May 23, 87
  Troy 23, 86
GROVER
  W. Arthur 24, 88
GRYTE
  Carl Campbell 27, 94
  Carl 26, 94
  Daniel Gillespie 27, 94
  Stephen 27, 94
GUTHRIE
  Richard 29, 101

H

HANCOCK
  Chelsea Lynn 62, 171
  Glen 62, 171
  Jonathan Glen 62, 171
HANLEY
  Jason Michael 58, 161
  Michael 58, 161
  Robyne Lynn 58, 161

HARMER
  Sharon Barrie 21, 81
HARRIS
  Maida. See Olive
  Olive 37, 117
HASTINGS
  Catherine 15, 68
HAWKINS
  Gladys 30, 102
HAYES
  Margaret 37, 116
HAYWARD
  Erin 59, 163
  James 59, 163
  Lauren 59, 163
  William 59, 163
HEALY
  Helen 41, 127
HEASTON
  Katherine 20, 79
HEDEN
  Elsa 51, 147
HENNEBURY
  Elizabeth 31, 105
HENNESSEY
  Catherine 46, 135
  Connor Robert 46, 135
  Daniel Drake 46, 135
  Robert 46, 135
HERRIGTON
  Kathy. See Kathy What-
    more
HERRING
  Adah 24, 89
HERSEY
  Allyson 15, 68
  David 15, 68
  Kenneth 15, 67
  Melissa 15, 67
HETHERINGTON
  Gerald 44, 131
  Greg 44, 131
  Lisa 44, 131
HICKEN
  Reta Florence 36, 114, 201
HICKMAN
  Gordon Richard 62, 171
  James Gordon MacRae
    62, 171
  Joanne Catherine 62, 171
  Nancy Suzanne 62, 171
HIGGINBOTHAM
  Basil 23, 86
  Cindy Lynn 23, 86
  Hope 23, 86
  Marilyn 23, 86
  Mary Hannah 23, 86
  Michael 23, 86
  Patricia Ann 23, 86
HILDEBRAND
  Merle 94
HILDEBRANDT
  Merle 27
  Steve 27, 94
HILL
  Elizabeth 31, 105
  Irene Douglas 51, 145
  Libby. See Elizabeth
HINCKLEY
  Barbara 64, 176
  James 64, 176
  Joan 64, 176
  Lianne 64, 176
HOEFLICH
  Margaret Ann 30, 103
HOFFMAN
  Ella 43, 129
HOLIDAY
  Bob 27, 95
  Jonathan 27, 95
  Ryan 27, 95
HOLMES
  Carl. See Donald Carlyle
  Donald Carlyle 50, 144
  Glen 50, 144
  John Allison 50, 144
  Paul. See Richard
  Richard 50, 144
  Ronald George 50, 144
  Shirlene Marilyn 50, 144
HONG
  Caleb 43, 129
  Gabriel 43, 129
  Kessely 43, 129
  Se June 43, 129
  Ted 43, 129
HOPKINS
  Gerard De LeMarr 32,
    106
  Jean Louise 32, 107
  Joan Eleanor 32, 106
HORN
  Hatto Heinrich 22, 83
HORNMOEN
  Kimberley Ann 25, 90
HOWARD
  Vera 14, 66
HOWELLS
  Virginia Lee 30, 102
HULSEY
  Lauryn Marie 19, 77
  Ron 19, 77
HUME
  Cathy Lynn 17, 73
  Donald William 17, 73,
    179
  Ethan William 18, 73
  John William 17, 73, 178
  Kieren Blaine 18, 73
  Samuel 17, 73, 181

I

IRWIN
  Adam 158
  Bill. See William
  Billy-Jo 57, 158
  Bobby-Sue 57, 158
  Ceylor Alyse 19, 77
  Jackie 158
  Jason 57, 158
  Robert Albert 19, 77
  Travis 158
  William 57, 158
ISAAC
  Allison Margaret 57, 161
  James Joseph 57, 161
IVY
  Marion 42, 127

J

JAASTAD
  Randine 41, 127
JACKSON
  Edward 37, 115
JAMES
  Christy Breanna Pierce 19, 78
  Harrison 36, 113
  Mary Elaine 50, 143
  Michael 36, 113
  Mike. See Michael
JARDINE
  Annie 64, 175
JENKINS
  William Albert 44, 130
JENSEN
  David Arnold 16, 69
  Michael Allan 16, 69
JIMENEZ
  Delia 30, 103
JOHNSON
  Elizabeth 63, 175
JOLLIMORE
  Baylee 54, 152
  Karl 54, 152
  Logan 54, 152
JONES
  Debra Lori 25, 90
JORDAN
  Ann 32, 108
  Grace 32, 108
  Jack. See John P.
  John P. 32, 108
  Margaret 33, 108

K

KAYS
  Pam 56, 157
KEITH
  Ida Louise 22, 83
KELLOGG
  David Dwight 40, 120
  Dwight Alva 39, 120
  Jenny Elizabeth 40, 121
  Kim 40, 120
KELLY
  Douglas 28, 96
  Kara Edna 28, 96
  Tawny Justine 28, 96
KERMODE
  Cole David 39, 119
  Keegan Douglas 39, 119
KIDD
  George 41, 124
KIEF
  Amelia M. 32, 107
  David Lawrence 32, 107
  Joseph Lawrence 32, 107
  Karen Murchison 32, 107
  Kathryn Marie 32, 107
  Lawrence C. 32, 107
KING
  Herman 64, 176
KIRK
  Bradley 58, 161
  Chris 32, 107
  Hunter Stewart 58, 161
KITCHCOCK
  Irene Lois 14, 67
KITCHEN
  Douglas 23, 86
KNOLLS
  Linda Kaye 16, 69
KNOX
  James 60, 167
KOAZK
  Cathy 28, 96
KONEVICH
  Mary Catherine 16, 69
KRAMARCZYK
  Dylan Reginald Simon 26, 93
  Kent Matthew 26, 93
  Marcus 26, 93
  Mike. See Marcus
  Ruth Ann 26, 93

L

LADNER
  Arthur 36, 113
  Cal. See Claude W.
  Claude W. Ladner 36, 114
  Helen Ladner 36, 114
  Hugh Ladner 36, 114
LAFERTE
  Janet LaFerte 45, 133
LAIRD
  Velda Laird 35, 113
LAKE
  Kathryn Lake 114
LAMB
  Sharleen Lamb 45, 133
LAMBOURN
  Genie Lambourn 43, 129
LAMONT
  Mary Lamont 18, 74
  Masie. See Lamont: Mary Lamont
LANDRY
  Marie Landry 52, 150
  Tray Landry 23
LANE
  Bob Lane 34, 111
  Darlene Lane 34, 111
  Edith Marguerite Elizabeth Lane 51, 146
  Emily Lane 34, 111
  Laurie Lane 34, 111
LAROUSE
  Sharon Larouse 28, 96
LARSEN
  Amy Lyn Larsen 42, 127
  Anders Thomas Larsen 42, 127
  Barbara Larsen 127
  Christine Larsen 41, 127
  Christopher Larsen 41, 127
  Edward Larsen 42, 127
  Eric Larsen 18, 41, 127
  Erika Larsen 42, 127
  Heide Marie Larsen 41, 127

John Larsen 42, 127
Ludwig Larsen 41, 127
Malcolm Larsen 42, 127
Michael Eric Larsen 18, 75
Robert Larsen 42, 127
Todd Ludwig 41, 127
LAU
  Lora 21, 82
LAYBOLT
  Linda 58, 162
LEA
  Clifford Hayden 45, 132
  Dorothy 45, 133
  Forrest 51, 145
  George Garth 51, 145
  Glenda Ferne 45, 133
  John 45, 132
  Mary Jane 45, 133
  Paul Dingwell 45, 132
  Paul 45, 132
LEBLANC
  Ninian 36, 114
LEE
  Caroline Ruth 18, 76
  Erica 14, 67
  Erin 14, 67
  George 29, 102
  Justin Ryan 14, 67
  Nils 14, 67
LELIEVRE
  Joseph Gerard Hebert 48, 139
  Kim James 48, 139
LESLIE
  Tim. See Timothy
  Timothy 26, 92
LETHBRIDGE
  Alice 33, 108
LICHTER
  Monica 30, 104
LILY
  Kathy 47, 136
LIND
  Mary Ann 29, 101
LINLEY
  Marjorie 32, 107
LITTLE

Alice Jean 29, 102
Eva Rose 30, 102
Hubert 29, 102
LIVINGSTONE
  Fred 52, 150
LIVOCK
  Norma A. 51, 147
LOCKART
  May 52, 149
LOTT
  Edna 28, 95
  Naomi 27, 94
LUTRELL
  Rick 19, 78
LYGON
  Valeria Mavis 19, 77
LYLE
  Alma Susan 71
LYNSKEY
  Glen Arthur 22, 83
  Torin Stewart 22, 83
  William John 22, 83

M

MACALLISTER
  Lynn Marie Murchison 32, 107
  Robert 32, 107
  Robert Murchison 32, 107
  Sandra Murchison 32, 107
  Thomas 32, 107
MACARTHUR
  Sandra 54, 153
MACAUSLAND
  Elmer 53, 151
  Kale 53, 151
  Laura 53, 151
  Logan 53, 151
  Tyler 53, 151
MACCALLUM
  Marin 46, 135
MACCAULL
  Donovan 53, 151
  George 53, 151
  Randy 53, 151
  William 53, 151

MACDONALD
  Alexander Blair Ronald 49, 141
  Angus A. 31, 104
  Arthur 52, 150
  Benjamin Luke 36, 114
  Blair Robert 49, 141
  Catherine Pauline 49, 141
  Christy 14
  Daniel 52, 149
  Donald 26, 52, 94, 150, 177
  Douglas 43, 128
  Douglas Matheson 60, 166
  Eileen 52, 149
  Faye 52, 150
  Grace Elizabeth 49, 142
  Hugh Wallace 60, 166
  Ian 36, 114
  James 51, 146
  Janet Murchison 60, 166
  Jerry 52, 150
  Joel 36, 114
  John Alex 60, 166
  Jon Miller 36, 114
  Kate. See Mary Catherine
  Keith Thomas 49, 141
  Kenneth Gordon 60, 166
  Kenneth 16, 70
  Kirsten 36, 114
  Lorna May 56, 156
  Malcolm D. 40, 123
  Marion 61, 168
  Mary Ann 61, 97, 169, 221
  Mary Catherine 49, 142
  Mary Jane 40, 122
  Mary Nichol 60, 166
  Mildred Christine 51, 147
  Mitchell 52, 150
  Paul 49, 142
  Rae Ann 52, 150
  Rhonda 52, 150
  Roma 52, 150
  Ronald 52, 150
  Sarah Anne 49, 142
  Susan 36, 114

Thayne 43, 128
MacDougall
　Deneen 45, 132
　Donald. See Parker
　Everett James 44, 132
　Everett Noel Gregory 45, 132
　Marion Euphemia 35, 111
　Parker 40, 122
　William Everett Noel 45, 132
MacEachern
　Catherine 49, 142
MacEwen
　Charles Edward 33, 109
　Gabrielle Rebecca 33, 109
　Harvey 33, 109
　John Harvey 33, 109
　Margaret Roseanne 33, 109
　Peggy. See Margaret Roseanne
　Robert Hugh 33, 109
　Ted. See Charles Edward
MacGregor
　Elsie 17, 72
MacInnis
　Dickie. See Lucinda
　Edna 55, 155
　Lucinda 45, 133
　Margaret Isbel 45, 132
MacIntosh
　Barry 31, 105
　William 31, 105
MacKay
　Aaron Mark 52, 149
　Alexander 52, 113, 148
　Brendan Matthew 52, 149
　Brian Gordon 58, 162
　Christie Ann 52, 148
　Clive 52, 149
　Clive Milton 52, 148
　Dana Harold 58, 162
　Deborah 52, 149
　Dorothy 24, 88
　Earl 24, 88
　Emily 35, 52, 113, 149, 213
　Ernest 52, 150
　George 52, 148, 149
　Glen 53, 150
　Harold Gordon 58, 162
　Harvey 24, 88
　Hugh Samuel 52, 148, 212
　James A. 53, 150
　John Scott 58, 162
　Kenneth Ira 58, 162
　Lauchlin 53, 150
　Lois Leanne 58, 162
　Paul Arthur 52, 148
　Pearle 52, 148
　Ralph 52, 148
　Robert 52, 149
　Ruth 52, 149
　Sadie. See Sarah E.
　Sarah E. 52, 148
　Scottie. See Ralph
　William 52, 148
MacKenzie
　Barbara Etta 53, 150
　Charlotte 53, 150, 214
　Effie. See Euphemia
　Euphemia Catherine 53, 151
　Euphemia 29, 100, 179, 190
　Garth 54, 153
　George Clifton 53, 151
　Gladys 53, 151
　Harriet 44, 130
　Hattie. See Harriet
　James Andrew 55, 155
　John Gunn 53, 150
　Margaret E. 53, 150
　Margaret 45, 132
　Margie 30, 103
　Mary Ella 55, 155
　Mitchell 54, 153
　Norma Adelaide 53, 151
　Phemie. See Euphemia Catherine
　Roberta M. 53, 151
　Samuel Martin 53, 151
　Sarah A. 53, 151
　Sheila Marlene 16, 70
　Shirley Dianne 16, 70
　Tyler 54, 153
Mackie
　Jack 53, 152
　James 53, 152
　Jason 53, 152
MacKie
　Bonnie. See Jessie Emma
　Boyce 48, 140
　Carolyn 48, 140
　Dorothy 48, 140
　Harold H. 48, 140
　Harold H. 56, 158
　Jean 48, 140
　Jessie Emma 56, 158
　Joyce. See Carolyn
　Wilbur 48, 140
MacKinnon
　Archibald 40, 122
　Dan. See Donald
　Donald 26, 74, 93
　Faye 34, 110
　Murdoch 16, 69, 70
　Sheila Mary 35, 111, 200
MacLaughlan
　Allan 50, 144
MacLean
　Allison Ivan 26, 92
　Angus William 48, 141
　Anna Elizabeth 49, 141
　Annie Euphemia 50, 144
　Ann 50, 145
　April 57, 161
　Arthur Martin 50, 143
　Blair. See Reginald
　Blair Joseph 25, 90
　Bonnie Ruth 26, 92
　Bradley Jonathan 25, 90
　Carl Lydell 34, 110
　Catherine 48, 141
　Cathy 149
　Charles Bryan 50, 144
　Cheryl Marie Campbell 40, 121
　Clarence 51, 147; see also Edwin
　Darlene Catherine 34, 110
　Darrell Lloyd 34, 110
　Donald 51, 145

Donald MacLeod 50, 145
Earl 51, 145
Edwin Kenneth 51, 147
Edwin 51, 146
Ella. See Margaret
Emma Angela 26, 93
Ernest Clinton 51, 146
Euphemia 27, 94, 184
Evan 50, 144
Flora Catherine 50, 144
Garfield 52, 150
George Lane 51, 146
Glen 51, 147
Haywood William 34, 110
Herbert Vickerson 51, 145
Hugh MacMillan 51, 145
James Kenneth 50, 143
James 52, 149
Jean. See Catherine
Jeff 34, 110
Jennifer 34, 110
Jessica Ruth 26, 92
Joshua Scott 26, 92
Justin Merle 26, 93
Kenneth 48, 140
Laura Jean 26, 92
Laura 51, 52, 149
Lester 34, 110
Lloyd Winston Robbins 34, 111
Mac. See Malcolm
Malcolm Evan Jacob 25, 90
Malcolm 51, 145
Margaret B. 48, 140
Margaret Estelle 62, 171
Margaret 48, 141
Mark 34, 110
Marvin 34, 110
Mary Beth 26, 92
Mary Emma Lynn 25, 90
Mary Margaret 40, 121
Matthew James 26, 92
Melanie Ella Audrey 25, 90
Michael 50, 143
Mitchell Brandon 26, 93
Monica Jill 25, 90
Peggy. See Margaret Estelle
Reginald 51, 147
Rena Myrtle 51, 145
Robert 50, 145
Roderick Thomas 50, 144
Roger. See Clarence
Russell 52, 149
Ruth Agnes 49, 142
Ruth Laura 51, 146
Ruth 51, 146
Samuel Martin 48, 140
Sarah Janette 48, 140
Sarah Jean 50, 144
Scott Allison 26, 92
Sharon Lynn 34, 110
Shawn 34, 110
Sinclair. See William
Sterling 34, 110
Steven Richard 50, 144
Susan 51, 145
Thomas Richards 48, 141
Topanga Sea 23, 86
Vic. See Herbert Vickerson
Wade 23, 86
Wallace Henry 50, 144
Wanda 52, 150
William 48, 57, 161
William Sinclair 57, 160
Woodrow. See Earl
MACLEOD
Alexander 44, 60, 130, 139, 165
Alice 60, 165
Allan Kenneth 19, 77
Allistair. See Angus
Angus Alexander 16, 71
Angus Keith 56, 156
Angus 17, 71, 164
Angus Murchison 60, 166
Angus Norman 40, 123
Anne Bernice 18, 75
Ann 49, 60, 165
Bobbie. See Robert Martin
Bruce 17, 60, 72, 166
Caitlin Ayn 19, 76
Caitlin Marie 19, 76
Callie Leah 19, 76
Cameron Donald 20, 79
Carleton 61, 168
Carrick Ian 19, 76
Cassie. See Catherine Florence
Catherine Florence 62, 171
Catherine 37, 115, 181, 182, 202
Charles Douglas John 60, 166
Cheryl Ann 49, 142
Christine 24, 89
Christy 57, 160, 216; see also Christine
Clara. See Edith
Colin 56, 156
David Campbell 20, 79
David 17, 44, 71, 130, 178
Dawson Lauder 20, 79
Devin 54, 154
Dianna Jean 50, 143
Donald Andrew 56, 156
Donald Campbell 20, 78
Donald 17, 44, 71, 130, 145
Donald Malcolm 56, 156
Donald M. 60, 165
Douglas 17, 72
Edith 56, 110, 157
Elaine 17, 71
Elva. See Mary
Euphemia 32, 108, 197
Everett. See : Donald
Flora 16, 71
Florence Eleanor 56, 157
Gordon. See Walter
Gwendolyn 56, 158
Harold Walton 56, 157
Heather May 49, 143
Ian 17, 71
Isabel 40, 41, 121, 125, 130, 181
Janice Helen 56, 157
Jeffrey 56, 156
Jessie 44, 130

Joan Agnes 50, 143
John 37, 44, 56, 60, 115, 130, 156, 166
Jonathan 56, 156
Julie Anne 20, 78
Karen 17, 72
Karla 16, 70
Kate 56, 156
Katherine Ella 49, 143
Kaylee 56, 156
Kelli Margaret 16, 70
Kenneth 54, 153
Kerry Lynn 19, 77
Kevin 56, 158
Lauren Ellie 20, 79
Laurie Ann 19, 77
Leah Alyse 19, 76
Lee 17, 72
Mabel 16, 71
Madeline 17, 72
Malcolm 60, 165, 181
Malcolm Murchison 60, 165
Margaret Catherine 37, 115
M. Arthur 44, 130
Mary Ferguson 19, 78
Mary Louise 56, 157
Mary 17, 55, 72, 156
Mary Martin 44, 131
Nancy 56, 157
Neil 63, 175
Norman Conner 19, 76
Norman 18, 75
Norman Scott 18, 76
Norman Stewart 18, 76
Pat 17, 72
Pauline Jessica 50, 143
Randy 56, 157
Richard Keith 56, 156
Roberta Ruth 49, 143
Robert 51, 146
Robert Martin 56, 157
Robin 56, 157
Roger 44, 130
Ross 17, 72
Ruth 49, 60, 165
Shawn Allen 19, 76
Sinclair. See William
Timothy Ross 156
Waldo Keith 16, 70
Walter A. 60, 165
Walter 16, 71
Wayne 16, 71
Weston George 49, 142
Willard Campbell 17, 55, 71, 155
William Gordon 32, 108
William 17, 72
MACMILLAN
  Donald 23, 86
  Tiffany 23, 86
  Wilhelmina 51, 145
MACNEILL
  Edith Anne 37, 115
MACPHAIL
  Gregory Scott 61, 167
  Scott John 61, 167
MACPHEE
  Bessie Goss 46, 111, 134
MACPHERSON
  Betty Helena 51, 145
  Bonnie Lynn 61, 167
  Catherine 18, 75, 107
  Chester 23, 87
  Christina Belle 24, 88
  Daniel 22, 84
  Dolly. See Donalena
  Donald Alexander 60, 167
  Donalena 24, 88, 183
  Elizabeth 60, 165
  Euphemia 24, 87
  Gloria June 24, 87
  Janet Florence 22, 84
  Jenny. See Janet Florence
  Jessie 60, 166
  J. 172
  Joyce 23, 87
  Kathy Ann 61, 167
  Malcolm Archibald 22, 84
  Malcolm James 22, 84, 182
  Mamie. See Mary
  Mary Ann 24, 88
  Mary 24, 88
  Neil 22, 84
  Phemie. See Euphemia
  Sandra Elinor 60, 167
  Sarah Catherine 23, 87
  Wallace William 51, 145
MACQUEEN
  Barcley 61, 168
  Katherine 61, 168
  Mary C. 61, 168
  William Alexander 61, 168
MACRAE
  Adelaide 53, 151
  Andrew 53, 152
  Anne Mary 24, 89
  Ann 53, 152
  Anthony 53, 152
  Austin 53, 152
  Christina Mary 26, 94
  Cindy 53, 152
  George 53, 152
  Janet Catherine 62, 170
  Judith Ann 62, 171
  Kenneth John 62, 170
  Marie 53, 152
  Michelle 53, 152
  Norman 53, 151
  Sherry 59, 164
MACSWAIN
  Christa 23, 86
MAHAR
  Logan Alexander 61, 167
  Randy 61, 167
MAILMAN
  Patti 62, 170
MAIN
  Lillian Burt 18, 74
MALLOY
  Bill 33, 108
MANCHON
  Alexander Stewart 21, 81
  Melissa Maria 21, 81
  Michael Angelo Manuel 21, 81
  Nicholas Velandi 21, 81
MANN
  Willene S. 114
MARCHESSAULT
  Marie-Claude 38, 117

MARENT
  Gabrielle Isabella 19, 76
MARKS
  Bessie May 63, 175
MARSHALL
  Andrew 59, 164
  Barett Jay 59, 164
  Emilyne 59, 164
  Jocelyn 59, 163
  John 59, 164
  Matthew 59, 164
  Robert 59, 163
MARTIN
  Adam 57
  Alexander MacLeod 48, 139
  Alexander 17, 73
  Annie Campbell 44, 130
  Annie Mae 44, 132
  Annie 46, 134, 209
  Arlene 47, 138
  Barbara. See also Doris Martin
  Barry Malcolm 45, 133
  Billy. See William Alexander; William Barry; William Hugh
  Billy-Jo 57
  Bobby-Sue 57
  Brenda 57, 158
  Bruce 43, 51, 129, 147
  Buster. See Alexander MacLeod
  Catherine Grace 55, 155
  Catherine 17, 36, 42, 48, 55, 71, 115, 127, 140, 155
  Cheryl 44, 45, 131, 134
  Christy Ann 48, 139
  Clayton Lloyd 45, 133
  Daniel 44, 131
  David 34, 36, 111, 114
  Debbie. See Deborah Ann
  Deborah Ann 46, 136
  Debra Anne 45, 133
  Denis 43, 129
  Donald Irwin 45, 133
  Donald 35, 45, 52, 113, 134, 149
  Donna Mary 46, 134
  Doris 43, 44, 129, 131
  Doug. See John Douglas
  Douglas 43, 129
  Edith Dianne 47, 137
  Elaine 44, 131
  Eleanor Katherine 57, 159
  Emily Campbell 36, 113
  Emily Christine 47, 138
  Emily 44, 48, 51, 147
  Emily Mildred 34, 46, 110, 135
  Emma 48, 139
  Ernest 36, 114
  Erwin 57, 158
  Etta 55, 155
  Euphemia 32, 107, 197
  Evelyn 44, 131
  Flora Ann 32, 108
  George 36, 114
  Harold Neil 55, 155
  Heather 44, 131
  Holly Alana 47, 137
  Hugh James 46, 134
  Hugh 32, 41, 43, 98, 107, 108, 109, 115, 126, 129, 180, 181, 196
  Hunter Joseph 47, 136
  Jackie 57
  James Albert Beers 51, 147
  James Boyce 47, 137, 210
  James Campbell 51, 147, 193, 210
  James 51, 147
  Jason 58
  Jean 57, 159
  Jennifer Lynn 45, 133
  Jesse William 47, 136
  Joanne Lynn 47, 137
  John Arthur 43, 129
  John Campbell 35, 37, 112, 115, 200, 206
  John Donald 55, 57, 155, 158, 214
  John Douglas 46, 136, 209
  John 41, 44, 126, 131, 148
  John Samuel 44, 129, 207
  John W. 46, 134
  Joyce. See Annie
  Julie 57, 158
  June 51, 57, 147, 159
  Karen 36, 115
  Kendra Diane 47, 136
  Kevin 43, 129
  Leida Jane 45, 132
  Leslie 45, 134
  Linda 51, 147
  Lloyd George 57, 158
  Lloyd 45, 133, 208
  Lois 43, 129
  Loren Boyce 47, 138
  Mac. See MacLeod Martin
  MacLeod 44, 131
  Malcolm Campbell 57, 158
  Malcolm 57, 133, 159
  Marabel 44, 131
  Margaret Cecelia 57, 159
  Margaret Christine 36, 114
  Margaret Irene 37, 115
  Margaret 41, 57, 126, 159
  Marilyn Anne 48, 139
  Marion Emily 48, 56, 140, 158
  Marjorie Donalda 35, 113
  Marjorie 52, 148, 211
  Mary Bethany 45, 133
  Mary Emily 44, 130, 207
  Mary Noreen 47, 136
  May Bertha 42, 127
  Molly. See Mary Noreen
  Muriel. See Catherine
  Muriel 36, 115
  Neil 42, 127
  Robert Winston 47, 137
  Ronald 57, 158
  Ryan 43, 129
  Sadie. See Sarah Catherine; Sarah
  Samuel Angus 57, 159, 215
  Samuel Hugh 57, 158

Samuel 41, 44, 126, 130, 131, 140, 151
Sarah Catherine 36, 114
Sarah Margaret 41, 44, 126, 127, 130
Sarah 44, 53, 131, 150
Travis 57
Troy Douglas 47, 136
Wallace James 57, 159
William Alexander 44, 131
William Barry 45, 133
William Hugh 47, 136

MATHER
Nicola Claire 56, 156

MATHESON
Alexander 48, 60, 140, 167
Allan 60, 166
Annie 60, 166
Catherine 48, 60, 141, 166
Christine Anne 60, 167
Donald J. 60, 166
Florence 48, 141
James Craig 60, 166
Katie. See Catherine
Margaret Mary 61, 168
Ruth 48, 141

MATHIES
Martin 37, 115

MATTAPOISETT
Walter 114

MAYNARD
Catherine 41, 125
Eva 41, 125
Harry 41, 125
Margaret 41, 125

MAYNE
Neil Campbell 24, 89
William C. 24, 89

McCULLY
Alan 43, 129
Charles 44, 129
Karen 43, 129
Lucas 43, 129
MacKenzie 43, 129
Megan 43, 129
Samuel 43, 129

Susan 44, 129

McGRATH
David 59, 163
Kelly Erin 59, 163
Laura Helen 59, 163
Steven Joseph 59, 163

McGREGOR
Marlene 28, 95

McGREW
Carol 42, 128

McINNIS
Arthur 18, 74
William 18, 74

McKEE
Ann Elizabeth 58, 161

McKENNA
Kathy 43, 129

McKENZIE
David Ryan 38, 118
Effie See Euphemia MacKenzie
John Ryan 38, 117
Keira Grace 38, 118
Rebecca Leslie 38, 118

McKENZIE FLEMING
Elizabeth Anne 38, 118

McLAUGHLIN
Randise Gail 21, 82
Randy. See Randise Gail

McMAHON
Jessica Lane Diana 50, 143
Kyle Weston John 50, 143
Tara 50, 143

McNAUGHT
Muriel 53, 150

MEARS
Andrew 20, 80

MEEN
Elysia Dhyana 21, 81

MELLISH
Clarence William 22, 84
Elsie May 23, 85
John Thomas 22, 84
Margaret Florence 22, 84
Ruth Amelia 22, 25, 84, 89

MELVIN
Dale Philip 20, 80
Isabelle Anne 20, 80

Olivia 20, 80, 177

MERKEL
Bonnie Eve 58, 162
Laurel Jean 58, 162
William Philip 58, 162
William Stewart 58, 162

MEYER
Susan Faye 18, 75

MILLAR
William 63, 174
William M. 63, 174

MILLER
Charlotte Louise 39, 119
Deborah 43, 129
Jack Thomas 39, 119
Stephen 39, 119
Steve. See Stephen

MILNE
Gary Kenneth 48, 139

MOEN
Tracy 28, 96

MOORE
Delphia 30, 102
Harris Penna 58, 162
H. June 59, 162
Jenna 53, 152
Mabel 58, 162
Marcus 54, 152
Roger 53, 152

MORRISON
Donald A. 60, 167
Donna 60, 167
Dorothy Margaret 40, 122
Edith 20, 79
Gordon 40, 122
Neil Ross 60, 167

MOSES
Donald 59, 163

MOURIS
Joanna 36, 114
Joe 36, 114
Margaret Catherine Johanna 36, 114

MUNN
Blair Douglas 23, 85
Bob. See Robert Alexander
Boyd 22, 85

Lincoln Merrill 22, 85
Lindsay Margaret 22, 85
Lisa Margaret 22, 85
Merrill 22, 85
Penny Michelle 22, 85
Robert Alexander 22, 84
Ronald Boyd 22, 85
Ronnie. See Robert Alexander
MURCHISON
  Annie Campbell 61, 62, 168, 170
  Annie Catherine 63, 171
  Ann 31, 61, 104, 169
  Brian 31, 105
  Carl 31, 105; see also David Carlson
  Charles 61, 169
  Christianna 61, 168
  Christy. See Christianna
  David Carlson 31, 105
  Deborah 31, 105
  Donald 31, 32, 60, 61, 74, 99, 104, 106, 123, 165, 169, 218
  Donna 31, 105
  Dorothy 63, 172
  Earl 31, 105
  Edna Florence 63, 172
  Euphemia 28, 30, 31, 32, 41, 60, 98, 99, 104, 105, 106, 123, 165
  Flora 61, 168
  George 30, 104
  Glenn 31, 105
  Gordon 31, 105
  Grace. See also Euphemia
  Harriet Elizabeth 63, 172
  Heather Anne 31, 105
  Irene 31, 105
  Isabell 32, 105
  James Campbell 61, 168
  James Donald 18, 62, 74, 170
  James 27, 32, 61, 94, 106, 168
  James Pringle 31, 105
  Jamie. See James Pringle
  Janet 14, 30, 65, 66, 104, 166
  Jessie. See Janet
  John Alexander 30, 104
  John Malcolm 61, 63, 169, 172
  John Neil 31, 63, 105, 172, 180, 194
  John Ronald 61, 170
  Joseph 32, 106
  Katie MacDonald 61, 168, 219
  Laurie Bruce 31, 105
  Leonard 62, 171
  Leslie 31, 105
  Lloyd 31, 105
  Louise 61, 169
  Mac. See Malcolm
  Malcolm 31, 104, 165
  Margaret Ann 63, 172, 214
  Margaret 60, 62, 165, 170
  Mary Isabella 32, 107
  Mary 60, 61, 166, 169
  Michael 32, 105
  Murdoch Pringle 31, 105
  Murdock M. 32, 106
  Muriel 61, 63, 169, 172
  Myrtle 31, 105
  Neil 29, 30, 31, 61, 99, 100, 104, 105, 168, 180
  Nellie 31, 105
  Peter James 32, 106
  Peter 30, 31, 98, 104, 179, 180, 193
  Peter Simon 61, 169, 220
  Phemie. See Euphemia
  Randy 31, 104
  Robert 31, 105, 107
  Ross 31, 105
  Sadie. See Sarah
  Samuel Alexander 62, 171, 222
  Samuel 61, 169
  Sarah 31, 104
  Simon Malcolm 31, 104
MURNAGHAN
  Bill. See William Roy
  Jorel James Roy 48, 139
  Sherry. See Sheryl Lee
  Sheryl Lee 48, 139
  William Roy 48, 139
MURPHY
  Albert 17, 73
  Mary Elizabeth 25, 89
  Olivia Anne 21, 82
  Sheila 14, 67
MUSIKA
  Shelley 59, 163
MYERS
  Cameron John 46, 135
  Clinton 46, 135
  Joanne 58, 162
  Wayne 58, 162

N

NAMEE
  Ruth Constance 58, 161
NAUGLER
  Elaine 38, 118
NAYLOR
  Walter 53, 151
NEAL
  Peggy 16, 69
NEIMER
  Doris 33, 109
NICHOLSON
  Donald Glen 55, 156
  Donald Gordon 23, 55, 87, 156
  Donald Matthew 23, 87
  Douglas 55, 156
  Gordon. See Donald Gordon
  Lea 55, 156
  Mary Christine 23, 87
  Raymond Donovan 23, 87
NOLET
  Allan 142
NORDGREN
  Anika 20, 80
  Eric Terrance 20, 80
  Flynn Eric 20, 80

NORRIS
Allison 27, 95
Danna 27, 95
David 27, 95
Destanne 27, 95
Jacklyn 27, 95
James 27, 95
Kevin 27, 95
Leah 27, 95
Tekarra 27, 95
Treanne 27, 95
NOVAK
Patrick 21, 83

O

OAKES
Vivan Eileen 47, 136
OAKLEY
Andrew 59, 163
O'CONNER
Frances 59, 163
O'HARA
Frances 26, 91
O'LAUGHLIN
Noreen 40, 121
OLMSTEAD
Kathryn 30, 102
ORNENSTIEN
Ron 63, 172
O'ROURKE
Bernard 52, 149
Matthew MacKay 52, 149
Sarah Jean 52, 149

P

PAIGE
Sharon 16, 69
PALERMA
Esther Avallana 40, 121
Tet. See Esther Avallana
PARK
Mary Ellen 31, 104
PARKS
Ella May 57, 159

PATTERSON
David 56, 157
PAYNE
Jeffrey William 49, 143
John 49, 143
Nathan Miller 49, 143
PAYNTER
Allyson 54, 153
Ashley 54, 153
Bradley 55, 154
Brenda 55, 155
Brian 54, 153
Christopher 36, 113
Crystal 36, 113
Daniel Norris 36, 113
Daniel 54, 153
Dawn 36, 113
Dawson 54, 153
Douglas 55, 154
Garth Martin 36, 113
Gary. See James
George Wesley 53, 151
Gladys 54, 152
Glen 55, 154
Grant 36, 113
Herbert 54, 153
James Garth 36, 113
James 35, 113
Joan 55, 154
Johnathan 54, 153
Kaylynn 55, 154
Kendall 36, 113
Kyle 54, 154
Leslie John 36, 113
Martin 36, 54, 154
Merle 55, 154
Muriel 53, 151
Norma 54, 153
Pam 36, 113
Rachel 35, 36, 113
Ronald 55, 154
Ryan 54, 154
Stephen 54, 153
Tracy 54, 154
Vera 55, 155
William 54, 153
PENDERGAST
Elizabeth 49, 142

Liz. See Elizabeth
PENNY
Georgina 22, 85
PETTERSON
Brent 21, 82
Matthew James 21, 82
PHILLIP
Joseph 43, 128
Kathy 43, 128
PHILLIPS
Dennis 54, 154
John 55, 154
Megan 55, 154
PICKARD
Barbara Jean 49, 141
Deborah Lynn 49, 141
Doris Ruth 49, 141
Ellen Carolyn 48, 141
George 48, 141
George Thomas 48, 141
Keith. See George
PICKERSGILL
Alexander James 26, 93
David Kyle 26, 93
Kyle. See David Kyle
PIERCEY
Roy 59, 163
PIPER
Diane Lynn 20, 80
POIRIER
Alyson 59, 163
Andrew 59, 163
Robert 59, 163
POLLOCK
Ian 58, 162
John 58, 162
Joshua Hart 58, 162
POTTER
Ross 57, 161
POWER
Adam David 23, 86
David Augustine 23, 86
Kelly Rose May 23, 86
PRONOVOST
Marcel 39, 119, 204
PROULX
Jonathan 59, 162
Roland 58, 162

PRYER
  James 43, 129

Q

QUALLS
  Victoria 20, 78
QUIGLEY
  Catherine 42, 127
  John Henry 42, 127
  Michael 42, 127
QUON
  Brian 24, 87
  Jacquelin 24, 87
  John 24, 87
  Lori Ann 24, 87

R

RAMBERT
  Sue 29, 101
RAMIREZ
  Alex 19, 77
  Brandon David 19, 77
  Danielle Alyssa 19, 77
  Jacob Allen 19, 77
  Jenna Brianne 19, 77
  Levi Samuel 19, 77
  Tara Karissa 19, 77
RAMSAY
  Natashia 53, 152
  Nathan 53, 152
  Ronald 53, 152
REAVES
  Brittany Leeanne 19, 78
  Joshua 19, 77
  Kelly Michael 19, 77
REDMOND
  Brooke Katharine 38, 118
  Elizabeth Florence 38, 118
  Grace Leslie Faith 38, 118
  Jack Christopher Fleming 38, 118
  Keith Christopher 38, 118
REEVE
  John 27, 95
  Tony 27, 95
REEVES
  David 55, 154
  Jeremy 55, 154
  Rachael 53, 151
  Richard 55, 154
  Ryan 55, 154
REID
  Susan Alma 17, 71
REIZ
  Jeni Ann 18, 75
RENN
  Jim 23, 85
  Shannon 23, 86
REYNOLDS
  Adrian Hiram 24, 87
  Arthur Stroud 24, 88
RHODENHIZER
  Ann Denise 47, 138
RICE
  Allan 50, 144
  Barry 50, 144
  Eleanor 50, 144
  Elmer 50, 144
  George Harrison 50, 144
  Marilyn 50, 144
  Shirley 50, 144
  Wilber 50, 144
  Wilmot 50, 144
RICHARDS
  Donald 64, 175
  Farrell B. 64, 175
ROBBINS
  Aaron 35, 112
  Alexander 35, 111
  Allyson Lynn 35, 112
  Benjamin Mildred 112
  Bill. See William
  Brennan Timothy Joseph 33, 109
  Christopher Hugh 33, 109
  Christopher 34, 111
  Corrie 34, 111
  David Alan 35, 112
  David Martin 34, 111
  Donald Lloyd 33, 109
  Donnie. See Donald Lloyd
  Ellen Marion 34, 110
  Elwood. See Harry
  Flo. See Florence Ellen
  Florence Ellen 34, 110, 199
  Garrett William 34, 110
  Gary Elwood 35, 112
  Griffon Donald Lloyd 33, 109
  Harry 35, 111
  Helen Anne 33, 109
  Henry Lloyd 33, 108
  Hugh Martin 33, 108, 109, 198
  Jacqueline Goss 34, 111
  James Henry Lloyd 33, 108
  James Sandford 35, 112
  Jeffrey David 35, 112
  Jennifer Marie 33, 109
  Jill 33, 108
  John Campbell 34, 46, 110, 135, 199
  Jonathan 33, 108
  Joseph Lloyd 33, 109
  Joyce Lorraine 34, 110
  Karen Lynn 35, 112
  Kathy 35, 111
  Kirsten 34, 111
  Leslie Harold 33, 109
  Lloyd Winston 34, 111
  Marilyn Grace 34, 110
  Mark 35, 112
  Meagan Patricia 35, 112
  Melinda 35, 112
  Pam. See Pamela Marie
  Pamela Marie 33, 109
  Paula 33, 108
  Peter Sandford 35, 112
  Phil. See Philip John
  Philip John 34, 110
  Preston Sanford 35, 112
  Rebecca Charlotte 35, 112
  Robbie. See Robert
  Robert 35, 111
  Sherri Lynn 33, 109
  Sterling. See Alexander
  Terry. See Teryl Hugh

Teryl Hugh 33, 109
Tonia Gloria 35, 112
William 33, 108, 110
ROBERTSON
  Winifred Georgina Anne 21, 81; also see Win
ROGERS
  Alfreda 44, 131
  Ethel Letitia 29, 100
ROMAN
  Christina Campbell 29, 102
  Lolly Story 29, 102
  Robert Ernest 29, 101
  Shirley Jeanne 29, 102
ROSS
  Abigail Bertha 41, 124, 125
  Alexander 61, 168
  Ann 61, 168
  Craig 61, 168
  Eleanor 60, 167
  Eliot 61, 168
  Judy 61, 168
  Lorna 61, 168
  Mary Isabel 60, 167
  Mary 61, 168
  Peggy 61, 168
  William Neil 60, 167
  William 22, 83
ROWE
  Pearle 50, 144
ROWELL
  Bradford Vaughn 24, 88
  James R., Jr. 24, 88
  John Cidney 24, 88
  Russell James 24, 88
RUMMENS
  Carolyn 19, 78
RUSINOSKI
  Jennifer A. 114
RYCHEL
  Katherine 44, 129
  Madeline 44, 129
  Timothy 44, 129

S

SAINT
  Aiden James 19, 78
  Andrew Michael 19, 78
  Bryson 20, 78
  Gavin MacLeod 19, 78
  Matthew Paul 19, 78
  Paul Michael 19, 78
SALANARDI
  Wiescia 20, 79
SAMWAYS
  Mollie 55, 154
SANDALL
  Betty. See Mary Elizabeth
  Mary Elizabeth 20, 79
SANGSTER
  Chris 29, 102
  Teague Colin 29, 102
SCHAFFNER
  L.L. 61, 169
SCHLESS
  Caroline Gray 18, 76
SCHMIDTKE
  Linda 63, 172
SEARA
  Susie 47, 136
SEXTON
  Jeffrey 58, 162
SHARKEY
  James 56, 157
SHARPE
  Linda 54, 152
SHARUN
  Karen Lee 39, 119
SHAW
  Beth. See Margaret Elizabeth
  Dorothy Christina 47, 137
  Ian Ernest 49, 142
  John Allan 49, 142
  Jonathan Alexander 49, 142
  Madeline Donalda Anne 49, 142
  Margaret Elizabeth 49, 142
  Margaret 17, 73
  Mildred 15, 68
  Paul Thomas 49, 142
SHELBY
  Philip 30, 104
  Stewart 31, 104
SHERWOOD
  Ardyth 46, 134
SHORE
  Carol 50, 144
SIEMS
  Carleen Louise 16, 69
SIMMONS
  Donald 51, 147
SINCENNES
  Benjamin Samuel 37, 117
  Emily Elizabeth 37, 117
  Nicholas Alexander 37, 116
  Pierre Romeo 37, 116
SLAWINSKI
  John 33, 108
SLAWKINSKI
  Robert 32, 108
  Sarah 32, 108
SMITH
  Alexander Daniel Pierre 62, 171
  Ann Brew 32, 106
  Catherine Jane 62, 170
  Charles 63, 172
  Cynthia Anne 62, 170
  David 62, 63, 171, 173
  Donald Campbell 32, 106
  Donald Edward 32, 106
  Donald M. 63, 173
  Donald 14, 67
  Dorothy 14, 67
  Irwin. See Malcolm
  James 14, 67
  Jessi-Lynn Elizabeth 62, 170
  John Neil 63, 173
  Kenneth. See Winston Kenneth
  Lucas. See Peter Winston
  Malcolm 62, 171
  Mary-Lynn 62, 171

Peter Winston 62, 171
Pierre. See Alexander Daniel Pierre
Robert 14, 67
Susan Gail 62, 171
Wade Winston 62, 170
Wanda 57, 158
Warren 14, 67
Winston Kenneth 62, 170
Winston 62, 170

SMYTH
Ann Michele 20, 80
Kelly 17, 73

SNOW
Mary 46, 135

SOMERS
Margaret 54, 153

SOPER
Elizabeth 52, 149

SORENSEN
Barbara J. 63, 172

SPOUSA
Claude 37, 115

SPOWART
David 35, 112

STANFORD
Aaron 16, 69
Megan Ashley 16, 69

STAVERT
Albert 54, 152
Christopher 54, 152
Davis 54, 152
Ella Mabel 22, 84
Gary 54, 153
Jean 54, 153
Lowell 54, 153
Reta 54, 152
Shanae 54, 153
Sharon 54, 153
Wendell 54, 152
Willa 54, 152

STEELE
Candace G. 114

STEEVES
Lorne 45, 133
Monty 45, 133
Regan 45, 133
Roberta 45, 133
Robert 45, 133
Shane 45, 133

STEPHENS
Clayton 17, 73

STEVENSON
Clifford 31, 105
Garth 31, 105
James 31, 105
Jim. See James

STEWART
Aaron Michael 21, 81
Abigail Bertha Ross 41, 125
Abigail Jean 21, 82
Alan 41, 123, 125, 181
Alexander 40, 41, 81, 123, 124
Allan Campbell 18, 39, 75, 120
Allan Robertson 21, 81
Allan 21, 81, 82
Alyssa Jane 17, 73
Amy Leanne 21, 83
Angus John 20, 79
Anne. See also Elizabeth Anne
Annie 41, 124
Arlene 41, 124
Ashley 22, 83
Baden Powell 41, 124
Barbara Alexander 58, 161
Benjamin Campbell 20, 80
Benjamin 21, 82
Bernard 22, 83
Berta. See Roberta Lillian
Bessie. See Elizabeth May
Beverly 41, 125
Braeden John 17, 73
Cam. See Edison Campbell
Campbell 41, 124
Carroll 41, 125
Catherine Marie 21, 82
Catherine Melissa 20, 80
Catherine 40, 123
Cathy. See Catherine Melissa
Charlie Angus 20, 79
Christy Ann 22, 83
Christy 40, 123
Claudia Piper 22, 83
Cliff. See Robert Clifford
Colin John 21, 82
Dan. See Donald
Daniel Maynard Ross 22, 83
Daniel 22, 83
David Alexander 20, 80
David Allan 20, 80
Deborah Ann 57, 161
Dickie. See Richard
Donald. See also Daniel
Donald Alexander 41, 124
Donald Arthur 21, 81
Donald Campbell 20, 79
Donald 18, 22, 40, 41, 74, 84, 123, 124
Donnie. See Donald
Edison Campbell 20, 79, 177, 181, 204
Edith Joyce 57, 161
Effie. See Euphemia Margaret
Elizabeth Anne 20, 80
Elizabeth May 57, 160
Emily 21, 41, 82, 125
Eric Donald 20, 79
Euphemia Margaret 18, 74
Fay. See Mary
Gail Charlene 57, 161
Georgia Mary 21, 80
Georgina Anne Campbell 21, 81
Hayley 21, 82
Hazel Irene 58, 162
Hazel Mae 18, 75
Hazel 59, 163
Heather Ruth 22, 83
Henry Daniel 22, 83
Ian James 21, 82
Ira Alexander 57, 160
James Alexander 58, 161
James Alex 18, 74

James Allan 21, 82
James 41, 82, 123, 165
Janet Euphemia 18, 62, 74, 170
Jean Shirley 58, 162
Jeffrey Grant 58, 161
Jesse Alexander James 21, 82
J.J.. See John James
John Alexander 21, 82, 180
John Goodwill 18, 74
John James 59, 163
John N. 41, 124
John Ralph 57, 161
John Sandall 20, 79
John 17, 21, 41, 73, 124
Katherine Ellen 58, 161
Kayla 22, 83
Kenneth Esplin 21, 82
Kimberly Ruth 58, 162
Laney Rose 20, 79
Lawrence 41, 125
Lesley Margaret 58, 161
Logan James 21, 83
Lulu Christina 58, 162
Mabel F. 18, 74
MacLeod 41, 125
Malcolm Campbell 18, 74
Malcolm Hector Murchison 18, 74
Margaret Priscilla 18, 74, 180
Margaret 41, 124
Maryl Elaine 20, 79, 181
Mary 59, 163
Maynard 41, 124
Michael Jeffrey 58, 161
Morgan Allen 20, 80
Nathan James 21, 82
Neil Donald 41, 124
Neil 41, 124
Richard 22, 84
Roberta Jean 22, 83
Robert Alexander 57, 160
Roberta Lillian 41, 124
Robert Clifford 20, 80
Robert James 57, 160

Robert Livingstone 21, 81
Robert 61, 168
Roderick MacLean 18, 74
Ross 41, 124
Ruth 22, 41, 124; see also Hazel Stewart
Sadie 18
Sally. See Sarah
Sandy. See : John Sandall; Alexander
Sara Elizabeth 58, 161
Sarah 56, 157
Shawna Lee 20, 80
Sheldon 17, 73
Simon 41, 124
Sterling James 58, 161
Todd Donald 21, 81
Travis 22, 83
STICKLE
Chet 27, 95
Ellie. See Gabrielle
Gabrielle 28, 95
Jamie Paige 27, 95
Kelly 28, 95
Marc 27, 95
Roderick 28, 95
Ronald 27, 95
Teresa 27, 95
Teri. See Teresa
STORY
Helen 29, 101
STOWE
Alan Walker 31, 104
George 30, 104
SWIM
Mark 33, 108
SWOGGER
Alfred Dallas 61, 168
Alfred D. 61, 168
Flora Elizabeth 61, 168
Malcolm M. 61, 168

T

TARRAS
Andrea Leigh 39, 119
Gordon Alfred 39, 119

Jefferson James 39, 119
TAYLOR
Anthony 47, 138
Bonita Ruth 51, 146
Ernest Disney 51, 146
Karen Leigh 51, 146
Linda 51, 146
Malcolm 51, 146
Richard 51, 146
TEMPLETON
Linda Marie 19, 78
TESSNEER
Evelyn 40, 121
TEXARA
Ben 42, 127
Jake 42, 127
Ken 42, 127
THOMAS
Andrew 41, 127
Charles 45, 133
Helen 64, 176
Laurie Anne 45, 133
Michael Charles 45, 133
THORBOURN
Jay 22, 83
THORNTON
Audrey Cecilia 21, 81
TILLER
Faith Barbara 35, 112
TOMSON
Arin 58, 161
TRAINOR
Lucille 61, 169
TRAXLER
Carol 43, 129
TRODDEN
Norma 37, 116
TROLANDER
Harold 64, 175
TRUDEAU
Douglas 43, 128
Justin 43, 128
TURNER
Ruth 33, 108
TYSON
Jill 29, 101

U

Ulchek
Brody 39, 119
Jared 39, 119
Steven 39, 118

Ungar
Michael 38, 117
Mike. See Michael

Ungar Campbell
Megan Marcellina 38, 117
Scott 38, 117

V

Varico
Katie 27, 94
Larry 27, 94
Robbie 27, 94

Vaughn
Emily Meagan 35, 111
James 35, 111
Kathryn 35, 111
Paul Robbins 35, 111

Vickers
Paul 63, 172

Vining
David 15, 68
Jacqueline 15, 68
Jessica 15, 68

Volk
Marjorie 36, 114

Volker
Lorie 45, 133
Vanessa Lorraine 45, 133

W

Wade
Sherri 62, 170

Walker
David 24, 88
John 24, 88
Robert 24, 88

Ward
Gerald Ralph 57, 161

Warner
Floyd 61, 169

Warren
Sheila Lucy 25, 91

Weaver
Robert 24, 88

Weber
Amelia Nicolle 26, 92
Corey Campbell 26, 92
Debra-Jo 32, 106
Francois 26, 92

Weeks
Beryl June 59, 163
Blair. See Gordon
Chantal Marie 59, 163
David Kevin 59, 162
Douglas Steven 59, 163
Gordon 59, 163
John Earle 59, 163
Megan Sarah 59, 163
Myron MacDonald 59, 162
Nancy Jean 59, 163
Paul Wayne 59, 163
Wendy Faye 59, 163
Will David 59, 162

Weethmouth
C.A. 37, 115

Weir
Betty. See Elizabeth
Elizabeth 24, 88

Whatmore
Kathy 33, 109

Wheeler
Beatrice Ann 63, 175
Beatrice 63, 174
George Herbert 63, 174
Gerard Heath 63, 175
John Vere 63, 174, 175
John William Vere 63, 175
Leslie 56, 157
Lucy May 63, 174
Mary Evelyn 63, 175
Munroe Kenneth 56, 157
Paul 56, 157
Stephen 56, 157
Susan 56, 157
Wendy 56, 157

White
Derek Stephen 48, 138
Emily 48, 139
Gail. See Emily
Hal. See Loren Harold
Joseph Harold 47, 138
Loren Harold 47, 138
Patricia Catherine 48, 139
Patsy. See Patricia Catherine
Shawn Martin 48, 138
Verlie Pauline 63, 175

Whitehead
Wendy 54, 153

Whiteway
April 35, 111
Billy. See William
Matthew 35, 111
Michael 35, 111
Sara 35, 111
William 35, 111

Wickstrom
Mariel Ilona Jean 28, 96

Wildy
Karla 36, 113
Lily Catherine 36, 113

Wiley
Joyce 61, 168

Wilkinson
Erin C. 20, 79

Williams
Andrew James 39, 119
Benjamin Michael 39, 119
Carlene Marie 39, 119
Collin Michael 39, 119
Elizabeth. See also Julie Elizabeth
Julie Elizabeth 39, 119
Katherine Anne 38, 117
Kathy. See Katherine Anne
Kelly Victoria Elaine 39, 119
Kimberley Sandra 39, 118
Mark David 39, 119
Mitchell Benjamin 39, 119

Ronald Edgar 38, 117
Ronald 38, 118
Winton. See Ronald
WILSON
  Cliff 114
  James 23, 87
  Jim. See James
WINDSOR
  Andrew 62, 170
  Tobias Franklin 62, 170
WINTERS
  Kalyn Marie 26, 91
  Kyle Ray 26, 91
  Ray. See Raymond
  Raymond 25, 91
WISMER
  Evelyn 14, 67
WOLTERS
  Grant 35, 112
  Isaac 35, 112
  Peter 35, 112
WOOD
  George 48, 139
  Lisa 29, 101
WOODWORTH
  Caroline Campbell 32, 107
  Neil Smith 32, 107
  Robert Merrill 32, 106
WRIGHT
  Amanda Christine 47, 136
  Douglas 46, 136
  Michael Douglas 47, 136
WYLAND
  Claude LeRoy 24, 88
  Leslie 24, 88
  Rosamund 24, 88
  Roy. See Claude LeRoy
  Ruth M. 24, 88
  Vivian 24

Y

YEO
  Ernest 57, 159
YORK
  Clyde 59, 162
YOUNG
  Benjamin Mildred 35
  Rhonda Mildred 35, 112
YOUNGSTON
  Ann. See Annabella D.
  Annabella D. 46, 136

Z

ZAKLUKIEWEIZ
  Amanda 51, 147
  Kirsten 51, 147
  Roger 51, 147
  Stephanie 51, 147
  Wendy 51, 147
ZIMMERMAN
  Daryl 44, 131
  Earl 44, 131
  Patricia 44, 131

www.ingramcontent.com/pod-product-compliance
Lightning Source LLC
Chambersburg PA
CBHW081742100526
44592CB00015B/2261